TEACHER'S EDITION 2

English

No Problem!

Maria H. Koonce
Adult ESOL
Broward County Schools, FL

William J. Koonce
Adult ESOL
Nova Community School, FL

New Readers Press

English—No Problem!®
English—No Problem! Level 2 Teacher's Edition
ISBN 978-1-56420-352-6

Copyright © 2004 New Readers Press
New Readers Press
A Publishing Division of ProLiteracy
1320 Jamesville Avenue, Syracuse, New York 13210
www.newreaderspress.com

Printed in the United States of America
9 8 7 6 5 4 3 2

All proceeds from the sale of New Readers Press materials
support literacy programs in the United States and worldwide.

Acquisitions Editor: Paula L. Schlusberg
Developer: Mendoza and Associates
Project Director: Roseanne Mendoza
Project Editor: Pat Harrington-Wydell
Content Editor: Rose DeNeve
Production Director: Heather Witt-Badoud
Designer: Kimbrly Koennecke
Cover Design: Kimbrly Koennecke
Cover Photography: Robert Mescavage Photography

Distributed By:
Grass Roots Press
Toll Free: 1-888-303-3213
Fax: (780) 413-6582
Web Site: www.grassrootsbooks.net

Authors

Maria H. Koonce
Adult ESOL
Broward County Schools, FL

William J. Koonce
Adult ESOL
Nova Community School, FL

Contributors

National Council Members
Audrey Abed, *San Marcos Even Start Program, San Marcos, TX*
Myra K. Baum, *New York City Board of Education (retired), New York, NY*
Kathryn Hamilton, *Elk Grove Adult and Community Education, Sacramento, CA*
Brigitte Marshall, *Oakland Adult Education Programs, Oakland, CA*
Teri McLean, *Florida Human Resources Development Center, Gainesville, FL*
Alan Seaman, *Wheaton College, Wheaton, IL*

Reviewers
Sabrina Budasi-Martin, *William Rainey Harper College, Palatine, IL*
Linda Davis-Pluta, *Oakton Community College, Des Plaines, IL*
Patricia DeHesus-Lopez, *Center for Continuing Education, Texas A&M University, Kingsville, TX*
Gail Feinstein Forman, *San Diego City College, San Diego, CA*
Carolyn Harding, *Marshall High School Adult Program, Falls Church, VA*
Trish Kerns, *Old Marshall Adult Education Center, Sacramento City Unified School District, Sacramento, CA*
Lydia Omori, *William Rainey Harper College, Palatine, IL*
Debe Pack-Garcia, *Manteca Adult School, Humbolt, CA*
Pamela Patterson, *Seminole Community College, Sanford, FL*
Catherine Porter, *Adult Learning Resource Center, Des Plaines, IL*
Jean Rose, *ABC Adult School, Cerritos, CA*
Eric Rosenbaum, *Bronx Community College Adult Program, Bronx, NY*
Laurie Shapero, *Miami-Dade Community College, Miami, FL*
Terry Shearer, *North Harris College Community Education, Houston, TX*
Abigail Tom, *Durham Technical Community College, Chapel Hill, NC*
Darla Wickard, *North Harris College Community Education, Houston, TX*

Pilot Teachers
Connie Bateman, *Gerber Adult Education Center, Sacramento, CA*
Jennifer Bell, *William Rainey Harper College, Palatine, IL*
Marguerite Bock, *Chula Vista Adult School, Chula Vista, CA*
Giza Braun, *National City Adult School, National City, CA*
Sabrina Budasi-Martin, *William Rainey Harper College, Palatine, IL*
Wong-Ling Chew, *Citizens Advice Bureau, Bronx, NY*
Renee Collins, *Elk Grove Adult and Community Education, Sacramento, CA*
Rosette Dawson, *North Harris College Community Education, Houston, TX*
Kathleen Edel, *Elk Grove Adult and Community Education, Sacramento, CA*
Margaret Erwin, *Elk Grove Adult and Community Education, Sacramento, CA*
Teresa L. Gonzalez, *North Harris College Community Education, Houston, TX*
Fernando L. Herbert, *Bronx Adult School, Bronx, NY*
Carolyn Killean, *North Harris College Community Education, Houston, TX*
Elizabeth Minicz, *William Rainey Harper College, Palatine, IL*
Larry Moore, *Long Beach Adult School, Long Beach, CA*

Lydia Omori, *William Rainey Harper College, Palatine, IL*
Valsa Panikulam, *William Rainey Harper College, Palatine, IL*
Kathryn Powell, *William Rainey Harper College, Palatine, IL*
Alan Reiff, *NYC Board of Education, Adult and Continuing Education, Bronx, NY*
Brenda M. Rodriguez, *San Marcos Even Start, San Marcos, TX*
Juan Carlos Rodriguez, *San Marcos Even Start, San Marcos, TX*
Joan Siff, *NYC Board of Education, Adult and Continuing Education, Bronx, NY*
Susie Simon, *Long Beach Adult School, Long Beach, CA*
Gina Tauber, *North Harris College, Houston, TX*
Diane Villanueva, *Elk Grove Adult and Community Education, Sacramento, CA*
Dona Wayment, *Elk Grove Adult and Community Education, Sacramento, CA*
Weihua Wen, *NYC Board of Education, Adult and Continuing Education, Bronx, NY*
Darla Wickard, *North Harris College Community Education, Houston, TX*
Judy Wurtz, *Sweetwater Union High School District, Chula Vista, CA*

Focus Group Participants
Leslie Jo Adams, *Laguna Niguel, CA*
Fiona Armstrong, *New York City Board of Education, New York, NY*
Myra K. Baum, *New York City Board of Education (retired), New York, NY*
Gretchen Bitterlin, *San Diego Unified School District, San Diego, CA*
Patricia DeHesus-Lopez, *Center for Continuing Education, Texas A&M University, Kingsville, TX*
Diana Della Costa, *Worksite ESOL Programs, Kissimmee, FL*
Frankie Dovel, *Orange County Public Schools, VESOL Program, Orlando, FL*
Marianne Dryden, *Region 1 Education Service Center, Edinburgh, TX*
Richard Firsten, *Lindsay Hopkins Technical Center, Miami, FL*
Pamela S. Forbes, *Bartlett High School, Elgin, IL*
Kathryn Hamilton, *Elk Grove Adult and Community Education, Sacramento, CA*
Trish Kerns, *Old Marshall Adult Education Center, Sacramento City Unified School District, Sacramento, CA*
Suzanne Leibman, *The College of Lake County, Grayslake, IL*
Patty Long, *Old Marshall Adult Education Center, Sacramento City Unified School District, Sacramento, CA*
Brigitte Marshall, *Oakland Adult Education Programs, Oakland, CA*
Bet Messmer, *Santa Clara Adult School, Santa Clara, CA*
Patricia Mooney, *New York State Board of Education, Albany, NY*
Lee Ann Moore, *Salinas Adult School, Salinas, CA*
Lynne Nicodemus, *San Juan Adult School, Carmichael, CA*
Pamela Patterson, *Seminole Community College, Sanford, FL*
Eric Rosenbaum, *Bronx Community College Adult Program, Bronx, NY*
Federico Salas, *North Harris College Community Education, Houston, TX*
Linda Sasser, *Alhambra District Office, Alhambra, CA*
Alan Seaman, *Wheaton College, Wheaton, IL*
Kathleen Slattery, *Salinas Adult School, Salinas, CA*
Carol Speigl, *Center for Continuing Education, Texas A&M University, Kingsville, TX*
Edie Uber, *Santa Clara Adult School, Santa Clara, CA*
Lise Wanage, *CASAS, Phoenix, AZ*

Contents

Unit 1   Time for a Change 10

◆ Vocabulary: Finding a job • Interviews and applications
◆ Language: Using *can, cannot,* and *can't* • Present tense of *be* and *have*
◆ Pronunciation: Sentence stress • Intonation in statements and questions
◆ Culture: Interviews in the US

Unit 2   New Beginnings. 22

◆ Vocabulary: Moving and feelings • Activities • Volunteer jobs • Places
to volunteer • Immigration
◆ Language: Simple past tense of regular verbs • Simple past tense of irregular verbs
◆ Pronunciation: Sounds of simple past-tense endings • Sounds of *o*
◆ Culture: Measurements in the US

Unit 3   Balancing Your Life 34

◆ Vocabulary: Responsibilities and feelings • Health • Sports and leisure activities
◆ Language: Compound sentences with *and* or *but* • *Do* and *does* in Yes/No questions
and answers
◆ Pronunciation: Pauses and intonation in compound sentences • Sounds of *i*
◆ Culture: Being too busy

Unit 8   Understanding Yourself 94

◆ Vocabulary: Words to describe people • Words to describe relationships
◆ Language: Reflexive pronouns • Future with *will* (review) and *going to*
◆ Pronunciation: Sounds of *u* • Sounds of *b* and *v*
◆ Culture: Marriage in the US

Unit 9   It Takes a Team 106

◆ Vocabulary: Celebrations • Skills for working with other people
◆ Language: Direct and indirect object pronouns • Simple past tense of regular and irregular verbs (review)
◆ Pronunciation: Sound of the *–tion* ending • Sounds of *r*
◆ Culture: Celebrations in the US

Scope and Sequence

Unit Number and Title	Global Unit Theme (across all levels)	Unit Topic/Skill	Lesson-Specific Life Skills	Vocabulary	Language
Unit 1 Time for a Change	Life stages: Personal growth and goal setting	Dealing with change	L1: Ask family or friends for help L2: Find out about job applications L3: Learn about job interviews in the US	Finding a job Interviews and applications	Using *can*, *cannot*, and *can't* Present tense of *be* and *have*
Unit 2 New Beginnings	Making connections	Coming together	L1: Talk about daily actions and skills Take a phone message L2: Talk about helping in your community L3: Calculate liquid and solid measurements	Moving and feelings Activities Volunteer jobs Places to volunteer Immigration	Simple past tense of regular verbs Simple past tense of irregular verbs
Unit 3 Balancing Your Life	Taking care of yourself	Finding balance	L1: Talk about your responsibilities L2: Talk about health problems and feelings L3: Talk about sports and hobbies	Responsibilities and feelings Health Sports and leisure activities	Compound sentences with *and* or *but* *Do* and *does* in Yes/No questions and answers
Unit 4 Making a Plan for Your Money	Personal finance	Making a budget	L1: Look at income and expenses L2: Learn about checking and savings accounts L3: Talk about saving money	Budgets and banking	*Will, have to,* and *must* *Wh-* questions and answers
Unit 5 Bargain Shopping	Consumer awareness	Getting a good deal	L1: Identify clothing and prices L2: Identify clothing L3: Talk about shopping on the Internet	Shopping Places to shop Clothing Electronics	Comparative adjectives Compound sentences with *and . . . too* and with *or*

Culture	Pronunciation	Tasks and Unit Project	EFF Skill (The basic communication skills—read with understanding, convey ideas in writing, speak so others can understand, listen actively, and observe critically—are taught in every unit.)	SCANS Skills (The basic skills of reading, writing, listening, and speaking are taught in every unit.)	Technology
Interviews	Sentence stress Intonation in statements and questions	T1: Make a job ladder T2: Write your job history T3: Talk about your strengths UP: Complete an application form	Reflect and evaluate	Organize and maintain information Self-management	Type your basic information worksheet on the computer, or use the Internet to look for your dream job
Measurements	Sounds of simple past-tense endings Sounds of *o*	T1: List your skills T2: Make a poster for a class party T3: Sharing your culture UP: Plan an international party	Cooperate with others	Work with cultural diversity Arithmetic	Leave a phone message for your teacher
Being too busy	Pauses and intonation in compound sentences Sounds of *i*	T1: Explain a schedule change T2: Chart your activities T3: Find community activities UP: Make a presentation about your life	Solve problems and make decisions	Manage time Responsibility	Take photos of other learners giving presentations
Living with parents Family life	Sounds of *ch* and *sh* Syllable stress	T1: Track your spending T2: Make a savings plan T3: Make a chart of your spending UP: Make a budget	Plan Use math to solve problems and communicate	Manage money	Use a calculator
Shopping	Sounds of *th* Sounds of *s* and *st*	T1: Compare as you shop T2: List clothing sizes T3: Compare ads UP: Find a bargain	Learn through research	Acquire and evaluate information Apply technology to task Arithmetic	Find shopping links and products of interest on the Internet

Scope and Sequence

Unit Number and Title	Global Unit Theme (across all levels)	Unit Topic/Skill	Lesson-Specific Life Skills	Vocabulary	Language
Unit 6 Equal Rights	Protecting your legal rights	Protecting your legal rights	L1: Talk about qualifications and challenges L2: Prepare for a job interview L3: Learn how to deal with discrimination	Rights in the workplace Equality and discrimination	Modals *may, should, could, would* Present continuous (review) Past continuous
Unit 7 Paying Taxes	Participating in your new country and community	Understanding paychecks and taxes	L1: Understand your paycheck L2: Learn about W-4 forms L3: Learn about government tax forms	Paychecks Taxes	Verbs followed by infinitives Order of adjectives
Unit 8 Understanding Yourself	Lifelong learning	Learning your strengths	L1: Find out about your strengths and weaknesses L2: Discuss relationships L3: Talk about helping neighbors	Words to describe people Words to describe relationships	Reflexive pronouns Future with *will* (review) and *going to*
Unit 9 It Takes a Team	Celebrating success	Celebrating success	L1: Talk about strategies for success L2: Talk about teamwork L3: Discuss ways to celebrate	Celebrations Skills for working with other people	Direct and indirect object pronouns Simple past tense of regular and irregular verbs (review)

Culture	Pronunciation	Tasks and Unit Project	EFF Skill (The basic communication skills—read with understanding, convey ideas in writing, speak so others can understand, listen actively, and observe critically—are taught in every unit.)	SCANS Skills (The basic skills of reading, writing, listening, and speaking are taught in every unit.)	Technology
Equal rights and the law	Sounds of *a* Reductions	T1: Write a thank-you letter T2: Prepare for a job interview T3: Discuss discrimination UP: Complete a discrimination complaint form	Resolve conflict and negotiate	Understand systems Problem solving Self-esteem	Visit the Equal Employment Opportunity Commission web site and share something interesting from it with other learners
Taxation	Sounds of *e* Sounds of *t* and *d*	T1: Read paychecks T2: Fill out a W-4 form T3: Make a list of tax forms UP: Practice completing a 1040EZ form	Use math to solve problems and communicate	Interpret and communicate information Understand systems	Find the latest forms and information at the IRS web site
Marriage	Sounds of *u* Sounds of *b* and *v*	T1: Evaluate jobs for your skills T2: Describe good relationships T3: Solve a problem UP: Complete a skills inventory	Cooperate with others	Manage human resources Acquire and evaluate information Self-management	Find an online skills inventory, complete the inventory, and share it with other learners
Celebrations	Sound of the *-tion* ending Sounds of *r*	T1: Describe successful team planning T2: Write a group speech about teamwork T3: Write a speech about success UP: Present a success story	Guide others	Participate as member of a team Exercise leadership Sociability	Create a computer presentation, or write a speech on a word processor. Include color, pictures, and different fonts

About This Series

Meeting Adult Learners' Needs with *English—No Problem!*

English—No Problem! is a theme-based, performance-based series focused on developing critical thinking and cultural awareness and on building language and life skills. Designed for adult and young adult English language learners, the series addresses themes and issues meaningful to adults in the United States.

English—No Problem! is appropriate for and respectful of adult learners. These are some key features:
- interactive, communicative, participatory approach
- rich, authentic language
- problem-posing methodology
- project-based units and task-based lessons
- goal setting embedded in each unit and lesson
- units organized around themes of adult relevance
- contextualized, inductive grammar
- student materials designed to fit into lesson plans
- performance assessment, including tools for learner self-evaluation

Series Themes

Across the series, units have the following themes:
- Life Stages: Personal Growth and Goal Setting
- Making Connections
- Taking Care of Yourself
- Personal Finance
- Consumer Awareness
- Protecting Your Legal Rights
- Participating in Your New Country and Community
- Lifelong Learning
- Celebrating Success

At each level, these themes are narrowed to subthemes that are level-appropriate in content and language.

English—No Problem! Series Components

Five levels make up the series:
- literacy
- level 1 (low beginning)
- level 2 (high beginning)
- level 3 (low intermediate)
- level 4 (high intermediate)

The series includes the following components.

Student Book

A full-color student book is the core of each level of *English—No Problem!* Literacy skills, vocabulary, grammar, reading, writing, listening, speaking, and SCANS-type skills are taught and practiced.

Teacher's Edition

Each teacher's edition includes these tools:
- general suggestions for using the series
- scope and sequence charts for the level
- lesson-specific teacher notes with reduced student book pages
- complete scripts for all listening activities and Pronunciation Targets in the student book

Workbook

A workbook provides contextualized practice in the skills taught at each level. Activities relate to the student book stories. Workbook activities are especially useful for learners working individually.

 This icon in the teacher's edition indicates where workbook activities can be assigned.

Reproducible Masters

The reproducible masters include photocopiable materials for the level. Some masters are unit-specific, such as contextualized vocabulary and grammar activities, games, and activities focusing on higher-level thinking skills. Others are generic graphic organizers. Still other masters can be used by teachers, peers, and learners themselves to assess the work done in each unit.

Each masters book also includes scripts for all listening activities in the masters. (Note: These activities are not included on the *English—No Problem!* audio recordings.)

 This icon in the teacher's edition indicates where reproducible masters can be used.

Audio Recording

Available on CD and cassette, each level's audio component includes listening passages, listening activities, and Pronunciation Targets from the student book.

 This icon in the student book and teacher's edition indicates that the audio recording includes material for that activity.

Lesson-Plan Builder

This free, web-based *Lesson-Plan Builder* allows teachers to create and save customized lesson plans, related graphic organizers, and selected assessment masters. Goals, vocabulary lists, and other elements are already in the template for each lesson. Teachers then add their own notes to customize their plans.

They can also create original graphic organizers using generic templates.

When a lesson plan is finished, the customized materials can be printed and stored in PDF form.

This icon in the teacher's edition refers teachers to the *Lesson-Plan Builder,* found at www.enp.newreaderspress.com.

Vocabulary Cards

For literacy, level 1, and level 2, all vocabulary from the Picture Dictionaries and Vocabulary boxes in the student books is also presented on reproducible flash cards. At the literacy level, the cards also include capital letters, lowercase letters, and numerals.

Placement Tool

The Placement Test student booklet includes items that measure exit skills for each level of the series so that learners can start work in the appropriate student book. The teacher's guide includes a listening script, as well as guidelines for administering the test to a group, for giving an optional oral test, and for interpreting scores.

Hot Topics in ESL

These online professional development articles by adult ESL experts focus on key issues and instructional techniques embodied in *English—No Problem!,* providing background information to enhance effective use of the materials. They are available online at www.enp.newreaderspress.com.

Addressing the Standards

English—No Problem! has been correlated from the earliest stages of development with national standards for adult education and ESL, including the NRS (National Reporting System), EFF (Equipped for the Future), SCANS (Secretary's Commission on Achieving Necessary Skills), CASAS (Comprehensive Adult Student Assessment System) competencies, BEST (Basic English Skills Test), and SPLs (Student Performance Levels). The series also reflects state standards from New York, California, and Florida.

About the Student Books

Each unit in the student books includes a two-page unit opener followed by three lessons (two at the literacy level). A cumulative unit project concludes each unit. Every unit addresses all four language skills—listening, speaking, reading, and writing. Each lesson focuses on characters operating in one of the three EFF-defined adult roles—parent/family member at home, worker at school or work, or citizen/ community member in the larger community.

Unit Opener Pages

Unit Goals The vocabulary, language, pronunciation, and culture goals set forth in the unit opener correlate to a variety of state and national standards.

Opening Question and Photo The opening question, photo, and caption introduce the unit protagonists and engage learners affectively in issues the unit explores.

Think and Talk This feature of levels 1–4 presents questions based on classic steps in problem-posing methodology, adjusted and simplified as needed.

What's Your Opinion? In levels 1–4, this deliberately controversial question often appears after Think and Talk or on the first page of a lesson. It is designed to encourage lively teacher-directed discussion, even among learners with limited vocabulary.

Picture Dictionary or Vocabulary Box This feature introduces important unit vocabulary and concepts.

Gather Your Thoughts In levels 1–4, this activity helps learners relate the unit theme to their own lives. They record their thoughts in a graphic organizer, following a model provided.

What's the Problem? This activity, which follows Gather Your Thoughts, encourages learners to practice another step in problem posing. They identify a possible problem and apply the issue to their own lives.

Setting Goals This feature of levels 1–4 is the first step of a unit's self-evaluation strand. Learners choose from a list of language and life goals and add their own goal to the list. The goals are related to the lesson activities and tasks and to the unit project. After completing a unit, learners revisit these goals in Check Your Progress, the last page of each workbook unit.

First Lesson Page

While the unit opener sets up an issue or problem, the lessons involve learners in seeking solutions while simultaneously developing language competencies.

Lesson Goals and EFF Role The lesson opener lists language, culture, and life-skill goals and identifies the EFF role depicted in that lesson.

Pre-Reading or Pre-Listening Question This question prepares learners to seek solutions to the issues presented in the reading or listening passage or lesson graphic that follows.

Reading or Listening Tip At levels 1–4, this feature presents comprehension and analysis strategies used by good listeners and readers.

Lesson Stimulus Each lesson starts with a reading passage (a picture story at the literacy level), a listening passage, or a lesson graphic. A photo on the page sets the situation for a listening passage. Each listening passage is included in the audio recording, and scripts are provided at the end of the student book and the teacher's edition. A lesson graphic may be a schedule, chart, diagram, graph, time line, or similar item. The questions that follow each lesson stimulus focus on comprehension and analysis.

Remaining Lesson Pages

Picture Dictionary, Vocabulary Box, and Idiom Watch These features present the active lesson vocabulary. At lower levels, pictures often help convey meaning. Vocabulary boxes for the literacy level also include letters and numbers. At levels 3 and 4, idioms are included in every unit.

Class, Group, or Partner Chat This interactive feature provides a model miniconversation. The model sets up a real-life exchange that encourages use of the lesson vocabulary and grammatical structures. Learners ask highly structured and controlled questions and record classmates' responses in a graphic organizer.

Grammar Talk At levels 1–4, the target grammatical structure is presented in several examples. Following the examples is a short explanation or question that guides learners to come up with a rule on their own. At the literacy level, language boxes highlight basic grammatical structures without formal teaching.

Pronunciation Target In this feature of levels 1–4, learners answer questions that lead them to discover pronunciation rules for themselves.

Chat Follow-Ups Learners use information they recorded during the Chat activity. They write patterned sentences, using lesson vocabulary and structures.

In the US This feature is a short cultural reading or brief explanation of some aspect of US culture.

Compare Cultures At levels 1–4, this follow-up to In the US asks learners to compare the custom or situation in the US to similar ones in their home countries.

Activities A, B, C, etc. These practice activities, most of them interactive, apply what has been learned in the lesson so far.

Lesson Tasks Each lesson concludes with a task that encourages learners to apply the skills taught and practiced earlier. Many tasks involve pair or group work, as well as follow-up presentations to the class.

Challenge Reading

At level 4, a two-page reading follows the lessons. This feature helps learners develop skills that prepare them for longer readings they will encounter in future study or higher-level jobs.

Unit Project

Each unit concludes with a final project in which learners apply all or many of the skills they acquired in the unit. The project consists of carefully structured and sequenced individual, pair, and group activities. These projects also help develop important higher-level skills such as planning, organizing, collaborating, and presenting.

Additional Features

The following minifeatures appear as needed at different levels:

One Step Up These extensions of an activity, task, or unit project allow learners to work at a slightly higher skill level. This feature is especially useful when classes include learners at multiple levels.

Attention Boxes These unlabeled boxes highlight words and structures that are not taught explicitly in the lesson, but that learners may need. Teachers are encouraged to point out these words and structures and to offer any explanations that learners require.

Remember? These boxes present, in abbreviated form, previously introduced vocabulary and language structures.

Writing Extension This feature encourages learners to do additional writing. It is usually a practical rather than an academic activity.

Technology Extra This extension gives learners guidelines for doing part of an activity, task, or project using such technology as computers, photocopiers, and audio and video recorders.

Assessment

Assessment is completely integrated into *English—No Problem!* This arrangement facilitates evaluation of class progress and provides a systematic way to set up learner portfolios. The pieces used for assessment are listed below. You may use all of them or select those that suit your needs.

Check Your Progress

Found on the last page of each workbook unit, this self-check is tied to the goals learners set for themselves in the student book unit opener. Learners rate their progress in life and language skills.

Unit Checkup/Review

For each unit, the reproducible masters include a two-page Unit Checkup/Review. You can use this instrument before each unit as a pretest or after each unit to assess mastery. If it is used both before and after, the score differential indicates a learner's progress.

Rubrics for Oral and Written Communication

The reproducible masters include a general rubric for speaking and one for writing (Masters 8 and 9). You can use these forms to score and track learner performance on the unit tasks and projects. Copy the rubric for each learner, circle performance scores, and include the results in the learner's portfolio.

Forms for Evaluating Projects

For three projects (in Units 3, 6, and 9), the reproducible masters include a form on which you can evaluate learner performance. Make a copy for each learner, record your assessment, and add the form to the learner's portfolio.

Peer Assessment

Peer assessment helps learners focus on the purpose of an activity. Encourage learners to be positive in their assessments of each other. For example, ask them to say one thing they liked about a presentation and one thing they did not understand. Use the Peer Assessment Form (Master 12 in the reproducible masters) when learners are practicing for a performance. Peer assessment is best used to evaluate groups rather than individuals and rehearsals rather than performances.

Self-Assessment

Self-assessment is a way for learners to measure their progress. Use the self-check masters (Masters 10 and 11 in the reproducible masters) at the beginning of Unit 1 and at the end of Units 3, 6, and 9. Then save them in learners' portfolios.

Ongoing Assessment

These minirubrics and guidelines for specific tasks and projects in the student book are integrated into the teacher notes. They often focus on assessing one particular language or life-skill function. You can include the pieces you evaluate in learners' portfolios. After using these resources systematically for a few units, you will probably develop similar ways of assessing learners' progress on other parts of the unit.

Teaching Effectively with *English—No Problem!* Level 2

The following general suggestions for using level 2 of *English—No Problem!* can enhance your teaching.

Before beginning a unit, prepare yourself in this way:
- Read the entire set of unit notes.
- Gather the materials needed for the unit.
- Familiarize yourself with the student book and workbook pages.
- Prepare copies of masters needed for the unit.

Look for ways to express meaning clearly, using objects, pictures, gestures, and the most basic language structures and vocabulary. Avoid idioms and two-word verbs, which do not translate well. You can also help learners by slowing the instructional pace. Don't hesitate to repeat, recycle, and explore material in-depth.

Materials

The notes for each unit include a list of specific materials. These lists do not include the following, which are recommended for all or most units:
- large sheets of paper (butcher or flip-chart).
- magazines, newspapers, catalogs (to cut up).
- art supplies (scissors, glue, tape, colored pencils, markers, colored and plain paper, etc.).
- a "Treasure Chest" box or other container of prizes (new pencils, pens, erasers, rulers, stickers, hard candy, small candy bars, key chains, and things collected at conferences or found at dollar stores).

Grouping

Working in groups increases learner participation and builds teamwork skills important in the workplace.

Learners can be grouped randomly. Four or five on a team allows for a good level of participation. For increased individual accountability, assign roles to group members. These commonly include
- group leader, who directs the group's activities
- recorder, who writes group responses
- reporter, who reports the group's responses to the whole class
- timekeeper, who lets everyone know how much time is left for an activity

Groups and roles within groups can be changed as needed.

Talking about the Photos

Contextualized color photos are used as starting points for many unit activities. Talking about the photos with learners is a good way to assess prior knowledge and productive vocabulary. For every photo, follow one or more of these suggestions:

- Ask general questions about what learners see: Who are the people in the photo? What is their relationship? Can you say anything about their ages, jobs, or nationalities? Where are they? What's happening? What do you think is going to happen next? Encourage learners to explain their answers.
- As learners name items in the photos, write new vocabulary on the board or an overhead transparency.
- If a photo has a lot of detail, groups can compete to list the most items or to write the most sentences about it. Make this more challenging by showing the photo for 30 seconds and asking the groups to work from memory.

Reading Titles and Captions

Focusing on titles and captions helps learners create a context for the unit or lesson.

Lesson Titles Discuss vocabulary that appears in lesson titles and ask learners to talk about how the titles relate to the lessons. In some cases, you can ask learners to predict what will happen in the story.

Captions Use the captions to discuss the characters and the story. Ask questions like these: Do you know anyone like this or in this situation? What do you think the character will do?

Identifying and Analyzing Problems

The questions in What's the Problem? set up the central issue for the unit. Model responses by talking about how you would answer the question. Learners may think about the questions individually or discuss them with a partner or group. If they discuss the questions, ask volunteers to share ideas from their small groups. Then follow up with a class discussion.

The grammar structures taught in the unit often appear in the opening discussion. You can use the structures yourself in talking about the problem, but don't expect learners to use them yet.

Setting Goals

Write each goal on a large piece of paper. Then follow these steps:
- Post the goals around the room.
- Have learners read all the goals and decide which is the most important.
- Ask learners to go stand near the goal that is most important to them. Have them sign their names beneath the goal they've chosen.

- Remind learners throughout the unit to review their goal and monitor their progress toward achieving it.

Listening Comprehension

One lesson in each unit is driven by a listening passage, such as a recorded phone message, conversation, or commercial announcement. There are also other listening activities, including a dictation.

Ideally, you will have access to a cassette or CD player and will be able to use the *English—No Problem!* audio recording. The recording allows learners to hear a variety of native-speaker and non-native-speaker voices. For teachers who need or prefer to read the audio portions, scripts for listening passages and activities excluding Pronunciation Targets are printed on pages 118–119 of the student book. Complete scripts for the passages and for all student book listening activities are on pages 118–122 of this book.

In doing listening activities, the following sequence is recommended:
- Review and model the directions.
- Play the audio or read the listening script as often as learners want.
- After learners listen once, check for basic listening comprehension by asking *either/or* questions directly from the passage. (If the passage is long, play short sections and ask learners questions after each section.)

Comprehension Questions (Talk or Write)

Read the sentences. Have learners repeat. Read the sentences again. For *yes/no* questions, have learners use their *yes/no* cards for responses, especially in the early units.
- Pair learners to answer the questions.
- Make each pair responsible for reporting a question to the class by having one partner read the question and the other answer it.
- Discuss the questions. Answers are provided for all questions except personal ones, for which answers will vary according to learners' experience. When answers are given, learners may use different wording and structures, provided they capture the general concept.

Reading Comprehension

The readings in *English—No Problem!* are designed to be as useful as possible to adult English language learners. They are modeled on practical documents that adults want and need to read in everyday life. The reading lessons present the strategies and skills needed to successfully navigate such documents.

Attention Boxes The words in these unlabeled boxes are not active vocabulary, but learners will need them to understand the passage.

Reading Tips Each tip focuses on a reading strategy, for example, scanning for specific information or predicting content. Help learners apply these strategies to other student book and workbook readings.

In-Class Reading Follow these suggestions when learners read in class:

- Ask learners to read the passage silently first. They can mark any problem words, but they should not open their dictionaries at this point.
- Read the passage aloud so that learners can hear correct pronunciation of the words.
- Encourage learners to answer comprehension questions before dealing with new vocabulary. Have learners discuss questions in pairs or write answers individually before they answer.
- Review problem vocabulary and ask learners to read the passage aloud in pairs or in groups.

Vocabulary Practice

Spend plenty of time on each set of words introduced in the Picture Dictionaries and Vocabulary boxes.

Introducing Vocabulary These steps will help learners comprehend the words:

- Point to the words or pictures as you read them.
- Read the words in random order and have learners point to the words or pictures.
- Say each word again and have learners repeat.
- Write the words on the board or an overhead transparency. Point to the letters and have learners spell the words aloud.
- Act out any action words.
- Elicit definitions and sample sentences for vocabulary words learners already know. Write their ideas on the board. Have learners write their own definitions in pairs.
- Collect the definitions or ask volunteers to write one of their definitions on the board.
- If there is a line for "your word," have learners write another word that is new to them. If there is no line, have learners write new words in their notebooks. List the new words on the board or an overhead transparency. Introduce these words and their meanings as you did the Picture Dictionary and vocabulary words, using the steps above.
- Have them act out their own words.

Using Vocabulary Cards Use the Vocabulary Card Masters and your own card stock to make vocabulary cards for all Picture Dictionary and Vocabulary words. Consider duplicating the Vocabulary Card Masters in different sizes to accommodate various activities, e.g., a set of larger, laminated cards for whole-group activities, or individual sets for each learner. If you have a class set of scissors, have learners cut out their own cards.

Give learners plastic self-closing bags to keep their cards in, or use a hole punch and have learners put the cards on key rings or binder rings in their notebooks.

The sets of words and pictures can be used for a variety of activities like matching, alphabetizing, sorting, and categorizing.

Reinforcing Vocabulary Picture Dictionary and Vocabulary words are used often in the student book and the workbook. These activities use Vocabulary Card Masters to provide further reinforcement:

- Hold up a picture card. First ask *yes/no* questions (e.g., Is this an apple? Is this an orange?). Later ask, "What is this?"
- Hold up a word card and say, "Read this word."
- After you have practiced the new words, a more advanced learner may take your place showing the cards and asking questions. Or pass around the cards and have each learner ask the question, "What is this?"
- Use the vocabulary cards throughout the unit to review meaning, pronunciation, and form. Distribute the cards among the groups. Ask each group to pronounce a word, give any alternate forms, and create an example sentence.
- Use story writing to reinforce both meaning and use of vocabulary. First create a sample story that uses your own set of five words. Write the words on the board or an overhead transparency. Tell learners the story, or write it on the board too. Then give each group a set of five words and a large piece of paper. Some words may appear in more than one set, or you can include words from previous units. Ask each group to create a story using all of its words. Emphasize that although the story can be silly, it should make sense. It is not necessary to put a vocabulary word in every sentence.

Writing Activities

At this level, learners are moving from writing single sentences to writing short paragraphs. The writing activities in the student book emphasize supporting main ideas with related details and using correct paragraph form. Do not try to correct every mistake in learners' writing. Learners need to be aware of the *focus* of the writing activity, and your corrections should help them focus.

Writing well involves both fluency and accuracy. To help learners develop fluency, have them write often, but do not always collect and correct their writing. Rather, ask them sometimes to share their writing in groups and respond to the content. This helps them learn to communicate ideas effectively.

Class and Partner Chats

Follow these steps when introducing a Chat:
- Model the entire conversation as learners listen.
- Explain or mime meanings of unfamiliar words.
- Have learners listen and repeat. Then assign one learner a part to recite with you as a model for other learners.
- Have learners practice in pairs. Pair fluent learners with learners who have more difficulty.
- While learners are conversing in pairs or groups, circulate; join as many conversations as possible.

Role-Plays

Going beyond dialogue practice to role-playing reinforces the speaking skills developed in the conversation practice, but to be successful, learners at this level need to be given carefully structured and limited situations. Follow these steps:
- Describe a situation.
- Assign roles to specific learners.
- Have them act out the dialogue.

Encourage learners to think about the beginning and end of the conversation. Put commonly used phrases on the board so learners can use them for greeting, introducing, thanking, and saying good-bye. After learners finish, ask volunteers to perform role-plays for the class.

Grammar

The student book deliberately uses only essential grammatical terminology. Included in Grammar Talk are example sentences and questions to help learners arrive at the grammar concept deductively. Introduce a grammar point this way:
- Read the sentences to learners.
- Ask learners to repeat.
- Discuss the questions as a class. (Suggested answers are included in the teacher notes.)
- Elicit more example sentences and write them on the board or an overhead transparency.
- Discuss any specific issues related to the grammar point and answer learners' questions.

Pronunciation

Many adult ESL series give scant attention to pronunciation, but *English—No Problem!* gives it proper emphasis within an array of integrated skills.

Stress Word and sentence stress, which are so important for good English pronunciation, are often overlooked by learners themselves, who tend to focus on challenging sounds.

When teaching a new word, elicit the stress and number of syllables from learners. Use chants or songs to practice stress and rhythm. When learners are preparing to role-play, have them exaggerate syllable length and intonation. (Hiiiiiii! How've you beeeen lately?) Demonstrate how drawn-out syllables and question intonation can signal friendliness as well as provide important clues to meaning.

Voiced and Voiceless Sounds The words *voiced* and *voiceless* are not used in the student book, but the issue comes up in Unit 4 (voiceless sounds of *ch* and *sh*), Unit 5 (sounds of *th*), and Unit 7 (sounds of *t* and *d*). *Voiced* sounds produce a vibration in the voice box. They include all vowel sounds as well as most consonant sounds. Ask learners to touch their throats while pronouncing *go, run,* or *name*. They should feel a vibration in the throat. *Voiceless* sounds are softer and do not cause the voice box to vibrate. There are eight voiceless sounds in English: /f/, /s/, /th/ (as in *think*), /sh/, /ch/, /p/, /t/, and /k/.

The voiced/voiceless distinction is tied to several important issues in English pronunciation:
- Voiceless sounds followed by *s* produce an /s/ rather than a /z/ sound: *bets* vs. *beds*.
- Adding a regular past-tense ending to a verb that ends in a voiceless sound other than /t/ produces a /t/ rather than a /d/ sound: *tapped* (tapt) vs. *tagged* (tagd).
- Vowels are shortened before voiceless consonants: *rope* is shorter than *robe*.

Customizable Graphic Organizers

The teacher notes indicate when to use one of the Customizable Graphic Organizers in the reproducible masters. Gather Your Thoughts in the unit opener and the Class/Group/Partner Chats usually are done using one of these forms. Use the following procedure to customize these masters:
- Make one copy of the Customizable Graphic Organizer Master (chart, idea map, etc.) appropriate for the activity you are doing.
- Fill in the heads as shown in the student book.
- Duplicate enough copies for each learner or group, and distribute them.

After learners complete their graphic organizers, follow these steps:
- Draw a copy of the chart or idea map on the board or an overhead transparency.
- Fill in the appropriate headings.
- Ask learners to read the answers they recorded on their individual charts.
- Write the answers on the large chart.

Tried-and-True Techniques and Games for High Beginning Learners

Total Physical Response (TPR)

TPR is a method for teaching language based on the premise that if we physically act out what we are trying to learn, we are more likely to remember it than if we only read or hear about it. To adapt TPR to developing literacy skills using *English—No Problem!*, try the following procedure:
- When teaching Picture Dictionary or vocabulary words, identify words that can be acted out (e.g., *point, write, sign, walk*).
- Demonstrate each word by acting it out as you say it aloud.
- Have learners say the word as you act it out, then as they act it out.
- Use the Vocabulary Card Masters or write the words on flash cards. Show the cards to learners while saying the words. Ask learners to read each card and perform the action.
- Show the cards to students first in order and then out of order while students mime their meaning. Speaking is optional.
- Give learners vocabulary cards. As you act out each word, have learners hold up the corresponding card.
- Ask learners to copy the words from the vocabulary cards.

Spelling Dictations

Begin a learning session by doing a spelling dictation of vocabulary from the previous one:
- Select five to seven words for the dictation.
- Number the words and write a short line for each letter in the word on the board or on learners' papers (e.g., 1. _ _ _).
- Spell a word and have learners write it. Repeat the spelling as many times as necessary.
- Have learners exchange papers to correct each other's work.
- Review by saying a word and having learners spell it as you or a volunteer writes it on the board. Then ask all learners to read the words aloud together.

Jigsaw Reading

Jigsaws help learners practice all language skills and require real communication. This type of activity can be done with any piece of text that can be divided into four sections. Choose text with previously learned vocabulary. You may also want to use an illustration or photo for each section of text. Jigsaws work best when completed in one session. You may also find that they work best when used at the end of a unit.

Follow these steps:
- Prepare questions or a task that requires learners to synthesize information from all sections of the text (e.g., read about four people and decide which you would hire, read about four apartments and decide which you would rent, read about someone's life and identify the most important, happiest, and saddest events).
- Model a jigsaw for learners, walking them through each step.
- Put one section of the text in each corner of the room. Put learners in groups of four. Each person from a group goes to a different corner of the room to read the information there. (If your class does not divide evenly into groups of four, put five learnsers in some groups. Have two learners look at the same information in those groups.)
- Have each person learn the information in his or her corner. Then have learners return to their original groups to share the information. Learners should not take notes until they are back in their groups.
- Once learners return to their groups, they can complete the task or answer the questions together. Allow them time to read the task or questions and to practice telling their part of the story to one another.

Concentration

Make vocabulary cards for the unit vocabulary words with the definition on one card and the word on another. Model the steps below:
- Keeping words and definitions separate, learners arrange the cards in rows, facedown on the table.
- Taking turns, learners turn over one word card and one definition card.
- If the cards do not match, the learner turns them facedown again in the same place. A learner who finds a matching pair keeps the cards.

When all cards are matched, the learner with the most matches wins.

Twenty Questions

Give one learner a word card and have the others ask *yes/no* questions about the word. As the cardholder answers the questions, the other learners try to guess the word on the card. If after 20 questions no one has guessed correctly, the cardholder reveals the word, and play begins again with another learner holding a second word card. An easier variation of this game focuses on a particular beginning letter. After giving a learner a card, tell the class which letter the word begins with. Then play the guessing game with 20 questions.

Bingo

Use the generic bingo card (Master 1 in the reproducible masters) to review vocabulary for a unit. Duplicate the master and distribute one copy to each learner. Write unit vocabulary words on the board or an overhead transparency. (You will need 25 words.) Ask learners to choose words randomly and write a word in each square. Circulate to be sure they understand that they should write the words in random order.

Give each learner a pile of markers—dried beans, paper clips, pennies, or small squares of card stock. Then call out the words in random order and have learners place a marker on the word if it appears on their bingo card. The first learner to mark a row of five words down, across, or diagonally calls "Bingo!" and wins. Ask winners to read out the words they have marked and tell you the meanings.

Once learners understand the game well, have learners take turns calling out the words.

Unit 1: Time for a Change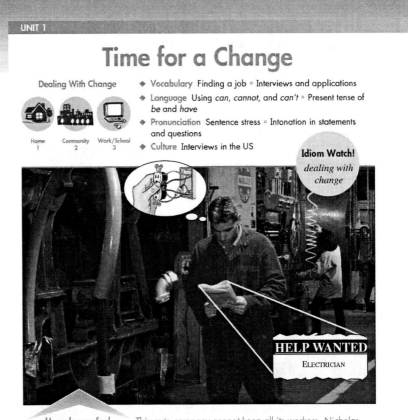

Materials for the Unit

- Pictures and other graphics showing what you do at work
- Customizable Masters 2–4, 6
- Generic Assessment Masters 10 and 11
- Unit Masters 13–18
- Vocabulary Card Masters for Unit 1

Self-Assessment

As you start the unit, give each learner a copy of the Speaking and Listening Self-Check and the Writing and Reading Self-Check (Generic Assessment Masters 10 and 11). Go over the items together. The completed forms will go into each learner's portfolio.

Time for a Change

Read the unit goals with learners. Then follow the suggestions on p. 5 for talking about the title.

- Introduce the expression *time for* using examples like *time for breakfast* or *time for a talk*.
- Ask learners to think of a time they had to make a decision to change their lives (e.g., getting married, moving away, buying a house).

Ask the questions below. Record learners' answers on a large sheet of paper.
- Why did you face a change?
- What did you do?
- Was the change good or bad?

Question

Read the question below the arrow.
- On the board or an overhead transparency, write three changes mentioned when you discussed the unit title.
- Talk about how some people might see those changes as positive and others as negative.

- Ask learners to tell you some positive things about change (e.g., exciting, fun). Then ask them to tell you some negative things (e.g., fear, loss).

Photo

Follow the suggestions on p. 5 for talking about the photo. Then ask these questions:
- Does Nicholas work in an office or a factory? *(factory)*
- Is he building cars or selling cars? *(building cars)*
- Can Nicholas wire houses or program computers? *(wire houses)*
- Can he be a manager or an electrician? *(electrician)*

Think and Talk

Ask learners to think individually about each question.
- Have learners answer questions 1 and 2 aloud. Be sensitive to learners' privacy when discussing questions 3 and 4.
- Write their answers on the board or an overhead transparency.

Possible Answers
1. He is walking to his job. He is looking at a newspaper. He feels worried.
2. He thinks that he will lose his job.
3. Answers will vary.
4. Answers will vary.

Picture Dictionary

Read the words in the student book. Follow the suggestions on p. 6 for introducing vocabulary.

Follow the suggestions on p. 6 for using vocabulary cards. Use the Vocabulary Card Masters for the words in the Picture Dictionary.

- Ask learners for examples of jobs and skills.
- List responses on the board or an overhead transparency.

Gather Your Thoughts

- Show learners some graphics that illustrate what you do (e.g., a flyer from your school advertising English classes, a picture of a teacher in front of a class).
- Ask learners to bring to class something that illustrates the job they have and the job they would like to have (e.g., an ad, a flyer, or a page from a manual or catalog).
- Post two large pieces of paper with the headings *My Job* on one and *My Dream Job* on the other.
- Create two displays with learners' illustrations. Help learners label their illustrations as they post them.

Draw the chart in the student book on the board or an overhead transparency. Fill in the two heads *My Skills* and *Dream Job*.

- Ask for volunteers to begin filling in the chart.
- After the chart is completed, have learners add vocabulary by looking at the chart. Encourage them to illustrate the words, either by drawing or by cutting and pasting from magazines.

What's the Problem?

Follow the suggestions on p. 5 for identifying and analyzing problems. Model the issue in this way:

- Tell learners about a job change you experienced.
- Explain why you made the change.

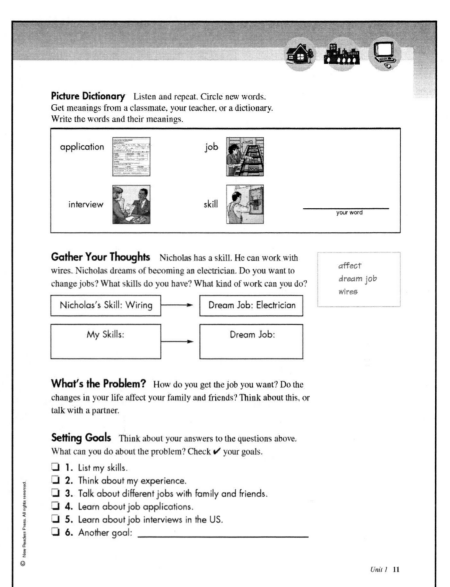

Picture Dictionary   Listen and repeat. Circle new words. Get meanings from a classmate, your teacher, or a dictionary. Write the words and their meanings.

application

job

interview

skill

_____ your word

Gather Your Thoughts   Nicholas has a skill. He can work with wires. Nicholas dreams of becoming an electrician. Do you want to change jobs? What skills do you have? What kind of work can you do?

affect
dream job
wires

Nicholas's Skill: Wiring → Dream Job: Electrician

My Skills: → Dream Job:

What's the Problem?   How do you get the job you want? Do the changes in your life affect your family and friends? Think about this, or talk with a partner.

Setting Goals   Think about your answers to the questions above. What can you do about the problem? Check ✔ your goals.

- ❏ 1. List my skills.
- ❏ 2. Think about my experience.
- ❏ 3. Talk about different jobs with family and friends.
- ❏ 4. Learn about job applications.
- ❏ 5. Learn about job interviews in the US.
- ❏ 6. Another goal: _____

Unit 1   **11**

- Tell them the skills you had.
- Tell them how you learned about the job you applied for.
- Tell them how your experience turned out.

Next, write these sentences on the board:

My dream job is to be a/an ___.
To get this job, I can _____.

Have learners complete the sentences based on their own experiences with change.

One Step Up

Ask learners to alter the sentences to describe other dreams (e.g., my dream life, place to live, partner).

Setting Goals

Follow the suggestions on p. 5 for setting goals. Ask learners to think about how they can deal with changes they must face.

One Step Up

Orally proficient learners can share their information with the class.

Use Unit Master 13 (Study Skill: KWL). Give a copy to each learner. Have learners complete the first two columns. Complete the third column at the end of this unit.

Lesson 1: Getting Help 🌐

Follow the suggestions on p. 5 for talking about titles. Then point out the lesson objectives listed below it.

Attention Box

- Write each word on the board or an overhead transparency.
- Encourage learners to help provide definitions, synonyms, related words, and illustrations to show meaning.
- List learners' suggestions, or put them into a word map on the board or transparency.

This vocabulary should be understood, but learners should not be expected to produce the words at this point.

Question

Read the question aloud and brainstorm answers with learners.

- Refer back to learners' answers from Gather Your Thoughts in the unit opener.
- Mention different circumstances that may cause a need for change (e.g., economic changes, job loss, divorce, health problems, marriage, birth, death).
- Talk about what people can do to prepare for each of those changes.
- Record learners' answers on the board or an overhead transparency.

Reading Tip

Read the tip aloud to learners.

- Ask learners to think about a change in their lives that they have already talked about in this unit.
- Then read the conversation aloud as learners follow silently.
- Ask for volunteers to read the parts of Nicholas and Elana.

Talk or Write

This exercise helps learners recognize important details.

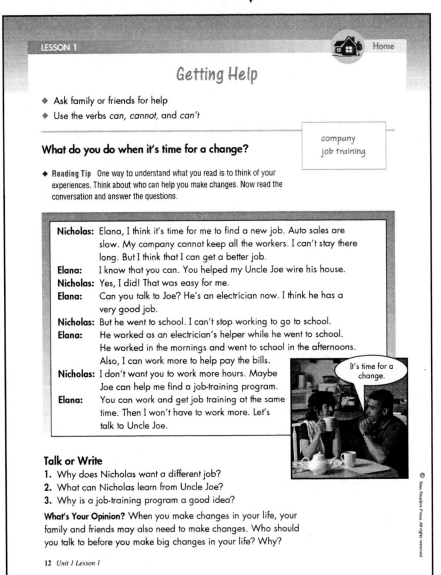

LESSON 1   🏠 Home

Getting Help

- Ask family or friends for help
- Use the verbs *can, cannot,* and *can't*

What do you do when it's time for a change?

company
job training

- **Reading Tip** One way to understand what you read is to think of your experiences. Think about who can help you make changes. Now read the conversation and answer the questions.

Nicholas: Elana, I think it's time for me to find a new job. Auto sales are slow. My company cannot keep all the workers. I can't stay there long. But I think that I can get a better job.
Elana: I know that you can. You helped my Uncle Joe wire his house.
Nicholas: Yes, I did! That was easy for me.
Elana: Can you talk to Joe? He's an electrician now. I think he has a very good job.
Nicholas: But he went to school. I can't stop working to go to school.
Elana: He worked as an electrician's helper while he went to school. He worked in the mornings and went to school in the afternoons. Also, I can work more to help pay the bills.
Nicholas: I don't want you to work more hours. Maybe Joe can help me find a job-training program.
Elana: You can work and get job training at the same time. Then I won't have to work more. Let's talk to Uncle Joe.

It's time for a change.

Talk or Write
1. Why does Nicholas want a different job?
2. What can Nicholas learn from Uncle Joe?
3. Why is a job-training program a good idea?

What's Your Opinion? When you make changes in your life, your family and friends may also need to make changes. Who should you talk to before you make big changes in your life? Why?

12   Unit 1 Lesson 1

Possible Answers
1. Nicholas thinks that he cannot stay long in his company, and he thinks that he can get a better job.
2. Nicholas can learn how to find a job-training program.
3. Nicholas could continue working while he gets training.

Extensions
1. Ask these additional questions:
   - How does Elana help her husband?
   - What is Nicholas's skill?
   - How did Uncle Joe become an electrician?

2. Discuss giving help to and receiving help from family and friends. This practice varies among cultures. Ask learners what is acceptable, not acceptable, and expected in their home culture.

What's Your Opinion?

Ask learners who they discuss their life changes with and why.

Vocabulary

Read the words in the student book. Follow the suggestions on p. 6 for introducing and reinforcing vocabulary.

Follow the suggestions on p. 6 for using vocabulary cards. Use the Vocabulary Card Masters for the words in the Vocabulary box.

Have learners add related words of their own. For example, they can list entry-level jobs.

<u>One Step Up</u>
Have learners as a group spell out each word as you write it on the board.

Partner Chat

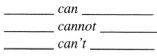 Use Customizable Master 2 (2-Column Chart). Follow the suggestions on p. 7 for customizing and duplicating the master. Make a copy for each learner.

- After the chat, ask two volunteers to tell what they learned about their partners.
- Write a sentence telling about each person's special skill (e.g., *Tran can complete job applications well. Silvio can speak three languages.*).

Grammar Talk

Follow the suggestions on p. 7 for introducing the grammar point.

<u>Answer</u>
Cannot and *can't* are the two negative forms of *can.*

<u>One Step Up</u>
Explain the following:
- *Can* is a *modal*. It is used to describe a physical ability, a skill, or a possibility, or to give permission.
- Modals do not add an *s* in the third person singular.

Write these structures on the board or an overhead transparency:

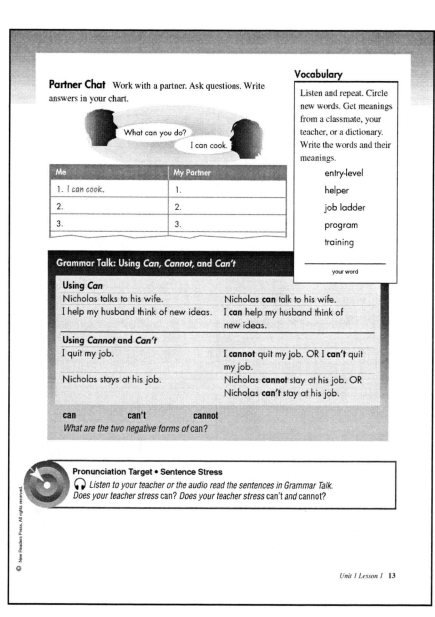

_____ *can* _____
_____ *cannot* _____
_____ *can't* _____

Then write this example sentence: *Juan can play the guitar.*
- Have a volunteer write one thing he or she can do and two things he or she cannot do.
- Tell learners to work in pairs and write their own sentences.
- Have them report to the class on what each partner can and cannot do.
- As a group, write sentences about what most people in the class can and cannot do, using subject pronouns.

Pronunciation Target

 Play the audio or read the Grammar Talk sentences. Emphasize the stressed *cannot* and *can't,* but do not emphasize *can.*

Assign Workbook pp. 4–5.

Use Unit Master 14 (Grammar: Bingo Game) now or at any time during the rest of the unit.

Activity A

Have learners look at the charts they completed for Partner Chat on p. 13.

Ask volunteers to tell things their partners can and cannot do.

Activity B

Structure the activity in this way:
- Read the four *cause* sentences to learners. Then read the four *effect* sentences.
- Have individual learners read each of the sentences.
- Reread Nicolas and Elana's conversation on p. 12 for learners.
- Have two volunteers read the same conversation aloud.
- Have learners answer the questions.

Answers

2. c   3. d   4. a

Activity C

Learners may draw the chart in their notebooks. If you prefer, use Customizable Master 2 (2-Column Chart). Follow the suggestions on p. 7 for customizing and duplicating the master and distributing the copies. Make a copy for each learner.

Extension
- Ask for one or two volunteers to dictate sentences to you as you write them on the board.
- Underline all the verbs and the modal *can*.

Task 1
- Write these prompts on the board or an overhead transparency:
  Dream Job: _____
  Training: _____
  Entry-Level Job: _____
  Skills: _____
- Pair learners who have similar interests.
- Ask each partner to create his or her own job ladder.
- Encourage volunteers to read their notes to the class.

14 Unit 1 *Lesson 1*

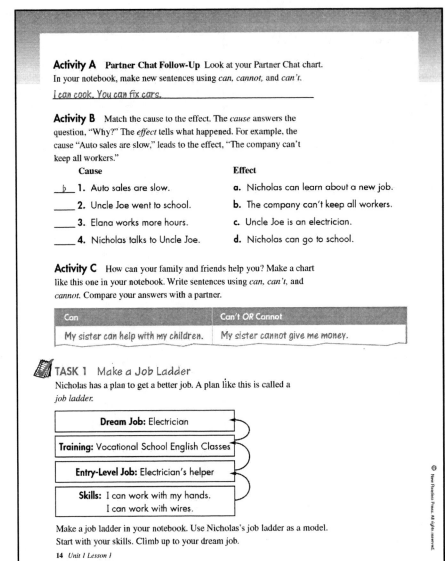

Activity A **Partner Chat Follow-Up** Look at your Partner Chat chart. In your notebook, make new sentences using *can, cannot,* and *can't.*

I can cook. You can fix cars.

Activity B Match the cause to the effect. The *cause* answers the question, "Why?" The *effect* tells what happened. For example, the cause "Auto sales are slow," leads to the effect, "The company can't keep all workers."

Cause	Effect
_b_ **1.** Auto sales are slow.	**a.** Nicholas can learn about a new job.
____ **2.** Uncle Joe went to school.	**b.** The company can't keep all workers.
____ **3.** Elana works more hours.	**c.** Uncle Joe is an electrician.
____ **4.** Nicholas talks to Uncle Joe.	**d.** Nicholas can go to school.

Activity C How can your family and friends help you? Make a chart like this one in your notebook. Write sentences using *can, can't,* and *cannot.* Compare your answers with a partner.

Can	Can't OR Cannot
My sister can help with my children.	My sister cannot give me money.

TASK 1 *Make a Job Ladder*
Nicholas has a plan to get a better job. A plan like this is called a *job ladder.*

Dream Job: Electrician
Training: Vocational School English Classes
Entry-Level Job: Electrician's helper
Skills: I can work with my hands. I can work with wires.

Make a job ladder in your notebook. Use Nicholas's job ladder as a model. Start with your skills. Climb up to your dream job.

14 *Unit 1 Lesson 1*

Lesson 2: Finding Jobs 🔆

- Follow the suggestions on p. 5 for talking about titles. Then point out the lesson objectives listed below it.
- Explain that in this lesson learners will learn how to complete a job application.

Attention Box

Read the words to learners, pointing or miming to convey meaning when possible. Then do the following:

- Write each word on the board or an overhead transparency.
- Encourage learners to help provide definitions, synonyms, related words, and illustrations to show meaning.
- As learners respond, list their suggestions on the board or an overhead transparency or put the suggestions into a word map.

This vocabulary should be understood, but learners should not be expected to produce the words at this point.

Question

Read the question aloud and brainstorm answers with learners.

- Ask learners to define the word *scan*. One meaning might be *to read quickly for important points.*
- Tell learners to scan the form to answer the question.
- Write their answers on the board or an overhead transparency.

Reading Tip

- Allow learners ample time to scan the form and then read it carefully.
- Point out the title of the form and the heads *Personal Information* and *Job History.* Ask questions to make sure learners understand what the two parts of the application are.

Talk or Write

In this exercise, learners practice scanning for information.

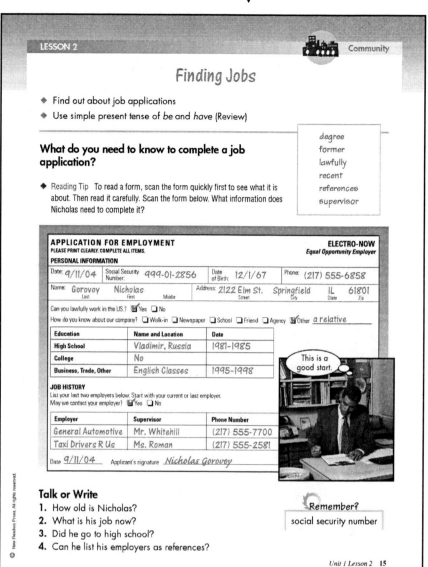

Answers
1. Nicholas is 36 years old.
2. His job now is with General Automotive.
3. Yes.
4. Yes, he can list his employers as references.

- When did he complete the application?

One Step Up
Ask these additional questions:
- What is Nicholas's social security number? *OR* What is 999-01-2856?
- When is his birthday?
- What is his address?
- Can he lawfully work in the US?
- How did he learn about this company?

Vocabulary

Read the words in the student book. Follow the suggestions on p. 6 for introducing and reinforcing vocabulary.

Follow the suggestions on p. 6 for using vocabulary cards. Use the Vocabulary Card Masters for the words in the Vocabulary box.

Class Chat

Use Customizable Master 3 (3-Column Chart) to create the Bingo cards. Make one copy for each learner.
- To play the game, have learners follow the directions in their books.
- Give the winner a prize from your treasure box.

Grammar Talk

Follow the suggestions on p. 7 for introducing the grammar point.

Remind learners of other things they have learned about the verb *be*:
- *Be* is used for definitions, locations, descriptions, places of origin, and age.
- The verb *be* is irregular.
- The contracted forms are *I'm, he's/she's, you're, we're, they're.*
- To form negative sentences, add *not* after the verb form (e.g., *They are not happy.*).
- The negative contractions are *isn't* and *aren't.*

Remind learners of other things they have learned about the verb *have*:
- The verb *have* is irregular.
- The third person singular form is *has.*
- In US English, the verb *have* is not normally contracted when it refers to possession.
- To form the negative, use the helping verb *do* plus the negative *not* before the verb, (e.g., *I do not have a good job. She doesn't*

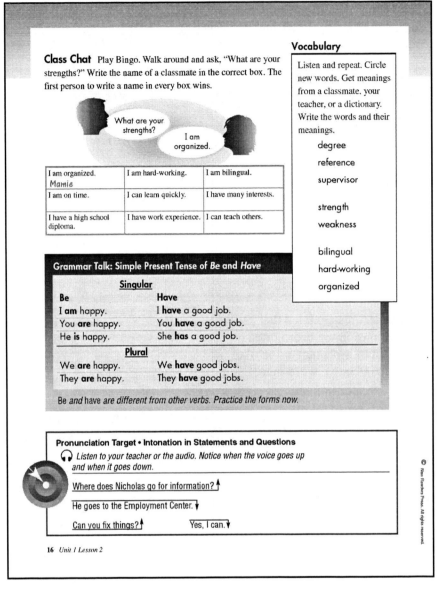

have a good job.).
- The negative contractions are *haven't* and *hasn't.*

One Step Up
For additional practice with *be* and *have*, do the following:
- Encourage learners to use the verb *be* in present-tense statements about Nicholas. Use these examples:
Nicholas is good with electric wiring.
Nicholas is from Russia.
- Have learners change the sentences orally to apply to themselves (e.g., "I am good with computers. I am from Chile.").

- Change to plural any sentences that apply to more than one learner.
- Practice the same sentences using contractions.
- Help learners to form negative sentences.

Follow these steps again using the verb *have.*

Pronunciation Target

Play the audio or read the sentences, emphasizing the rising and falling intonation.

 Assign Workbook pp. 6–7.

Activity A

Have learners review their job ladders from Task 1 to answer the questions. Then have partners practice asking and answering the questions.

Activity B

- Remind learners they will talk about good experiences and bad experiences.
- Review the list of Nicholas's experiences and goals shown in the student book. Then have learners pair up to talk about their own lives.
- Create a class chart on the board or an overhead transparency outlining learners' good and bad experiences.

Attention Box

Read the phrase and its definition to learners, pointing or miming to convey meaning if necessary. This phrase should be understood, but learners should not be expected to produce it at this point.

Task 2

Use Customizable Master 4 (4-Column Chart). Follow the suggestions on p. 7 for customizing and duplicating the master and distributing the copies. Make one copy for each learner.

One Step Down

Help less advanced learners write their own chart heads from the student book and complete the chart with their own job history.

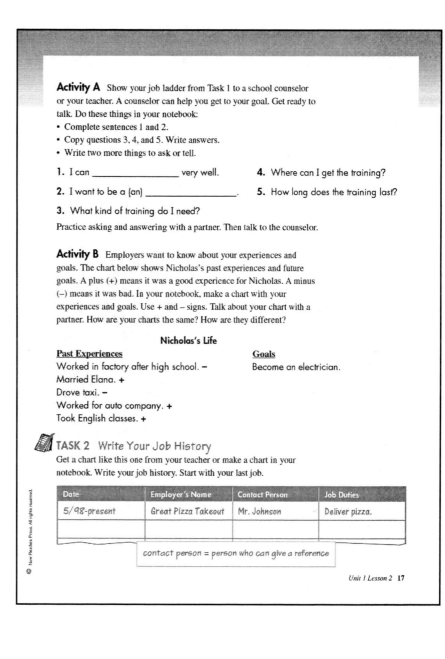

Activity A Show your job ladder from Task 1 to a school counselor or your teacher. A counselor can help you get to your goal. Get ready to talk. Do these things in your notebook:
- Complete sentences 1 and 2.
- Copy questions 3, 4, and 5. Write answers.
- Write two more things to ask or tell.

1. I can _____ very well.

2. I want to be a (an) _____.

3. What kind of training do I need?

4. Where can I get the training?

5. How long does the training last?

Practice asking and answering with a partner. Then talk to the counselor.

Activity B Employers want to know about your experiences and goals. The chart below shows Nicholas's past experiences and future goals. A plus (+) means it was a good experience for Nicholas. A minus (–) means it was bad. In your notebook, make a chart with your experiences and goals. Use + and – signs. Talk about your chart with a partner. How are your charts the same? How are they different?

Nicholas's Life

Past Experiences
Worked in factory after high school. –
Married Elana. +
Drove taxi. –
Worked for auto company. +
Took English classes. +

Goals
Become an electrician.

TASK 2 Write Your Job History
Get a chart like this one from your teacher or make a chart in your notebook. Write your job history. Start with your last job.

Date	Employer's Name	Contact Person	Job Duties
5/98-present	Great Pizza Takeout	Mr. Johnson	Deliver pizza.

contact person = person who can give a reference

Unit 1 Lesson 2 **17**

Lesson 3: Good News! www

Follow the suggestions on p. 5 for talking about the title.

- Give some examples of *good news;* ask learners for more.
- Give some examples of *bad news;* ask learners for more.
- Tell learners they will learn how to act in a job interview in the US.

Attention Box

- Write each word on the board or an overhead transparency.
- Encourage learners to help provide definitions, synonyms, related words, and illustrations to show meaning.
- As learners respond, list their suggestions or put the suggestions into a word map on the board or transparency.

This vocabulary should be understood, but learners should not be expected to produce the words at this point.

Question

- Read the question above the photo.
- Brainstorm possible answers with learners (e.g., learn about the type of job it is; learn about the requirements and the skills and experience needed; select the clothes you will wear; practice an interview conversation with a friend or family member).
- List learners' answers on the board or an overhead transparency.

Listening Tip

Read the tip aloud with learners.

🎧 Play the audio or read the listening script on p. 118 twice. Follow the suggestions on p. 5 for listening comprehension.

- As learners listen to the conversation the first time, have them write any new or difficult words in their notebooks.

LESSON 3   Work/School

Good News!

◆ Learn about job interviews in the US
◆ Prepare for a job interview

How can you do well in an interview?

ambitious
industry
sir
start
technical

◆ Listening Tip 🎧 Writing difficult words can help you understand what you hear. Listen to the conversation. You can read the words on page 118. Write difficult words in your notebook. Find the words in a dictionary or ask your teacher questions. Then listen again.

Nicholas is at a job interview. The interviewer thinks he can be good for the company.

Talk or Write
1. Where is Nicholas?
2. Why does he want a new job?
3. When can he start?
4. Why is this a good job for Nicholas?

18 Unit 1 Lesson 3

- After they listen, ask learners if any of their difficult words are in the Attention Box.
- If any new words are not in the Attention Box, list them on the board or a transparency.
- Help learners find definitions, synonyms, related words, or illustrations for the new words.

Talk or Write

This exercise helps learners better understand a conversation.

Answers
1. Nicholas is at a job interview.
2. He wants to become an electrician.

3. He can start in two weeks.
4. This is a good job for Nicholas because the company has a job-training program and excellent benefits.

One Step Up

🎧 Read the listening script or have learners listen to the audio a third time. Then ask partners to role-play the conversation.

18 Unit 1 *Lesson 3*

Vocabulary

Read the words in the student book. Follow the suggestions on p. 6 for introducing and reinforcing vocabulary.

Follow the suggestions on p. 6 for using vocabulary cards. Use the Vocabulary Card Masters for the words in the Vocabulary box.

Some words can be acted out.
- Distribute vocabulary cards for the words *eye contact, pay, confident, interested in,* and *polite.*
- Ask some learners to act out each word while the other learners try to guess it.

Attention Box

Read the words and phrases to learners, pointing or miming to convey meaning if necessary. This vocabulary should be understood, but learners should not be expected to produce the words at this point.

In the US

Write each idea on a separate card. Then do the following:
- Put learners in pairs.
- Give each pair an idea card.
- Ask one partner to act the wrong way while the other partner acts correctly.
- Have other learners tell which way of acting is the correct way.

<u>One Step Up</u>

Have learners explain *why* the way they acted is correct or incorrect.

Compare Cultures

Use Customizable Master 6 (Venn Diagram).
- Title the diagram *How to Prepare for a Job Interview.*
- Write *US* and *My Home Country: _____* as heads at the top of the two circles.
- Write *Both* where the circles overlap.
- Make a copy of the master for each learner and distribute the copies.

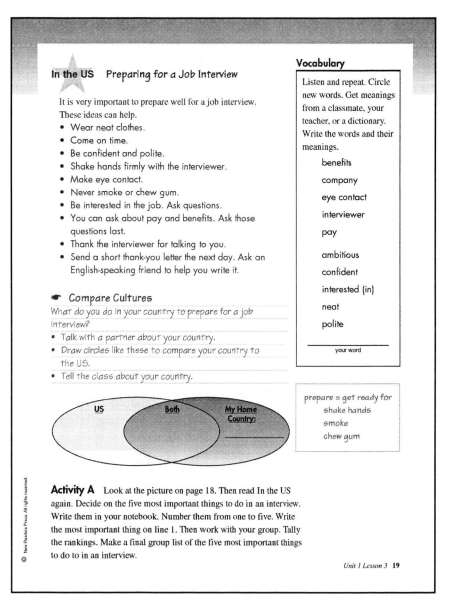

In the US   Preparing for a Job Interview

It is very important to prepare well for a job interview. These ideas can help.
- Wear neat clothes.
- Come on time.
- Be confident and polite.
- Shake hands firmly with the interviewer.
- Make eye contact.
- Never smoke or chew gum.
- Be interested in the job. Ask questions.
- You can ask about pay and benefits. Ask those questions last.
- Thank the interviewer for talking to you.
- Send a short thank-you letter the next day. Ask an English-speaking friend to help you write it.

Compare Cultures

What do you do in your country to prepare for a job interview?
- Talk with a partner about your country.
- Draw circles like these to compare your country to the US.
- Tell the class about your country.

US   Both   My Home Country:

Vocabulary

Listen and repeat. Circle new words. Get meanings from a classmate, your teacher, or a dictionary. Write the words and their meanings.

benefits

company

eye contact

interviewer

pay

ambitious

confident

interested (in)

neat

polite

_____
your word

prepare = get ready for
shake hands
smoke
chew gum

Activity A   Look at the picture on page 18. Then read In the US again. Decide on the five most important things to do in an interview. Write them in your notebook. Number them from one to five. Write the most important thing on line 1. Then work with your group. Tally the rankings. Make a final group list of the five most important things to do to in an interview.

Unit 1 Lesson 3 **19**

- Tell learners to write the name of their home country on the blank line.

To complete the activity, follow these steps:
- Put learners in pairs. Have them talk about their countries and add information to their circles.
- Ask volunteers to tell the class how people prepare for job interviews in their home countries.
- Have partners interview each other about their respective customs and take notes.

Activity A

- After each group finishes, compile the answers to make a list that includes all learners.
- Tally class responses on the board or an overhead transparency.

 Assign Workbook pp. 8–9.

Activity B
Help less advanced learners label their pictures as described in the student book.

Extension
Ask learners to think of a title for the class poster. Have a learner with good printing skills write it on the poster.

Activity C
• Assign a number to each small group so that voting can be done by number only.
• Tell learners that two persons in each small group will play the roles of job applicant and interviewer. The third person in the group can play the role of a second interviewer or other company employee, or participate only in the planning and scripting.
• Encourage learners to have fun and exaggerate while planning the role-play.

Activity D
• Put learners in groups.
• Review the directions in the student book to make sure learners understand the Give One, Get One activity.
• After learners write the questions in their notebooks, list the questions on the board.
• Have learners check their work or a partner's against the list on the board.

Extension
Ask learners if they can think of other good questions. Add the best ones to the list on the board and encourage learners to add them to the list in their notebooks.

Attention Box
Read the word and its definition to learners, pointing or miming to convey meaning if necessary. Point out that personal *strengths* are the topic of Task 3.

Activity B Look at catalogs and magazines. Cut out pictures of people dressed for your dream job. Make a class poster with the pictures. Write your name, your skills, and your dream job under the picture you selected. Hang your poster in the classroom.

Activity C With a small group, role-play a really bad interview. Look at the list of things to do in In the US. Try to do everything wrong. You can talk a lot or you can talk very little. Let the class select the worst interview and explain why it is the worst.

Activity D Work in a group. Play Give One, Get One:
• Each group member writes one question to ask in an interview.
• Send a group member to other groups to give a question to and get a question from each group.
• Write a list of questions in your group.
• Write all the questions in your notebook.
  1. What are the work hours?

One Step Up
Use the class poster to tell the class about your dream job.
Say these things:
My name is

_____

I can

_____

I have a dream job. It is

_____

I think I will be successful because I am

_____

TASK 3 Talk about Your Strengths
Read the list below. Check your strengths. With a partner, give examples of your strengths.

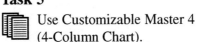
strengths = things that you do well

____ am organized	____ am hard-working
____ can teach skills	____ have many interests
____ speak two languages	____ can learn fast
____ come to work on time	____ _____
____ have job experience	(another strength)

In a chart like this one, write how you use the skills. Think carefully about your strengths. You don't have to write something about every skill in every column.

Skills	Family	Work	School	Community
I am organized.	I help my children get to school on time.			

This vocabulary should be understood, but learners should not be expected to produce the word at this point.

Task 3
Use Customizable Master 4 (4-Column Chart).
Customize the master by dividing a column in two to make a five-column chart. Write the five heads in the student book across the top of the chart. Then follow the suggestions on p. 7 for duplicating the master and distributing the copies.

Have pairs of learners help each other complete their charts.

Extension
On the board or an overhead transparency, compile a class chart for all learners. List all the ways learners use the skills in the four environments.

Use Unit Masters 15 (Game: Good and Bad Job Interviews) and 16 (Thinking Skill: Making Decisions) now or at any time during the rest of the unit.

Review Unit Skills
See p. 8 for suggestions on games and activities to review the vocabulary and grammar in this unit.

Unit 1 Project

Learners complete an application form.

Get Ready

Review what learners did in Tasks 1, 2, and 3, which built skills for the unit project. Then do the following:

• Help learners gather the information needed to complete the form in the student book. If necessary, ask them to bring the information from home to the next class session.

• Have learners fill in the form.

• Remind learners that they wrote a job history for Task 2.

Do the Work

Use Unit Master 17 (Unit 1 Project: Complete an Application Form). Distribute a copy to each learner. Have learners complete the form independently.

Present Your Project

• Have learners use the questions from Activity D on p. 20 in their interviews.

• Tell learners to use their job ladder (Task 1) and their list of strengths (Task 3) to answer interview questions.

• Have pairs of learners practice interviewing each other.

• Encourage learners to pretend they are going for a job interview for their dream job.

Ongoing Assessment

While learners are completing this activity, walk around the room and listen to their interviews. Try to listen to at least five different interviews. Make notes on how well learners perform on the following features:

a. Interview preparation: dress and information
   0 = no preparation
   1 = somewhat prepared
   2 = very well prepared

UNIT 1 Project

Complete an Application Form

Sometimes companies and schools want you to complete an application form at the interview. It can help to have an information form ready.

Get Ready

Complete this information form. Bring it with you to job interviews or school interviews.

PERSONAL:

Name: _____ Date of Birth: _____

Address: _____ Phone: _____

Emergency Contact: _____ Phone: _____

WORK EXPERIENCE: (List last job first.)

Dates	Company	Contact Person

EDUCATION/TRAINING:

High School: _____

Dates: _____

Technical School: _____

Dates: _____

Higher Education: _____

Dates: _____

Do the Work

Get the application form from your teacher. Complete the application. Use the information that you wrote in Get Ready.

Present Your Project

Have an interview party with your class. Practice interviewing for your dream job with your teacher or a counselor. Dress correctly to interview for this job. Use your information form to talk about your strengths. Explain why your strengths are important for this job.

Writing Extension In your notebook, write about your dream job. What is most exciting about the job? What seems most difficult? Why?

Technology Extra
Use a computer to type your basic information worksheet. Or use the Internet to look for your dream job. Can you find the average salary?

Unit 1 Project 21

---

b. Information and application form
   0 = not completed, or completed but with errors that interfere with meaning
   1 = some information, some errors
   2 = completed with no errors or few minor errors

c. Fluency and communicative ability
   0 = very poor
   1 = communicates haltingly
   2 = communicates clearly and with confidence

Assign Workbook p. 10 (Check Your Progress). Go over this self-assessment with learners. Be sure they understand how to complete it, especially the first part.

• Explain that the numbers represent a rating scale, with *1* being the lowest score and *5* being the highest.

• If learners have difficulty using the scale, explain that a *2* rating means *not very well, but improving* and that a *4* rating means *fairly well.*

Use Unit Master 18 (Unit Checkup/Review) whenever you complete this unit.

Unit 2: New Beginnings 🌐

Materials for the Unit

- Magnet and steel items
- Toy telephones or cellular phones
- Assorted flyers (optional)
- Picture of the Statue of Liberty (optional)
- Variety of household devices for measuring volume and weight (e.g., measuring cups and spoons, bathroom scales)
- American cookbooks and song-books (optional)
- Customizable Masters 3–6
- Generic Assessment Master 8
- Unit Masters 19–25
- Vocabulary Card Masters for Unit 2

New Beginnings

- Follow the suggestions on p. 5 for talking about titles. Then read the unit goals listed under the title.
- Tell learners this unit focuses on *coming together* by sharing talents and skills.

Explain the meaning of the expression *coming together* by doing the following:

- Bring a magnet and several steel items to class.
- Demonstrate how the magnet attracts the items.
- Discuss how some people can be like magnets. Do they attract good people or bad people? Why?
- Ask learners about personal examples of people who help them *come together* with others.

Question

Read the question below the arrow. List learners' responses on the board or an overhead transparency or put them into an idea map.

Photo

Follow the suggestions on p. 5 for talking about the photo. Ask questions like these:

- Who is Fotini?
- Where is she from?

22 Unit 2

- What is she doing?
- Who are the people waiting for her?
- How many granddaughters does Fotini have?
- Why is Ritza glad that her mother came to the US?

Think and Talk

- Ask learners to discuss the questions in pairs or small groups.
- Then have the groups report back to the class.

Answers

1. Fotini is in an airport.
2. Answers may vary. Possible answer: She is happy.
3. Answers will vary.

Picture Dictionary

Follow the suggestions on p. 6 for introducing and reinforcing vocabulary.

- Have individual learners act out the words that can be mimed while other learners try to guess the words.
- Follow the suggestions on p. 6 for using vocabulary cards. Use the Vocabulary Card Masters for the words in the Picture Dictionary.

Gather Your Thoughts

Use Customizable Master 5 (Idea Map). Follow the suggestions on p. 7 for customizing and duplicating the master. Make a copy for each learner.

- Have learners bring in photos of themselves in their home countries and in the US. Create a poster with all the photos.
- Have learners label their photos with descriptions of how they felt (e.g., I felt nervous when I first moved to the US. I felt excited at my sister's wedding in El Salvador.).

What's the Problem?

Follow the suggestions on p. 5 for identifying and analyzing problems.

Model the issue of change with these steps:

- Tell learners about a change in your life.
- Tell them the reason for the change.
- Tell how you felt about the change.

Ask learners to talk about the feelings they had when they came to the US.

- Write on the board or an overhead transparency sentences like the ones below. Use the past tense of regular and common irregular verbs.

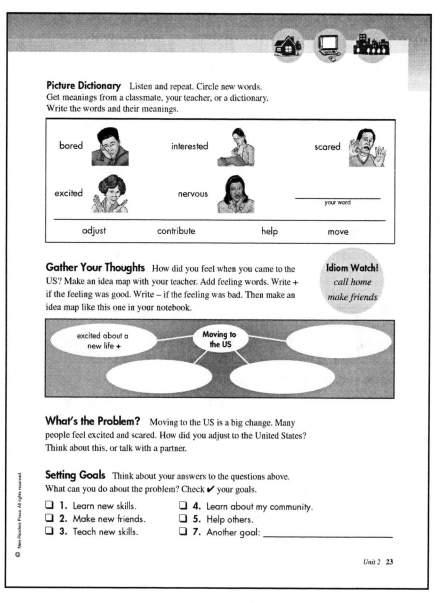

Picture Dictionary Listen and repeat. Circle new words. Get meanings from a classmate, your teacher, or a dictionary. Write the words and their meanings.

bored   interested   scared

excited   nervous   _____ your word

adjust   contribute   help   move

Gather Your Thoughts How did you feel when you came to the US? Make an idea map with your teacher. Add feeling words. Write + if the feeling was good. Write – if the feeling was bad. Then make an idea map like this one in your notebook.

Idiom Watch!
call home
make friends

excited about a new life +   Moving to the US

What's the Problem? Moving to the US is a big change. Many people feel excited and scared. How did you adjust to the United States? Think about this, or talk with a partner.

Setting Goals Think about your answers to the questions above. What can you do about the problem? Check ✔ your goals.

- ❏ 1. Learn new skills.
- ❏ 2. Make new friends.
- ❏ 3. Teach new skills.
- ❏ 4. Learn about my community.
- ❏ 5. Help others.
- ❏ 7. Another goal: _____

Unit 2 **23**

When I got my first job, I felt scared.
I moved to a small apartment.

- Have learners work in pairs.
- Ask them to write sentences about their own changes and feelings and about those of their partner.

Setting Goals

Follow the suggestions on p. 5 for setting goals.

- Remind learners to include things they can do to adjust to life in a new place and to contribute to their community.
- Have partners talk about their goals for this unit.

One Step Up
Orally proficient learners can share their information with the class.

Lesson 1: Adjusting to a New Country

Follow the suggestions on p. 5 for talking about titles.

- To convey the meaning of the title, write the following on the board or an overhead transparency:

  adjust to a new country = learn to live in a new country OR learn to feel at home in a new country

- Explain that in this lesson learners will list how they can use their skills at home, at work, and in the community. They will also learn to take a phone message.

Questions

Read the questions above the photo. To help learners understand and answer them, ask these additional questions:

- What do phone messages usually say? *(name, phone number, reason for call, when to call the person)*
- Do people speak slowly?
- Do they speak clearly?

Listening Tip

- Read the listening tip aloud.
- Tell learners that when listening to a phone message, they should always have a pen or pencil and paper.
- To help learners get ready to listen, have them write these cues in their notebooks:

  Name: _____

  Phone number: _____

  Message: _____

🎧 Play the audio or read the listening script on p. 118. Follow the suggestions on p. 5 for listening comprehension.

Talk or Write

This exercise helps learners become skilled at listening to phone messages.

Adjusting to a New Country

- ◆ Talk about daily actions and skills
- ◆ Take a phone message
- ◆ Use simple past tense (Review)

Is listening to phone messages difficult for you? Why?

- ◆ Listening Tip 🎧 One way to understand a phone message is to save the message and listen again. It is also good to take notes. Now you will hear a phone message. Get ready to write notes. You will need a pen and paper. First listen to the message. Don't write. Listen again. Take notes. Answer these questions. Check your answers with a partner. You can read the words on page 118.

I hope I can understand this message.

Fotini wants to understand the message. Then she can tell her daughter about it.

Talk or Write
1. Who called?
2. What did she want?
3. Where are the sisters?

24 Unit 2 Lesson 1

Answers
1. Raisa called.
2. She wanted to tell her mother and grandmother that she and Luisa are at school.
3. They are at school.

Picture Dictionary

Follow the suggestions on p. 6 for introducing and reinforcing vocabulary.

Have individual learners act out the words that can be mimed while other learners guess the words.

Follow the suggestions on p. 6 for using vocabulary cards. Use the Vocabulary Card Masters for the words in the Picture Dictionary.

Class Chat

Have learners copy the chart in their notebooks or use Customizable Master 3 (3-Column Chart). Follow the suggestions on p. 7 for customizing and duplicating the master. Make a copy for each learner.

Grammar Talk

Follow the suggestions on p. 7 for introducing the grammar point.

Answer

To make the simple past, add *-ed* to the base form of the verb.

Write on the board or an overhead transparency these additional verbs in simple present and simple past:

listen	*listened*
look	*looked*
stop	*stopped*
like	*liked*

Extension

On the board or an overhead transparency, write in random order the simple present of the verbs from the student book and the additional ones you have listed.

Have learners give the past form of each. Write it next to the present form.

One Step Up

For each verb, have learners suggest sentences to write on the board or an overhead transparency. They can use sentences from their Class Chat or create new ones.

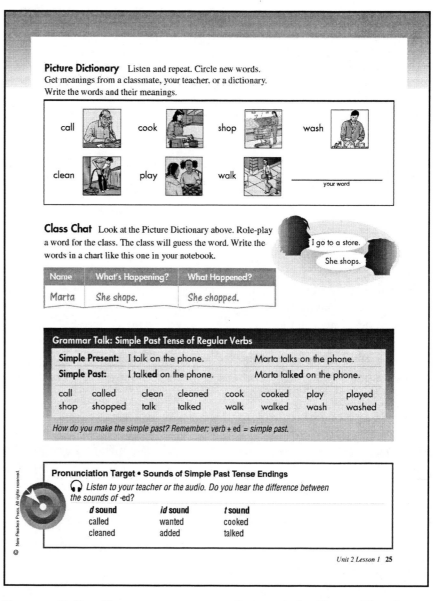

Picture Dictionary Listen and repeat. Circle new words. Get meanings from a classmate, your teacher, or a dictionary. Write the words and their meanings.

call cook shop wash

clean play walk _____ your word

Class Chat Look at the Picture Dictionary above. Role-play a word for the class. The class will guess the word. Write the words in a chart like this one in your notebook.

I go to a store.
She shops.

Name	What's Happening?	What Happened?
Marta	She shops.	She shopped.

Grammar Talk: Simple Past Tense of Regular Verbs

Simple Present:	I talk on the phone.	Marta talks on the phone.
Simple Past:	I talk**ed** on the phone.	Marta talk**ed** on the phone.

call	called	clean	cleaned	cook	cooked	play	played
shop	shopped	talk	talked	walk	walked	wash	washed

How do you make the simple past? Remember: verb + ed = simple past.

Pronunciation Target • Sounds of Simple Past Tense Endings

🎧 Listen to your teacher or the audio. Do you hear the difference between the sounds of -ed?

d sound	*id* sound	*t* sound
called	wanted	cooked
cleaned	added	talked

Unit 2 Lesson 1 **25**

Pronunciation Target

🎧 Play the audio or read the verbs in the Pronunciation Target, stressing the past-tense ending.

- Check individual learners to make sure they are able to discriminate between the three different sounds of the simple past ending.
- Say a verb in past tense and ask learners to say whether it sounds like *d, id,* or *t*.
- Have learners make a three-column chart in their notebooks, using the three headings in the Pronunciation Target. Then have them write other past-tense verbs in the correct columns.

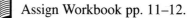 Assign Workbook pp. 11–12.

Activity A

Write the model sentences from the student book on the board or an overhead transparency.

Activity B

- Put learners in pairs. Provide each pair with two cellular phones or toy phones.
- Following the directions in the student book, have each pair act out calling each other and leaving messages.

Activity C

Play the audio or read the listening script below.

- Ask learners to take notes as they listen to the conversation.
- Then have partners discuss their notes and add some lines to the conversation.

Listening Script

Listen to Fotini and her daughter Ritza talk.

Ritza: Mom, are you sorry that you came to the United States?

Fotini: Oh, no. But sometimes I'm not sure that I can help.

Ritza: You help us so much! The girls and I are very happy that you are here.

Extension

Ask for volunteers to role-play the conversation between Fotini and Ritza.

Task 1

Use Customizable Master 4 (4-Column Chart). Follow the suggestions on p. 7 for customizing and duplicating the master. Make a copy for each learner.

One Step Down

Have the whole group do the activity together.

- Write the heads in four columns on the board or an overhead transparency.

Activity A   Class Chat Follow-Up Look at your Class Chat chart. In your notebook, write sentences about your classmates.

Marta talks on the phone. Marta talked on the phone.

Activity B Work with a partner. Leave a message, and listen to a message. Do these things:

1. **Partner A:** Write a note, call a friend, and leave a message to invite the friend to dinner.
2. **Partner B:** Listen to the message, and take notes.
3. **Partner B:** Leave a message. Partner A: take notes.

When you leave a message, say these things:

- Your name: _____
- Why you called: _____
- _____
- Call back? _____
- _____
- Your phone number: _____

When you take notes, write these things:

```
IMPORTANT MESSAGE
Name of caller: _____
Message: _____
Call back?   Yes   No
Phone Number: _____
```

Activity C Listen to Fotini and her daughter Ritza talk. Ritza wants to help Fotini adjust. Work with a partner. Write an ending for their conversation.

 TASK 1   List Your Skills

Make a chart like this one. Write all your special skills. How can you use your skills with your family, at work, and in your community?

Skills	Family and Friends	Work	Community
Cook	Teach the children to cook.	Give recipes to people at work.	Bring cakes to church.

26   Unit 2 Lesson 1

- Ask learners to respond orally. Write their skills in the correct columns.
- Help learners engage in a class discussion about how each one can use his or her skills in the community.

Use Unit Master 19 (Grammar: An Interview) now or at any time during the rest of the unit.

Lesson 2: Giving and Learning ☀www

- Follow the suggestions on p. 5 for talking about titles.
- Read the lesson objectives listed below the title.
- Explain that in this lesson learners will make a poster for a class party. They will also think about how they can help in their communities.

Attention Box

Read the words to learners, pointing or miming to convey meaning when possible. This vocabulary should be understood, but learners should not be expected to produce the words at this point.

Question

Read the question aloud.
- Emphasize that when people have many family and work responsibilities, they may not have time to volunteer.
- Many older people volunteer, especially after they retire from their jobs.
- People who have time may volunteer at hospitals, their churches, or their children's schools.

Reading Tip

- Ask learners what they think this flyer is about.
- Point out the title of the flyer.
- Ask learners if they recall the meaning of the verb *scan*. Then read the tip together.

Caption

- Have learners look at the flyer and photo and read the caption.
- Be sure they understand the meaning of the phrases *a little* and *a lot*. Use these phrases to ask questions related to learners' lives or your classroom.

Talk or Write

Have learners scan the flyer. Then have pairs answer the questions. This exercise builds skill in scanning for information.

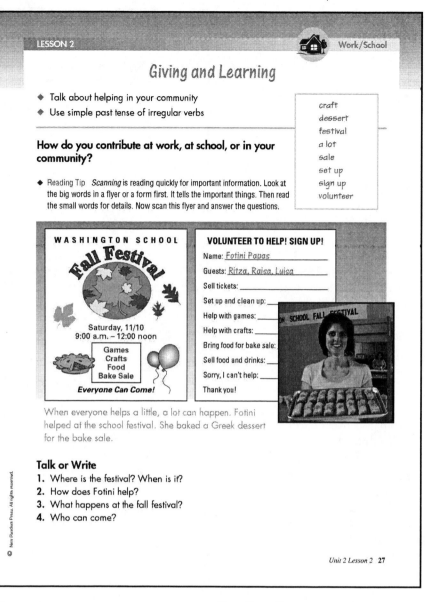

Unit 2 Lesson 2 27

Answers

1. The festival is at Washington School. It is in the fall, on Saturday, 11/10 (November 10), from 9:00 A.M. to 12:00 noon.
2. Fotini brings a Greek dessert for the bake sale.
3. They have games, crafts, food, and a bake sale.
4. Everyone can come.

Extension

Ask these additional questions:
- What other tasks can volunteers do?
- Did you ever go to a festival? If you did, where? When?

One Step Up

Bring other flyers to share with learners. Then do the following:
- Distribute the flyers, one to each small group.
- Have each group scan the information in their flyer.
- Assign a recorder in each group to take notes.
- Have a group reporter explain the group's flyer to the class.

Vocabulary

Follow the suggestions on p. 6 for introducing and reinforcing the vocabulary.

Act out each volunteer job after you write it. Have learners tell you what you are doing and where you would do this.

Follow the suggestions on p. 6 for using vocabulary cards. Use the Vocabulary Card Masters for the words in the Vocabulary box.

<u>One Step Up</u>
Have volunteers act out additional volunteer jobs while other learners guess what each job is.

Class Chat

- Assign each learner a volunteer job from the vocabulary list.
- Arrange learners' chairs in a circle. Ask for a volunteer to start the chat, following the directions in the student book.
- If learners have difficulty asking the question, tell them to refer to the place words in the vocabulary list.

Grammar Talk

Before introducing the past tense of irregular verbs, review the simple past of regular verbs, which learners studied in the previous lesson.

<u>Possible Answers</u>
Here are simple present and simple past forms of some other irregular verbs:

buy	*bought*
read	*read*
run	*ran*
speak	*spoke*
stand	*stood*
tell	*told*
think	*thought*
write	*wrote*

<u>Extension</u>
Help learners memorize the simple past forms of the verbs in their

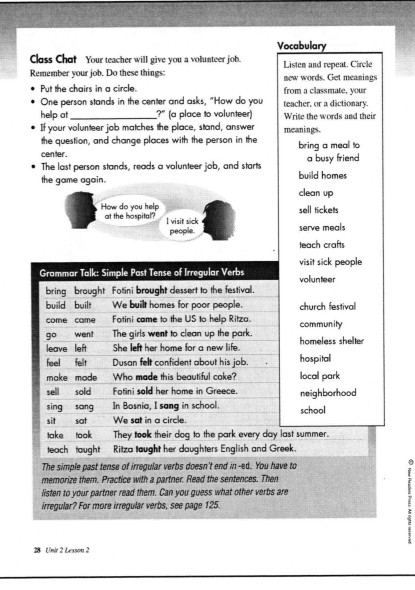

Class Chat Your teacher will give you a volunteer job. Remember your job. Do these things:

- Put the chairs in a circle.
- One person stands in the center and asks, "How do you help at _____?" (a place to volunteer)
- If your volunteer job matches the place, stand, answer the question, and change places with the person in the center.
- The last person stands, reads a volunteer job, and starts the game again.

How do you help at the hospital?

I visit sick people.

Grammar Talk: Simple Past Tense of Irregular Verbs

bring	brought	Fotini **brought** dessert to the festival.
build	built	We **built** homes for poor people.
come	came	Fotini **came** to the US to help Ritza.
go	went	The girls **went** to clean up the park.
leave	left	She **left** her home for a new life.
feel	felt	Dusan **felt** confident about his job.
make	made	Who **made** this beautiful cake?
sell	sold	Fotini **sold** her home in Greece.
sing	sang	In Bosnia, I **sang** in school.
sit	sat	We **sat** in a circle.
take	took	They **took** their dog to the park every day last summer.
teach	taught	Ritza **taught** her daughters English and Greek.

The simple past tense of irregular verbs doesn't end in -ed. You have to memorize them. Practice with a partner. Read the sentences. Then listen to your partner read them. Can you guess what other verbs are irregular? For more irregular verbs, see page 125.

Vocabulary

Listen and repeat. Circle new words. Get meanings from a classmate, your teacher, or a dictionary. Write the words and their meanings.

bring a meal to a busy friend

build homes

clean up

sell tickets

serve meals

teach crafts

visit sick people

volunteer

church festival

community

homeless shelter

hospital

local park

neighborhood

school

28   *Unit 2 Lesson 2*

books by facilitating the following activities:

- One learner says the simple present form and another tries to give the simple past without looking at the book.
- Have learners close their books. Write the simple present form of the verbs from the student book in random order on the board or an overhead transparency. Ask learners to call out the past form and write it next to each verb.
- Have learners keep their books closed while they suggest past-tense sentences for the verbs.

These can be either the sentences from their Class Chat charts from Lesson 1 or new ones. Write the sentences on the board or a transparency beside the appropriate present and past verb forms.

<u>One Step Up</u>
Have learners call out sentences using the past tense of the verbs they listed in the Grammar Talk. Write the sentences on the board.

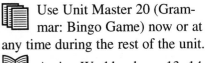 Use Unit Master 20 (Grammar: Bingo Game) now or at any time during the rest of the unit.

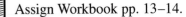 Assign Workbook pp. 13–14.

Pronunciation Target

Have learners copy the chart in their notebooks or use Customizable Master 4 (4-Column Chart). Follow the suggestions on p. 7 for customizing the master. Make a copy for each learner.

Play the audio or read the listening script below. Pause after each pair of words.

Listening Script

Listen for the different sounds of *o*.
shop, got
phone, broke
road, coach
low, throw

Extension

Ask learners to make a new chart in their notebooks with the same heads. Dictate the words in random order and have learners write them in the correct column.

One Step Up

Ask learners to look through the student book to find other words with *o* sounds and tell you in which column to write them.

Use Unit Master 21 (Phonics: Sounds of *o*) now or at any time during the rest of the unit.

Activity A

Write the model question and answer on the board or a transparency.

One Step Up

Ask volunteers to role-play.

Activity B

Remind learners there are more irregular verbs on p. 125 in their books.

Attention Box

This vocabulary should be understood, but learners should not be expected to produce the words at this point.

Activity C

Read aloud the list of ways to help.

Pronunciation Target • Sounds of *o*

Listen to your teacher or the audio.

Short *o*	Long *o*	Long *o*	Long *o*
shop	phone	road	low
got	broke	coach	throw

The letter *o* has different sounds in English. Copy this chart in your notebook.

Activity A Class Chat Follow-Up Use the sentences from the Class Chat. Write sentences in the simple past tense. Put a check ✔ by the irregular verbs.

How did you help at the hospital? I visited sick people.

One Step Up
Role-play something you did yesterday. The class can guess what you did.

Activity B Look at the volunteer flyer on page 27. Write things that volunteers did at the school festival. Use the past tense.

1. _They sold tickets._

2. _____

3. _____

4. _____

Activity C Think about these ways to help in your community. Write two more ways in your notebook. Check the most interesting thing to do.

- Clean up a public place.
- Walk in a walk-a-thon.
- Start a baby-sitting service with other parents.
- Organize an international party and invite friends and family.

international
invite
service

TASK 2 Make a Poster for a Class Party
Work with your class. Design a poster or a flyer for an international class party. Write these things on the poster: what the party is for, where the party is, what day and time the party is, and who to talk to about the party.

Extension

Have learners work in groups. Distribute a large sheet of paper and a marker to each group.

Ask learners to tell their groups about their own volunteer experiences: Where did they volunteer? What did they do? How did they feel?

One learner in the group records the answers, writing sentences. Another learner copies the sentences on large paper. A third learner reads the sentences to the class.

Extension

Have learners role-play a telephone call offering to help. Use this sample conversation:

Student A: Hello, I'm a parent. I'm calling because I want to help in my child's school.
Student B: That's great. Who is your child?
Student A: His name is Reggie Rivero, and he's in third grade.
Student B: Well, please give me your name and telephone number. I'll ask our assistant principal to call you.

Task 2

- Distribute poster board and other supplies.
- Encourage learners to illustrate the poster with their own artwork or with cutouts from magazines or catalogs.

Lesson 3: Sharing Cultures in the US

Introduce the words *sharing* and *culture* from the title.

- Act out *sharing* food with someone. Use an idea map to show aspects of *culture* (e.g., art, music, food, values).
- Point out the lesson objectives listed below the title.
- Tell learners that they will share a song from their culture. They will also calculate liquid and solid measurements and learn about immigration in the US.

Question

- Read the question aloud.
- Help learners brainstorm answers by drawing an idea map on the board. Write *Reasons for Coming to the US* in the center circle.
- Ask learners to give their own reasons. Write them in the surrounding circles.

Reading Tip

- Ask learners to define the word *context*.
- Tell learners to write any new words in their notebooks. Have them work in groups of three to find definitions for the words.
- Have each group share its list of new words with all learners.
- Assign a recorder from each group to write the group's new words on the board or an overhead transparency.

Extension

Talk about the cultural significance of the Statue of Liberty.

- Bring in a picture or drawing of the Statue of Liberty.
- Write the best-known part of the statue's inscription on the board or an overhead transparency:
  Give me your tired, your poor,
  Your huddled masses yearning
  to breathe free,
  The wretched refuse of your
  teeming shore.

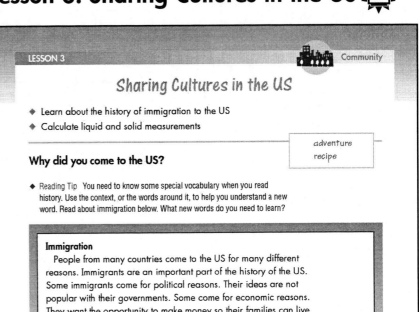

Send these, the homeless,
tempest-tost, to me,
I lift my lamp beside the
golden door!

- Read the inscription slowly and dramatically. Learners at this level may not understand many of the words, but you can demonstrate their power.
- Provide a simple paraphrase of the inscription for your learners.

Talk or Write

This exercise helps learners find context clues for what they read.

Answers

1. "Their ideas are not popular with their governments."
2. *Economic* means *related to money* or *about money.*
3. Two personal reasons for coming to the US might be to join family or to find adventure.

Extension

Ask these additional questions:

- Does everyone come to the US for the same reason? Explain.
- What are some other reasons for coming to the US?
- Why are immigrants important in the history of the US?

Vocabulary

Follow the suggestions on p. 6 for introducing and reinforcing vocabulary.

Follow the suggestions on p. 6 for using vocabulary cards. Use the Vocabulary Card Masters for the words in the Vocabulary box.

Attention Box

Read the word to learners, pointing or miming to convey meaning. This word should be understood, but learners should not be expected to produce it at this point.

In the US

- Show learners a number of household measuring devices.
- Ask learners if they already use conversion tables. What can they do with this information?

Extensions

1. Write on the board some simple metric measures like the ones below. Ask learners to convert each to a measurement in the US system.

   5 liters to gallons (*1.32 gallons*)
   10 grams to ounces (*0.35 ounce*)
   6 kilos to pounds (*13.23 pounds*)
   Continue doing sample conversions until all learners can perform them successfully.

2. To help learners apply this content to real-life situations, ask them to bring in recipes from their countries that list measurements in the metric system. Have learners work in groups to convert the measurements. If learners wish to exchange recipes, encourage and facilitate this cultural sharing process.

One Step Up

Assist learners in converting their recipes to US measurements.

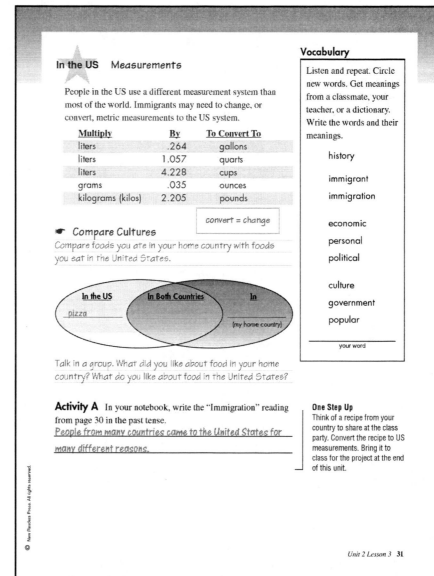

Compare Cultures

Make a copy of Customizable Master 6 (Venn Diagram). Then do the following:

- Title the diagram *Foods I Eat.*
- Write the following as heads at the top of the two circles:

   In _____ (My Home Country)
   In the US

- Write the head *In Both Countries* at the top of the overlapping part.

Follow the suggestions on p. 7 for duplicating the master. Give a copy to each learner.

- Have partners write the *In the US* part of their diagrams together.
- After individual learners complete their *Home Country* and *In Both Countries* sections, have them explain their diagram to their partner.
- Have volunteers share their charts with the class.

Activity A

As learners write the passage, circulate to assist anyone having difficulty with the past-tense forms.

Assign Workbook pp. 15–16.

Review Unit Skills

See p. 8 for suggestions on games and activities to review the vocabulary and grammar in this unit.

Attention Boxes

Read the words to learners, pointing or miming to convey meaning when possible. This vocabulary should be understood, but learners should not be expected to produce the words at this point.

Activity B

Have learners copy the chart in their notebooks or use Customizable Master 3 (3-Column Chart). Follow the suggestions on p. 7 for customizing and duplicating the master. Make a copy for each learner.

Extension

As learners share their answers in Activity B, write them on the board as sentences using the past tense (e.g., *In 1999 Ming Wu left China to come to the US to get married.*).

One Step Up

Encourage learners to use the World Map on pp. 122–123 in the student book to show where each of their famous immigrants came from.

Activity C

Have learners copy the chart in their notebooks or use Customizable Master 3 (3-Column Chart). Follow the suggestions on p. 7 for customizing and duplicating the master. Make a copy for each learner.

Activity D

After learners have calculated the conversions, do the conversions together on the board or an overhead transparency so learners can check their work.

Answers
1. 1 liter milk = 0.264 gallon
2. 3 kilos potatoes = 6.615 pounds
3. 300 grams cheese = 10.5 ounces

Task 3

- Tell learners their song can be very short. It can also be a poem

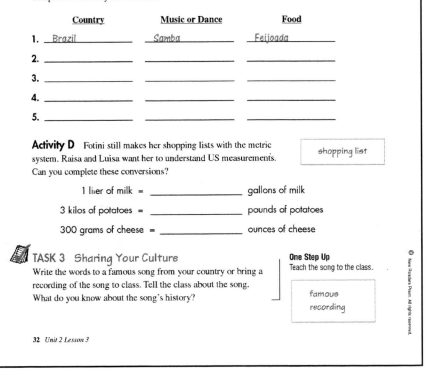

Activity B With your group, tell why you came to the US. In your notebook, make a chart for your group.

Date	Name	Reason for Coming to US
1. 1999	Ming Wu	to get married
2.		

One Step Up
Do you know a famous immigrant from your home country? Tell the class about that person.

Activity C Talk in a group of four or five students. Talk about music or dances from your home countries and other countries. Complete a chart in your notebook.

Country	Music or Dance	Food
1. Brazil	Samba	Feijoada
2.		
3.		
4.		
5.		

Activity D Fotini still makes her shopping lists with the metric system. Raisa and Luisa want her to understand US measurements. Can you complete these conversions?

shopping list

1 liter of milk = _____ gallons of milk

3 kilos of potatoes = _____ pounds of potatoes

300 grams of cheese = _____ ounces of cheese

TASK 3 Sharing Your Culture
Write the words to a famous song from your country or bring a recording of the song to class. Tell the class about the song. What do you know about the song's history?

One Step Up
Teach the song to the class.

famous recording

or verse from their country rather than a song.
- Some learners may prefer to bring a recipe rather than a song from their home country.

One Step Up

Encourage learners to teach their songs, but be sure any performance or teaching is done willingly.

Assessment

Use Generic Assessment Master 8 (Oral Communication Rubric) to evaluate the performances.

Extension

Bring some American cookbooks and songbooks to share with learners. You may want to select several recipes that are classics in the US, such as apple or pumpkin pie, brownies, meatloaf, or fried chicken. You can select some songs that are also classics from various eras and regions. If you enjoy singing and/or play a portable instrument, use your talent to further enliven this activity for your learners.

Use Unit Masters 22 (Thinking Skill: Pie Chart) and 23 (Life Skill: Share a Recipe) now or at any time during the rest of the unit.

Unit 2 Project

Learners plan an international party.

Attention Box

Read the word and its definition to learners, pointing or miming to convey meaning if necessary. This vocabulary should be understood, but learners should not be expected to produce the word at this point.

Get Ready

 Use Unit Master 24 (Unit 2 Project: Plan an International Party). Distribute a copy to each learner.

- Talk to learners about what they did in Task 1 (List Your Skills), Task 2 (Make a Poster for a Class Party), and Task 3 (Sharing Your Culture).
- Ask questions to encourage them to provide some of this information on their own.
- Help learners collect the songs that were presented for Task 3.
- Help all learners reach consensus about the date and time of their celebration.
- If learners are allowed to invite guests to the party, decide how many and help them create a guest list.
- Have learners work in national or cultural groups to plan their celebrations.

Do the Work

- Schedule regular meetings to continue the planning.
- Check regularly to make sure all learners understand their responsibilities.
- Have pairs of learners practice talking about their contributions to each other.
- Help learners successfully carry out their plans. Enjoy the celebration!

 Use Unit Master 23 (Life Skill: Share a Recipe). Give a

UNIT 2 Project

Plan an International Party

Plan an international celebration for your class.

Get Ready

In small groups, with other people from your home country, plan a celebration. Is it difficult for your class to have a party now? Select a date later in the school year, maybe before a vacation or at the end of school. Write things that each member of the group can contribute. Make a chart like this one.

celebration = party

Contribution	Describe	Name and Home Country
Food and recipe	empanadas (turnovers)	Felicia Gomez—Peru
Song or dance		
Photos with words		
Books and magazines		
Crafts		
Drinks/sodas		

Do the Work

1. Meet every week with your group to talk about the party plans. Use the chart from your teacher to make a time line.
2. Write recipes on the form your teacher gives you. Collect the class recipes and collect the songs from Task 3 (page 32).
3. Make a class book of recipes and songs from your home countries.
4. One or two students can volunteer to make a cover for the book.

Present Your Project

At the party, tell the class about what you contributed to the party.

Writing Extension Write your project presentation in your notebook.

Technology Extra
Leave a phone message for your teacher at your school. Tell what you liked best about the class party.

Unit 2 Project 33

---

copy to each learner to use in preparing the class book of recipes and songs.

Present Your Project

- Have learners tell everyone present about their contributions to the party.
- Distribute copies of the class book to learners.

Assessment

 Use Generic Assessment Master 8 (Oral Communication Rubric) to evaluate the presentations.

Writing Extension

Learners may want to write their presentations in their notebooks before their final presentations.

Technology Extra

Let learners know that you have received their messages.

Assign Workbook p. 17 (Check Your Progress).

Use Unit Master 25 (Unit 2 Checkup/Review) whenever you complete the unit.

Unit 3: Balancing Your Life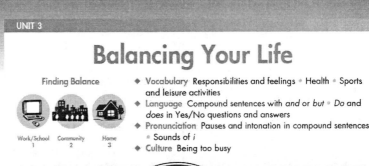

Materials for the Unit

- Three tennis balls
- Objects that represent three areas of life: family (e.g., a doll), work (e.g., a briefcase), and leisure (e.g., a ball)
- Articles, encyclopedias, and books on sports and leisure activities in different countries (optional)
- Newspaper articles, flyers, telephone books, and brochures from community centers about sports and leisure activities
- Picture that tells something about you and your life
- Towels (optional)
- Simple camera (optional)
- Customizable Masters 3–5
- Generic Assessment Masters 10–11
- Unit Masters 26–32
- Vocabulary Card Masters for Unit 3

Balancing Your Life

- Read the unit goals with learners. Then follow the suggestions on p. 5 for talking about the title.
- The theme of this unit is achieving a healthy balance of work and leisure in one's life.

One way to demonstrate the concept *balancing your life* is with juggling:
- Label three tennis balls *work, family,* and *leisure.*
- Demonstrate juggling for learners. Even if you cannot juggle well, your effort will inspire learners to try.
- Let everyone have fun juggling.
- If there are accomplished jugglers in the class, have learners vote for the best juggler.

As an alternative to juggling, bring to class objects that represent three areas of the learners' lives, e.g., a doll for family, a briefcase for work, a ball for leisure.

Another way to discuss *balancing your life* is by using a scale:

Is your life balanced?   Silvia Lopez feels tired, stressed, and sick.

- On the board or an overhead transparency, draw a simple, two-sided scale (e.g., the scale shown in representations of Justice).
- Mime a scale that is out of balance because the object on one side is heavier. Then mime a scale that is balanced because the objects on both sides weigh the same.
- Ask learners how this might apply to their lives.

Question

- Read the question below the arrow aloud for learners.
- Write three possible 24-hour schedules on the board.
- Compare the schedules. Which is most balanced?

Photo

Ask questions like these:
- How many children does Silvia have?
- What are they doing?
- How does Silvia feel?

Think and Talk

Have small groups discuss the questions and report back to the class.

Possible Answers
1. Silvia is cooking and watching her children.
2. She is tired, stressed, and sick.
3. No one is helping Silvia.
4. She wants to play tennis.
5. Answers will vary.

Picture Dictionary

Follow the suggestions on p. 6 for introducing and reinforcing vocabulary.

Have volunteers act out the words while other learners guess them.

Follow the suggestions on p. 6 for using vocabulary cards. Use the Vocabulary Card Masters for the words in the Picture Dictionary.

Gather Your Thoughts

- Model *responsibilities* for learners by describing your own. Use words from the Picture Dictionary to describe them (e.g., "I have many *responsibilities*. I *go to work* at the adult learning center. I also *do housework* at home, and I *care for my family*.").
- Then model *leisure activities* (e.g., "For leisure, I *exercise*. This helps me *relax*.").
- Ask volunteers to demonstrate how they *exercise*.
- Talk about how you feel about your *responsibilities* and *leisure activities*.

Use Customizable Master 5 (Idea Map). Follow the suggestions on p. 7 for customizing and duplicating the master. Make a copy for each learner.

- Have learners complete the idea map with their own feelings. Then have them discuss their ideas with a partner.
- Encourage learners to add vocabulary words to the map.
- Have them illustrate the words, either by drawing or by cutting and pasting from magazines.

Extension

Have learners bring in pictures or drawings of themselves doing the things they do for leisure. Create a display with the images and title it *Our Leisure Activities*. Have learners create captions for the pictures.

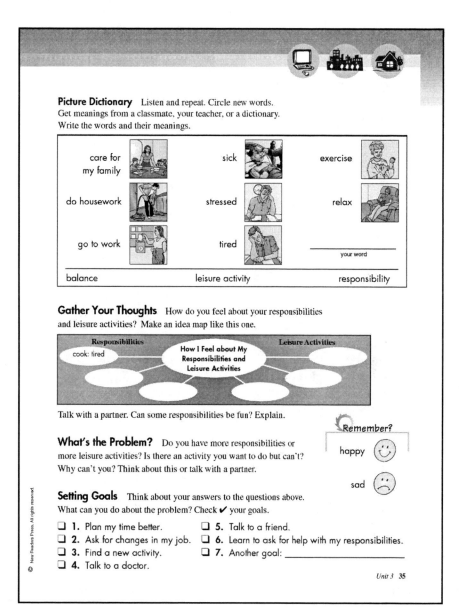

Picture Dictionary Listen and repeat. Circle new words. Get meanings from a classmate, your teacher, or a dictionary. Write the words and their meanings.

care for my family / sick / exercise / do housework / stressed / relax / go to work / tired / your word / balance / leisure activity / responsibility

Gather Your Thoughts How do you feel about your responsibilities and leisure activities? Make an idea map like this one.

Responsibilities — cook: tired / How I Feel about My Responsibilities and Leisure Activities / Leisure Activities

Talk with a partner. Can some responsibilities be fun? Explain.

What's the Problem? Do you have more responsibilities or more leisure activities? Is there an activity you want to do but can't? Why can't you? Think about this or talk with a partner.

Remember?
happy ☺
sad ☹

Setting Goals Think about your answers to the questions above. What can you do about the problem? Check ✔ your goals.

- ❑ 1. Plan my time better.
- ❑ 2. Ask for changes in my job.
- ❑ 3. Find a new activity.
- ❑ 4. Talk to a doctor.
- ❑ 5. Talk to a friend.
- ❑ 6. Learn to ask for help with my responsibilities.
- ❑ 7. Another goal: _____

Unit 3 **35**

What's the Problem?

Follow the suggestions on p. 5 for identifying and analyzing problems.

- Tell learners about something that you want to do but cannot.
- Tell why you cannot do it (e.g., too busy, not enough money).
- Tell how you feel about the situation (e.g. "I want to paint, but I can't because I'm too tired. I feel sad.")

Write the incomplete sentences below on the board or an overhead transparency:

_____ wants to _____, but _____.
_____ can't _____ because _____.
_____ feels _____.

Have learners complete the sentences in their notebooks, first about you and then about their partners.

Setting Goals

Follow the suggestions on p. 5 for setting goals.

Tell learners to think about things that they can do to improve their lives. Then have partners talk about their goals for this unit.

One Step Up

Orally proficient learners can share the information with the large group.

Lesson 1: Too Much Work!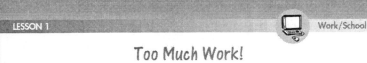

- Read the title aloud with learners and point out the lesson objectives below it.
- Explain that in this lesson learners will talk about their responsibilities at work or school. They will also learn how to ask for a change in a work schedule.

Attention Box

- Write *schedule* on the board or an overhead transparency and help learners pronounce it. Point out the *schedule* in their book.
- Ask for volunteers to describe a *nursing home*. Does anyone in the group work in a *nursing home* or visit someone there?
- Discuss other types of adult-care facilities in your community.
- Ask what work people do in a *laundry room*.
- Act out washing and folding laundry. Bring items such as towels to class to demonstrate the process, or use learners' sweaters or jackets.
- Ask volunteers to act out *laundry room* activities.

This vocabulary should be understood, but learners should not be expected to produce the words at this point.

Question

Read the introductory question and brainstorm answers with learners.

- Consider length of time and type of work.
- Record learners' responses on the board or an overhead transparency.

Reading Tip

Read the tip aloud with learners. Then do the following:

- Ask if any learners read a schedule at work. Some may need to interpret a schedule like this one to find their work hours each week.

Too Much Work!

◆ Talk about your responsibilities
◆ Use compound sentences with *and* or *but*

laundry room
nursing home
schedule

How much work is too much work?

◆ Reading Tip Learning to read schedules well is important. Now look at the schedule below. When does Silvia work?

Restful Nursing Home
Laundry Room Work Schedule

	S	M	T	W	TH	F	S
Silvia (Wash/dry)	6:00 a.m.–12:00 noon	6:00 a.m.–2:00 p.m.	6:00 a.m.–2:00 p.m.	6:00 a.m.–2:00 p.m.	6:00 a.m.–12:00 noon	6:00 a.m.–12:00 noon	
José (Fold/sort)		8:00 a.m.–4:00 p.m.	8:00 a.m.–4:00 p.m.	8:00 a.m.–4:00 p.m.	8:00 a.m.–4:00 p.m.	8:00 a.m.–2:00 p.m.	8:00 a.m.–2:00 p.m.
Julia (Wash/dry)	12:00 noon–6:00 p.m.	12:00 noon–8:00 p.m.	12:00 noon–8:00 p.m.	12:00 noon–8:00 p.m.	12:00 noon–6:00 p.m.		
Susan (Fold/sort)	8:00 a.m.–4:00 p.m.	8:00 a.m.–2:00 p.m.	8:00 a.m.–2:00 p.m.	8:00 a.m.–4:00 p.m.	8:00 a.m.–4:00 p.m.		
Miguel (Iron/deliver to rooms)	8:00 a.m.–4:00 p.m.	8:00 a.m.–4:00 p.m.	8:00 a.m.–4:00 p.m.	8:00 a.m.–2:00 p.m.			

> I feel sick, but I have to go to work.

Talk or Write
1. How many people work in the laundry room?
2. What do workers do in the laundry room?
3. When does Silvia work? How many hours does she work each week?

- Do they need to read every word? (*No, they need to look only for their own name and then note the hours they will work.*)
- For this schedule, tell learners to look only for the hours Silvia must work.
- When they read the Talk or Write questions, have them scan the schedule to find the answers.

Talk or Write

This exercise helps learners become skilled at reading schedules.

Answers
1. Five people work in the laundry room.
2. They wash and dry, fold and sort, and iron and deliver laundry.
3. Silvia works Sunday through Friday. She works 42 hours each week.

Extension
Ask these questions:
- What is the name of the nursing home?
- Is it "restful" for the laundry room workers?
- Who is it "restful" for?
- Who works as many hours as Silvia?
- Who works five days a week?
- Who works six days a week?

Picture Dictionary

Follow the suggestions on p. 6 for introducing and reinforcing vocabulary.

Have volunteers act out words that can be mimed while other learners try to guess the words.

Follow the suggestions on p. 6 for using vocabulary cards. Use the Vocabulary Card Masters for the words in the Picture Dictionary.

Class Chat

Use Customizable Master 3 (3-Column Chart). Follow the suggestions on p. 7 for customizing and duplicating the master. Make a copy for each learner.

- Ask two volunteers to model asking and answering questions.
- Then have learners walk around the room and talk with other classmates until they have filled in at least four rows of their chart.

Grammar Talk

Follow the suggestions on p. 7 for introducing the grammar point.

Extension

Depending on the abilities of your learners, share this information:

- *And* and *but* are conjunctions. Conjunctions can be used to connect two sentences to make a *compound sentence.*
- *And* means *added to, also,* or *at the same time.*
- *But* means *on the other hand* or *yet.*

Extension

Reinforce the meaning of *and* and *but* with this activity:

- Write the incomplete sentences below on the board or an overhead transparency:

  I _____, and I _____.
  I _____, and I feel _____.
  I _____, but I feel _____.

- Ask a volunteer to act out two activities that he or she does. Have learners guess the activities.

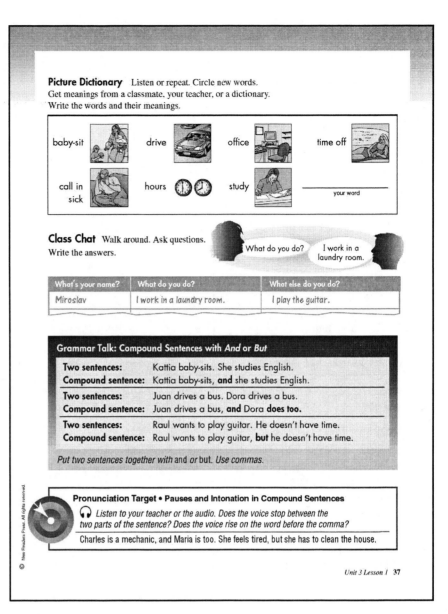

Unit 3 Lesson 1 37

- Write the activities on the blanks in the first sentence.
- Have another volunteer act out one responsibility and the way he or she feels about it. Have learners guess the responsibility and the feeling.
- Write the activity and the feeling on the blanks in one of the next two sentences. If the feeling is what someone would expect, write it in the *and* sentence. If the feeling is not what someone would expect, write it in the *but* sentence.
- Be sure learners understand that *but* signals oppositional facts.

Pronunciation Target

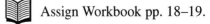 Play the audio or read the sentences, emphasizing the rhythm of rising and falling intonation.

- Pretend you are an orchestra conductor and lead learners in reading the sentences.
- Exaggerate the pause between the two parts of the compound structures.

Assign Workbook pp. 18–19.

Activity A

Extension

Have partners write a short story (i.e., a few connected sentences) with their sentences.

- Ask a few volunteers to dictate their stories to you as you write them on the board or an overhead transparency.
- Have the class read the stories as a shared reading activity.
- Use the stories for informal reading and writing extensions (e.g., *editing*: looking for/fixing errors; *word analysis*: underlining nouns, verbs, synonyms or antonyms; *comprehension*: *wh-* questions or *true/false* statements).
- Have one or both partners read aloud any stories not written on the board.

Activity B

Have two volunteers read the model sentences in the speech bubbles. Point out the use of *but* when *not* appears in the second part of a compound sentence.

Activity C

Have partners complete Silvia's note. Select learners to read the note aloud.

Answers

Can you change my <u>schedule</u>? I like my work at Restful Nursing Home, but I want to work only <u>five</u> days a week, from 6:00 to <u>12:00</u>. I need to <u>work</u> less because I also have to <u>study</u> English and <u>take care</u> of my family.

Task 1

Write on the board or an overhead transparency the following two sets of incomplete sentences:

___ works at ___.
___ works ___ hours a week.
___ works from ___ to ___.
___ goes to school at ___.
___ goes to school ___ hours a week.

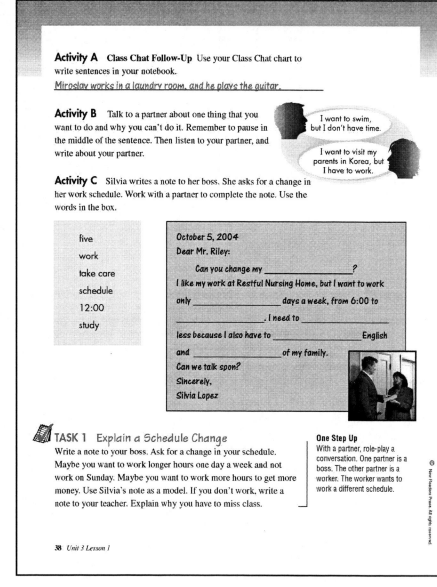

Activity A   Class Chat Follow-Up   Use your Class Chat chart to write sentences in your notebook.
Miroslav works in a laundry room, and he plays the guitar.

Activity B   Talk to a partner about one thing that you want to do and why you can't do it. Remember to pause in the middle of the sentence. Then listen to your partner, and write about your partner.

I want to swim, but I don't have time.

I want to visit my parents in Korea, but I have to work.

Activity C   Silvia writes a note to her boss. She asks for a change in her work schedule. Work with a partner to complete the note. Use the words in the box.

five
work
take care
schedule
12:00
study

October 5, 2004
Dear Mr. Riley:
    Can you change my _____?
I like my work at Restful Nursing Home, but I want to work only _____ days a week, from 6:00 to _____. I need to _____ less because I also have to _____ English and _____ of my family.
Can we talk soon?
Sincerely,
Silvia Lopez

TASK 1   Explain a Schedule Change
Write a note to your boss. Ask for a change in your schedule. Maybe you want to work longer hours one day a week and not work on Sunday. Maybe you want to work more hours to get more money. Use Silvia's note as a model. If you don't work, write a note to your teacher. Explain why you have to miss class.

One Step Up
With a partner, role-play a conversation. One partner is a boss. The other partner is a worker. The worker wants to work a different schedule.

___ goes to school from ___ to ___.

- Put learners in pairs.
- Have each learner complete one set of sentences about his or her partner.
- Select some learners to read aloud the sentences they wrote.

Have learners complete the task individually or in pairs.

- Encourage volunteers to read aloud the notes they wrote.
- Tell learners to use the Writing Checklist for Sentences on p. 126 to help them edit their notes.

Ongoing Assessment

Use the rubric below to evaluate this task. Make notes on how well learners perform on these criteria:

a. Mechanics
    0 = very weak
    1 = some errors
    2 = correct

b. Content
    0 = little information relevant to request
    1 = some relevant information
    2 = clear, convincing, and complete information

One Step Up

Have volunteers perform their conversations.

Lesson 2: Stressed! 🔆www🔆

- Read the lesson title aloud. Then read the lesson objectives below it.
- Explain that in this lesson learners will learn how to talk about their health problems. They will also learn how to chart their weekly activities.

Attention Box

- Read the words to learners, pointing or miming to convey meaning when possible.
- Also mime sore *throat* and *stomachache*. Write these words on the board or a transparency.
- Act out a patient with a *headache*. Mime the doctor writing out a *prescription*. Write these words on the board.
- Ask learners if they know what an antibiotic is. When does a doctor prescribe an antibiotic? *(when there is an infection)*

This vocabulary should be understood, but learners should not be expected to produce the words at this point.

Question

Read the introductory question aloud, and brainstorm answers with learners. Record their answers on an idea map on the board or an overhead transparency.

Listening Tip

Read the tip aloud.

🎧 Play the audio or read the listening script on p. 119. Follow the suggestions on p. 5 for listening comprehension.

Extension

Ask volunteers to identify and read the compound sentences in the listening script.

Talk or Write

This exercise helps learners practice focused listening.

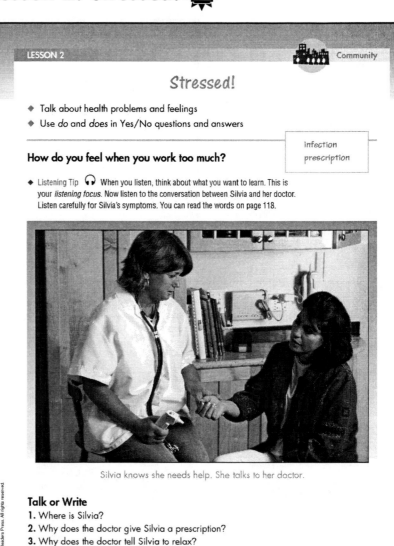

LESSON 2 Community

Stressed!

◆ Talk about health problems and feelings
◆ Use *do* and *does* in Yes/No questions and answers

infection
prescription

How do you feel when you work too much?

◆ Listening Tip 🎧 When you listen, think about what you want to learn. This is your *listening focus*. Now listen to the conversation between Silvia and her doctor. Listen carefully for Silvia's symptoms. You can read the words on page 118.

Silvia knows she needs help. She talks to her doctor.

Talk or Write
1. Where is Silvia?
2. Why does the doctor give Silvia a prescription?
3. Why does the doctor tell Silvia to relax?
What's Your Opinion? Will Silvia ask her family for help? Explain.

Unit 3 Lesson 2 **39**

- Have partners answer the questions and report back to the whole group.
- Have one partner read the question and the other answer it.

Answers
1. Silvia is at the doctor's office.
2. The doctor gives Silvia a prescription because Silvia probably has an infection.
3. The doctor tells Silvia to relax because Silvia works too much. Silvia needs to balance her life.

What's Your Opinion?

- Ask learners their opinions about sharing household chores and the responsibilities of husbands, wives, sons, daughters, and other relatives.
- Ask who works outside the house and who does not.

Vocabulary

Follow the suggestions on p. 6 for introducing and reinforcing vocabulary.

Follow the suggestions on p. 6 for using vocabulary cards. Use the Vocabulary Card Masters for the words in the Vocabulary box.

Have small groups use the new words to play "Symptom Charades":

- Each group receives vocabulary cards for all the symptom words in the Vocabulary box.
- Learners take turns acting out a symptom with facial expressions and body language.
- The group guesses the symptom.

One Step Up

Use the symptom words to write sentences on the board (e.g., *Carlos has a headache. Jamal has a sore throat.*). Have learners combine them into compound sentences (e.g., *Carlos has a headache, and Jamal has a sore throat.*).

Pronunciation Target

Play the audio or read the listening script on p. 119. Then do the following:

- Write these words in two columns on the board or an overhead transparency:

long *i*	short *i*
tired	sick
life	swim
night	

- Read the words aloud as you write, emphasizing the difference in the vowel sounds.
- Explain that the sound of long *i* is long and clear, while the sound of short *i* is short and unclear.
- Point out that a silent *e* at the end of a word often means the middle vowel is long (e.g., *life, bite, kite*). A consonant–vowel–consonant (*CVC*) pattern often means a short vowel (e.g., *bit, kit*).
- Have learners come to the board

and write one new word in the correct column as they say it.

Class Chat

Use Customizable Master 3 (3-Column Chart). Follow the suggestions on p. 7 for customizing and duplicating the master. Make a copy for each learner.

After all learners have spoken to one another, have volunteers read aloud what they wrote about another learner. Put the information into a class chart on the board or an overhead transparency.

Grammar Talk

Follow the suggestions on p. 7 for introducing the grammar point.

Answers

Use *does* with *he, she,* and *it.*

Long answers should follow this pattern:

  Yes, you do need more sleep.
  Yes, you need more sleep.
  No, you don't need more sleep.

Extension

Refer to the large Class Chat chart and ask *yes/no* questions about the information you collected (e.g, *Does Roberto have a fever? Do Maria and Teresa have headaches?*).

Have learners give short answers (e.g., *Yes, he does. No, they don't.*).

 Assign Workbook pp. 20–21.

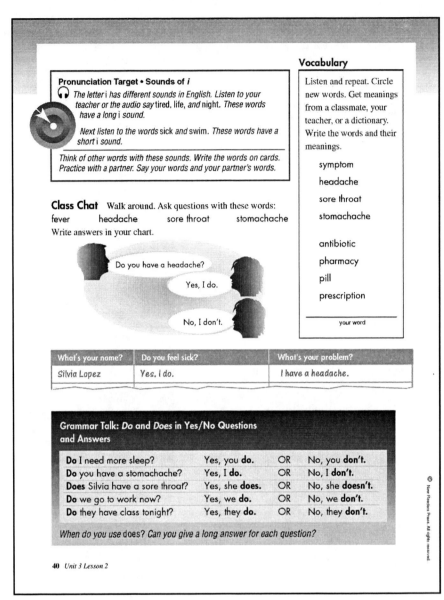

Pronunciation Target • Sounds of *i*

The letter *i* has different sounds in English. Listen to your teacher or the audio say *tired, life,* and *night.* These words have a long *i* sound.

Next listen to the words *sick* and *swim.* These words have a short *i* sound.

Think of other words with these sounds. Write the words on cards. Practice with a partner. Say your words and your partner's words.

Class Chat Walk around. Ask questions with these words:
fever   headache   sore throat   stomachache
Write answers in your chart.

Do you have a headache?
Yes, I do.
No, I don't.

What's your name?	Do you feel sick?	What's your problem?
Silvia Lopez	Yes, I do.	I have a headache.

Grammar Talk: *Do* and *Does* in Yes/No Questions and Answers

Do I need more sleep?	Yes, you **do**.	OR	No, you **don't**.
Do you have a stomachache?	Yes, I **do**.	OR	No, I **don't**.
Does Silvia have a sore throat?	Yes, she **does**.	OR	No, she **doesn't**.
Do we go to work now?	Yes, we **do**.	OR	No, we **don't**.
Do they have class tonight?	Yes, they **do**.	OR	No, they **don't**.

When do you use does*? Can you give a long answer for each question?*

Vocabulary

Listen and repeat. Circle new words. Get meanings from a classmate, your teacher, or a dictionary. Write the words and their meanings.

symptom
headache
sore throat
stomachache

antibiotic
pharmacy
pill
prescription

your word

Activity A

Write the sample sentences from the student book on the board or an overhead transparency. Have learners look at the charts they made for the Class Chat.

Activity B

Ask these questions about the pie chart:

- How many hours does Silvia spend doing housework? *(3)*
- How many hours does she take care of her children? *(4 + 2 = 6)*
- What do you think she can spend less time doing? *(Answers will vary.)*

Have partners discuss the questions in the student book.

Answers

1. She has no time to relax.
2. Answers will vary. Possible answer: Silvia does not balance her life. She has no time to relax or for leisure activities.

Activity C

- First have learners list their activities in their notebooks and estimate how much time they spend on each during a typical weekday.
- Assist individual learners in making their pie charts based on a typical day.
- Collect and display the pie charts for the whole group to compare.

Activity D

After learners write about their lives, tell them to use the Writing Checklist for Sentences on p. 126 to edit their writing.

Task 2

- First model the assignment. On the board or an overhead transparency, draw a large chart like the one in the student book. Then fill in a few examples from your own weekly schedule.
- Ask learners to complete their own charts in their notebooks.

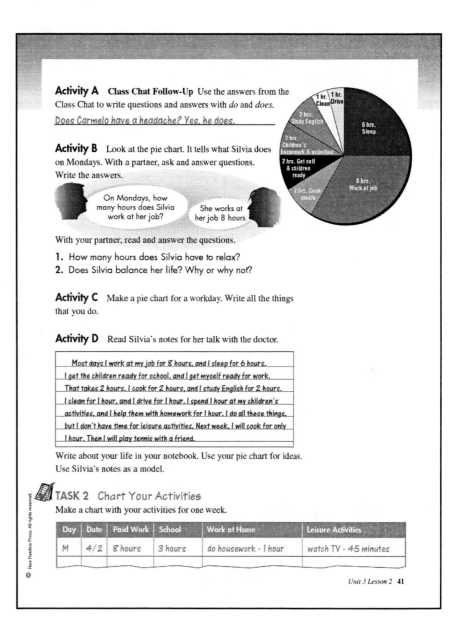

Activity A Class Chat Follow-Up Use the answers from the Class Chat to write questions and answers with *do* and *does*.

Does Carmelo have a headache? Yes, he does.

Activity B Look at the pie chart. It tells what Silvia does on Mondays. With a partner, ask and answer questions. Write the answers.

On Mondays, how many hours does Silvia work at her job?

She works at her job 8 hours.

With your partner, read and answer the questions.

1. How many hours does Silvia have to relax?
2. Does Silvia balance her life? Why or why not?

Activity C Make a pie chart for a workday. Write all the things that you do.

Activity D Read Silvia's notes for her talk with the doctor.

Most days I work at my job for 8 hours, and I sleep for 6 hours. I get the children ready for school, and I get myself ready for work. That takes 2 hours. I cook for 2 hours, and I study English for 2 hours. I clean for 1 hour, and I drive for 1 hour. I spend 1 hour at my children's activities, and I help them with homework for 1 hour. I do all these things, but I don't have time for leisure activities. Next week, I will cook for only 1 hour. Then I will play tennis with a friend.

Write about your life in your notebook. Use your pie chart for ideas. Use Silvia's notes as a model.

TASK 2 Chart Your Activities

Make a chart with your activities for one week.

Day	Date	Paid Work	School	Work at Home	Leisure Activities
M	4/2	8 hours	3 hours	do housework - 1 hour	watch TV - 45 minutes

Unit 3 Lesson 2 **41**

Use Unit Masters 26 (Grammar: Acting Out Feelings) and 27 (Thinking Skill: Compare and Contrast Daily Activities) now or at any time during the rest of the unit.

Lesson 3: Work and Play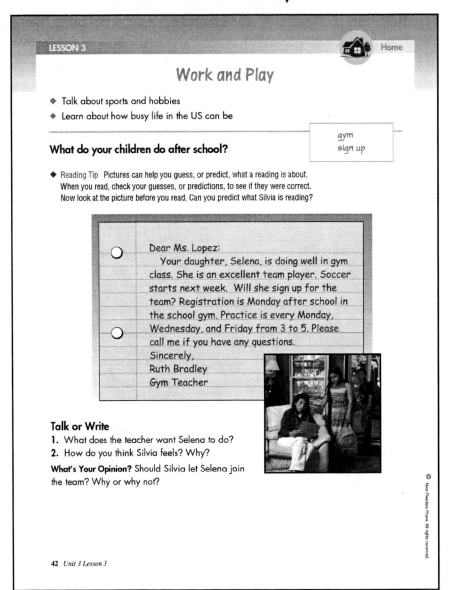

- Read the title aloud with learners and point out the lesson objectives below it.
- In this lesson, learners will talk about sports, hobbies, and the busy lifestyle of many Americans.
- They will also learn how to find out about sports and leisure activities in their community.

Attention Box

This vocabulary should be understood, but learners should not be expected to produce the words at this point.

Question

- Read the introductory question aloud.
- For learners who do not have children, ask, "What do children you know do after school?"
- Record learners' responses on an idea map on the board or an overhead transparency.

Extension

Ask these questions:
- What do children *need* to do after school?
- What do they *want* to do?
- Do children need balance in their lives?

Reading Tip

- Read the tip aloud with learners.
- Have learners look at the photo and then complete the reading silently.
- Read the note aloud to learners.

Ask these questions:
- What is the name of Selena's gym teacher?
- How is Selena doing in gym class?
- When is registration for soccer?
- When is soccer practice?

Talk or Write

This exercise helps learners make inferences from what they read.

Answers

1. The teacher wants Selena to join the soccer team.
2. Answers will vary. Possible answers: Silvia feels proud and happy that her daughter is doing well in gym class. She feels stressed that she will have to take Selena to soccer practice.

What's Your Opinion?

Have learners discuss the questions in small groups. Have a reporter from each group tell all learners what the group thought.

Extension

Have learners with children write sentences about their own families.

List these questions on the board or an overhead transparency:
- Do you help your children with homework? When?
- Are your children in sports or other activities? Explain.
- Do you drive your children to and from practice, games, or performances?
- Do you go to your children's practices, games, or performances?

If time permits, ask volunteers to read their sentences to the class.

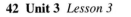

Picture Dictionary

Follow the suggestions on p. 6 for introducing and reinforcing the vocabulary.

- Act out each activity after you write it. Have learners tell you what you are doing.
- Ask learners to describe and act out some sports and hobbies that they are familiar with.
- Follow the suggestions on p. 6 for using vocabulary cards. Use the Vocabulary Card Masters for the words in the Picture Dictionary.
- Explain that the game we call *soccer* in the United States is called *football* in most other countries.

Extension

Choose a sport most of your learners are familiar with, and do a Language Experience activity.

- First discuss the selected sport.
- Have learners dictate a story describing the sport and a specific game or contest.
- Write the story on the board or an overhead transparency.
- Have learners read it chorally.
- Make one copy of the story for each small group.
- Cut each story into sentence strips and give each group one set.
- Have learners arrange the strips in the correct sequence.

Attention Box

Read the word to learners, pointing or miming to convey meaning if necessary. This word should be understood, but learners should not be expected to produce it at this point.

In the US

As a class, discuss the statement "Everyone is busy all the time!" Is it true in the US? Refer back to what learners wrote about their lives in Activities C and D in Lesson 2. Are they busy all the time?

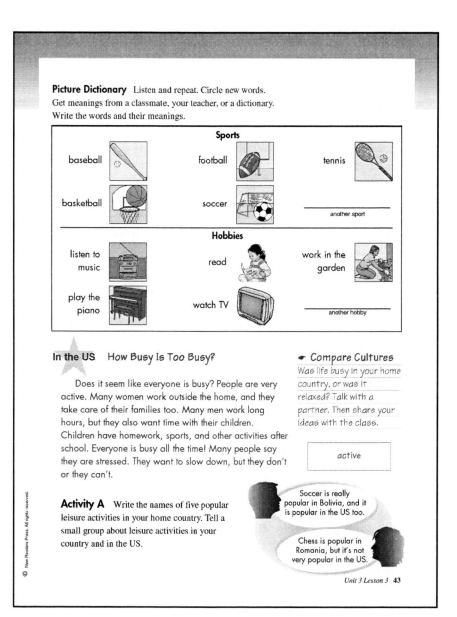

Compare Cultures

Have partners discuss life in their home countries and compare it to life in the US. Have volunteers share their thoughts with the class.

Activity A

- Bring in articles, encyclopedias, and books on sports and leisure activities in different countries, or take learners to the library to do the research.
- Group learners from the same country so they can help one another.
- Have a reporter from each group share the group's findings.

One Step Up

- Have learners write about the most popular sport or activity in their countries.
- Encourage learners to illustrate their reports.
- Ask volunteers to read the reports while the class tries to guess what country is being represented.

Use Unit Master 28 (Game: Find Your Match) now or at any time during the rest of the unit.

Assign Workbook pp. 22–23.

Activity B

- Write the model sentence on the board or an overhead transparency.
- Have learners walk around the room and talk with at least three other learners.

Extension
Help learners compile information on leisure activities to create a pie chart. Ask questions like these:
- How many classmates watch TV to relax?
- How many play sports?
- How many play musical instruments?

Collect this information by a show of hands. Then have small groups graph the most popular forms of relaxation among your learners.

Activity C

- As learners respond during the discussion, write their questions on the board or an overhead transparency.
- Ask volunteers to role-play conversations between Silvia and her family members.

Then ask these questions:
- How can asking questions help people solve problems?
- Have you ever solved a problem by asking questions?
- Why do people sometimes *not* want to ask questions?

Task 3

- To provide resources specific to this task, bring in print materials showing sports and other leisure activities (e.g., newspapers, flyers, phone books, brochures from community centers).
- Ask learners to do the same.

Make a copy of Customizable Master 4 (4-Column Chart). Label the columns with the heads *Activity, Location, Days and Times,* and *Cost.* Then make a copy for each learner.

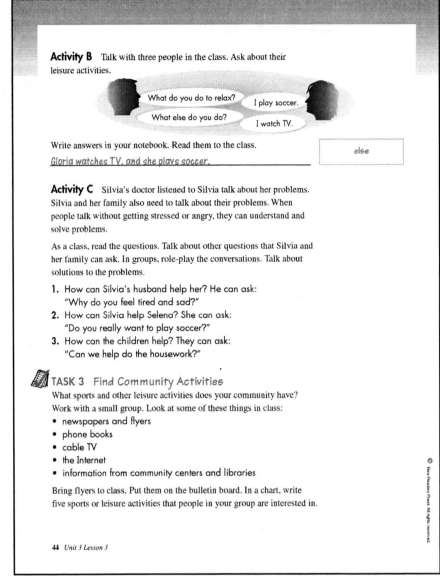

Activity B Talk with three people in the class. Ask about their leisure activities.

What do you do to relax?

I play soccer.

What else do you do?

I watch TV.

Write answers in your notebook. Read them to the class.

Gloria watches TV, and she plays soccer.

else

Activity C Silvia's doctor listened to Silvia talk about her problems. Silvia and her family also need to talk about their problems. When people talk without getting stressed or angry, they can understand and solve problems.

As a class, read the questions. Talk about other questions that Silvia and her family can ask. In groups, role-play the conversations. Talk about solutions to the problems.

1. How can Silvia's husband help her? He can ask: "Why do you feel tired and sad?"
2. How can Silvia help Selena? She can ask: "Do you really want to play soccer?"
3. How can the children help? They can ask: "Can we help do the housework?"

TASK 3 Find Community Activities
What sports and other leisure activities does your community have? Work with a small group. Look at some of these things in class:
- newspapers and flyers
- phone books
- cable TV
- the Internet
- information from community centers and libraries

Bring flyers to class. Put them on the bulletin board. In a chart, write five sports or leisure activities that people in your group are interested in.

44 *Unit 3 Lesson 3*

- Put learners in small groups and assist them in completing the task.
- Have learners enter at least five activities on their charts and provide detailed information for each one.
- Discuss the pros and cons of each activity. Consider these factors: *Interest level:* Are you interested in this activity? Would you enjoy it? *Location:* Is it close to your home? If not, is it easy to get to? *Time:* Is the time convenient? *Cost:* Can you afford it?

- Help learners prepare a bulletin-board display of local sports and leisure activities.
- Encourage learners who sign up for a local sport or activity to report back on their experience.

Use Unit Master 29 (Grammar: Bingo Game) now or at any time during the rest of the unit.

Review Unit Skills
See p. 8 for suggestions on games and activities to review the vocabulary and grammar in this unit.

Unit 3 Project 🌐

Learners prepare and give class presentations about their lives.

Get Ready

📑 Distribute a copy of Unit Master 30 (Unit 3 Project: A Presentation about Your Life) to each learner. Tell them they will use these cards in making notes for their speeches.

Talk to learners about what they did in Tasks 1, 2, and 3, which built skills for the unit project. Then do the following:

- Use the prompts in the student book to help them provide the information.
- Help learners compile the information they gathered in Tasks 1, 2, and 3 so that they can write their presentations.

Model the assignment using an example from your own life:

- Bring in a picture that tells something about you and your life.
- Explain what the picture means to you.

Do the Work

Encourage learners to read their notes silently several times. Have partners practice their presentations with one another.

Present Your Project

- Do not correct any errors as learners present. Rather, list common errors for future attention.
- Be alert for sensitive feelings and any reticence to discuss personal problems. Do not force participation.
- If some learners express frustration because their lives are not balanced, ask others to make suggestions for action plans. See whether learners are receptive to advice.

Assessment

📑 Use a copy of Unit Master 31 (Project Assessment Form) to record your assessment of each learner's presentation. Place the completed form in the learner's portfolio.

Writing Extension

Tell learners to use the Writing Checklist for Sentences on p. 126 for help in editing their sentences.

Technology Extra

If possible, bring a simple camera for learners to use. Have the photos developed and hang them in the classroom.

 Assign Workbook p. 24 (Check Your Progress).

📑 Use Unit Master 32 (Unit 3 Checkup/Review) whenever you complete the unit.

Self-Assessment

📑 Give each learner a copy of the Speaking and Listening Self-Check and the Writing and Reading Self-Check (Generic Assessment Masters 10 and 11). Go over the assessment together. The completed forms will become part of each learner's portfolio.

UNIT 3 Project

A Presentation about Your Life

Prepare a class presentation about you and your life.

Get Ready

Get five note cards from your teacher. On each card write about one of these things:

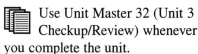
photo = photograph

1. Everything you do during one week
2. Your job (if you have one) or family responsibilities
   - where you work
   - what you do
   - your work schedule
3. What you like to do and why it is important to you
   - a food that you cook
   - a musical instrument that you play
   - a favorite sport or hobby
4. How you feel at different times of the week
   - what you like to do and why
   - what you don't like to do and why
5. What you will do to balance your life
   - what you want to do this year to balance your life
   - how you plan to reach that goal

Find a photo that shows an important part of your life.

Do the Work

Read your notes several times. Practice presenting alone. Then practice with a friend. Make eye contact. Speak in a loud voice. Speak slowly. Ask for suggestions. Practice again . . . and again.

Present Your Project

Tell the class about your life. Use your cards and your photo.

✏ **Writing Extension** Choose one of the five points above. Write sentences about it in your notebook.

💻 **Technology Extra**
Use a camera to take photos of other students doing their presentations. Your teacher will hang the photos in the classroom.

Unit 3 Project 45

Unit 4: Making a Plan for Your Money

Materials for the Unit
- Play money (bills and coins)
- Your photo ID
- Calculators
- Weather forecast (newspaper or Internet)
- Customizable Masters 2, 4, and 7
- Generic Assessment Master 9
- Unit Masters 33–38
- Vocabulary Card Masters for Unit 4

Making a Plan for Your Money
- Read the unit goals with learners. Then follow the suggestions on p. 5 for talking about the title.
- The focus of this unit is planning a family budget and using banking services.

Explore the idea of *making a plan for your money* in this way:
- Distribute play money so each learner has different amounts of money and denominations.
- Ask learners to think of something they can buy with the amount of money they have. How much do they think the item would cost?
- List the items and estimated prices for each on the board.
- Ask learners to select a more expensive item, something they really want even if they do not have enough money to buy it.
- List those items and their estimated prices on the board.
- Have learners work in small groups. Ask each group to put all their money together and make a plan to buy something from the list of items. The item should be something they can afford and that everyone in the group can share.

Then ask learners these questions:
- Do you have any money left over?
- If so, what can you do with it? *(divide it among group members, save it, donate it, etc.)*

Question
Read the question below the arrow. Write learners' answers on a large piece of paper and post them.

Photo
Follow the suggestions on p. 5 for talking about the photo. Then ask these questions:
- How many people are in the photo?
- Who do you think they are?

Have pairs or small groups discuss what they see in the photo. Then have them report their answers to the class.

Think and Talk
Ask learners to think individually about each question. Explain that learners can answer the first three questions aloud. Be sensitive to learners' privacy regarding question 4.

Answers
1. The people are Joseph Delva and his mother and father. They are in their living room at home.
2. He wants to move out of the family home and get an apartment.
3. He has to save money.
4. Answers will vary.

Vocabulary

Follow the suggestions on p. 6 for introducing and reinforcing vocabulary.

Follow the suggestions on p. 6 for using vocabulary cards. Use the Vocabulary Card Masters for the words in the Vocabulary box.

Gather Your Thoughts

- Draw an idea map on the board with the words *My Spending Plans* in the center circle.
- Ask several volunteers to answer the question, but be aware that some learners may consider this information private.
- Have each learner complete an idea map showing his or her spending plans.

What's the Problem?

Follow the suggestions on p. 5 for identifying and analyzing problems.

- Have partners talk about the question posed in the student book, "Why is it difficult to make a money plan, or a budget?"
- Draw two columns on the board or an overhead transparency Write the vocabulary words *Expenses* and *Income* as heads.
- Ask learners to tell you what some of their regular *expenses* are. Write these under *Expenses*.
- Ask them for ways they can earn *income,* or make money. Write these answers under *Income*.
- Discuss what happens if their expenses are higher than their income.
- Discuss what someone has to do to save money. Write these sentence openers on the board:

    I will ___.
    I have to ___.
    I must ___.

Have learners complete the sentences with ideas for saving money.

- Ask learners to make sentences about their partners.

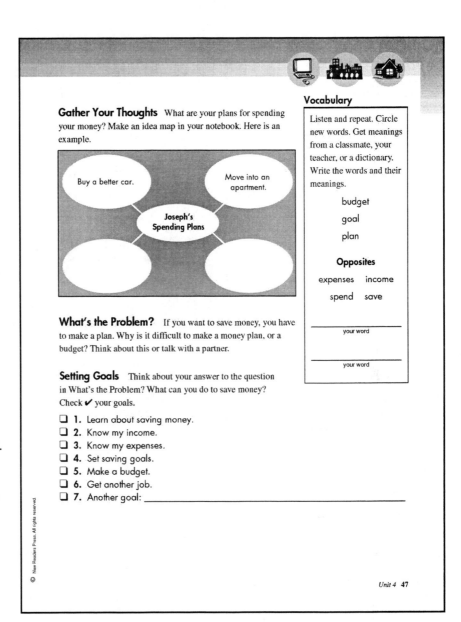

Gather Your Thoughts What are your plans for spending your money? Make an idea map in your notebook. Here is an example.

Buy a better car.

Move into an apartment.

Joseph's Spending Plans

What's the Problem? If you want to save money, you have to make a plan. Why is it difficult to make a money plan, or a budget? Think about this or talk with a partner.

Setting Goals Think about your answer to the question in What's the Problem? What can you do to save money? Check ✔ your goals.

- ❏ 1. Learn about saving money.
- ❏ 2. Know my income.
- ❏ 3. Know my expenses.
- ❏ 4. Set saving goals.
- ❏ 5. Make a budget.
- ❏ 6. Get another job.
- ❏ 7. Another goal: _____

Vocabulary

Listen and repeat. Circle new words. Get meanings from a classmate, your teacher, or a dictionary. Write the words and their meanings.

budget

goal

plan

Opposites

expenses   income

spend   save

_____
your word

_____
your word

Unit 4 **47**

- Have learners change the sentences to apply to more than one learner planning to do the same thing.
- If learners have difficulty, write sample sentences showing how the sentences change from *I will* to *You will* and *We will, have to,* and *must.*

Setting Goals

Follow the suggestions on p. 5 for setting goals.

- Remind learners they discussed saving money in What's the Problem?

- Tell them to review things they can do to make a budget plan. Have them talk with their partners about their goals for this unit.
- Orally proficient learners can share their goals with the class.

Lesson 1: Making a Plan ☀www

- Follow the suggestions on p. 5 for talking about the title.
- Read the lesson objectives aloud.
- Explain to learners that in this lesson they will track their spending.

Question

Read the question aloud with learners and brainstorm answers. Record learners' answers on the board or an overhead transparency.

Photo

Ask learners these questions:
- What is happening in the photo?
- What kind of work does Joseph do?
- What is he getting?

Attention Box

Read the word to learners, pointing or miming to convey meaning. This word should be understood, but learners should not be expected to produce it at this point.

Idiom Watch

Discuss the meanings of these expressions with learners.

Reading Tip

Focus learners' attention on the title of the reading and the meaning of the idiom *help dreams come true.* (One meaning might be to *make dreams become real.*) Then do the following:
- Read the paragraphs to learners as they follow along silently.
- Have them study the chart.
- Ask, "How does the chart help you understand the reading?"
- Have partners read the paragraphs again together.

Extension

Review the math terms *add* and *subtract.* Write sample addition and subtraction problems on the board.

Talk or Write

This exercise helps learners become skilled at analyzing a chart.

LESSON 1   Work/School

Making a Plan

- ◆ Look at income and expenses
- ◆ Use *will, have to,* and *must*

deposit

What is in a budget?

◆ Reading Tip A chart can help you understand what you read. Read the paragraph below the chart as your teacher reads it aloud. Then study the chart. How does the reading help you understand the chart?

Idiom Watch!
add up
down payment
keep track of

Here's your paycheck, Joseph.

Budget	
Income:	$2,093/month
− Expenses:	
= Savings:	
Savings Goals	
New Car:	$2,000 down payment
Apartment:	$1,600 deposit & first month's rent

A Budget Can Help Dreams Come True!

Making a budget, a plan for your money, is important. A budget will help you save your money. Making a budget can be difficult. You have to include your income, your expenses, and your savings goals. The first part is easy. You add up your income. This is how much money you earn each month. The next part is hard.

How much money do you spend each month? Keep track of all your expenses. Add them up. Then subtract them from your income. The money remaining is what you can save. Save a little money every month. Soon you will have the money you need to reach your goals.

Talk or Write
1. Joseph is making a budget. What are his savings goals?
2. Joseph thinks he can save $200 a month. How long will it take him to save money for a down payment on a car?
3. Why do you think it is hard to know your expenses?

48 *Unit 4 Lesson 1*

Answers

1. Joseph's goal is to save $3,600. He needs $2,000 for a down payment on a new car and $1,600 for a deposit and first month's rent for an apartment.
2. It will take him 10 months to save money for a down payment on a car.
3. Answers will vary.

Extension

Ask these discussion questions:
- What will a budget help you do?
- What do you need to put in a budget?
- What is the first step in making a budget?
- What is the second step?
- What is the third step?
- How can you know how much money you have left?
- How do you get money to reach your goals?
- How does the chart show you the steps to follow?

Picture Dictionary

- Follow the suggestions on p. 6 for introducing and reinforcing vocabulary.
- Follow the suggestions on p. 6 for using vocabulary cards. Use the Vocabulary Card Masters for the words in the Picture Dictionary.
- Have learners suggest related words. They can add types of *bills* (e.g., *water*), other math terms (e.g., *addition*), or words related to money (e.g., *cash*).

Partner Chat

Use Customizable Master 2 (2-Column Chart). Follow the suggestions on p. 7 for customizing and duplicating the master. Make a copy for each learner.

Compile a class list of bills on the board or an overhead transparency.

Grammar Talk

Follow the suggestions on p. 7 for introducing the grammar point. Then have learners use *will, have to,* and *must* to create additional sentences about things they will do or need to do.

Answers
Have to changes with different subjects. Use *have to* with *I, you, we,* and *they.* Use *has to* with *he, she,* and *it.*

Extension
Share this information with your learners according to their abilities:
- *Will* is used to talk about future time.
- The contraction is pronoun + *'ll* (*I'll, you'll, he'll, she'll, we'll, they'll*).
- *Have to* and *must* are modals. They express necessity. *Must* is usually stronger than *have to.*

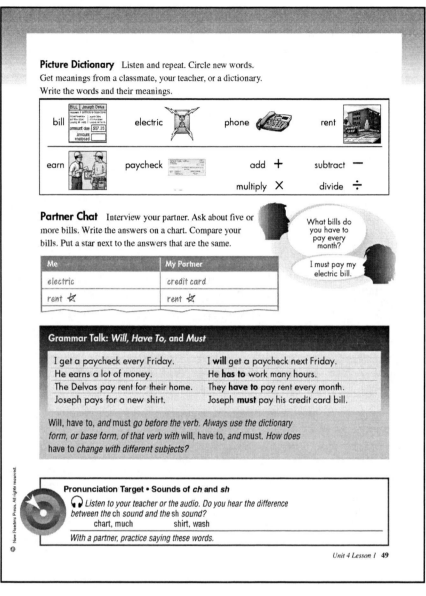

Pronunciation Target

Play the audio or read the listening script below.

Write *ch* and *sh* on the board or an overhead transparency. Ask a volunteer to come to the board. Then do the following:
- Ask learners to call out additional words with *ch* and *sh* sounds.
- Have the volunteer write those words in the correct column.
- Have learners pronounce all the words in chorus.
- Ask learners, "Do you hear a 'stop' when they pronounce the *ch* sound?" If not, have them hold an open hand in front of their mouths and pronounce the word *march*. They should feel a puff of air on their hands. Have them pronounce the word *marsh* to feel the difference in airflow.

Listening Script
Listen. Do you hear the difference between the sounds?
chart, much
shirt, wash

 Assign Workbook pp. 25–26.

Activity A

If this activity and the previous Grammar Talk are presented on different days, review the use of *will*, *have to*, and *must*.

Activity B

Use Customizable Master 4 (4-Column Chart). Follow the suggestions on p. 7 for customizing and duplicating the master. Make a copy for each learner.

- Write the word *estimate* on the board. Ask learners to *estimate*, or *guess intelligently*, what the temperature will be tomorrow.
- Show them a weather forecast so they can see how their estimate compares with a weather forecaster's estimate.
- Ask learners to estimate their monthly expenses in their notebooks. Assure them that this is private information they need not share.

Activity C

Answers
Big City Taxi: $1,853.40
Lawn Service: $240.00
Total Monthly Income: $2,093.40

Technology Extra

Help learners if they have difficulty using a calculator.

One Step Up
- Discuss the meaning of *gross income*, *net income*, and *take-home pay*.
- Have learners calculate their own income in their notebooks. Again, explain that this is private information they need not share.

Task 1

To help the students complete this task, draw a chart like this one on the board or an overhead transparency:

Activity A Partner Chat Follow-Up
Look at your Partner Chat chart. In your notebook, make new sentences with *will*, *have to*, and *must*.

Me	**My Partner**	**We Both**
I must pay my electric bill.	You have to pay a credit card bill.	We will pay rent.

Activity B
Some of your expenses are the same every month. Some of your expenses change from month to month. Look back at your Partner Chat list. List your bills in a chart like this one. Which type of expenses can you control, the expenses that stay the same or the expenses that change?

Expenses that Stay the Same		Expenses that Change	
Rent	$600.00	Telephone	$120.00
Car Insurance	$40.00	Food	$210.00

Activity C
Another part of your budget is your income. Your income is the money that is paid to you. It includes your paycheck and other money that you earn. Look at Joseph Delva's income. He has two jobs. What is his income?

Joseph's Income	Paychecks per Month	Multiply	Monthly Income
Big City Taxi—$463.35	4	463.35 x 4	
Lawn Service—$120.00	2	120.00 x 2	
		Total Monthly Income:	

Technology Extra
Check your answers with a calculator.

TASK 1 Track Your Spending
For one week, keep track of all the money that you spend and where you spend it. You may be surprised to see where it goes!

One Step Up
There is an old saying in English, "Watch your pennies and the dollars will take care of themselves." What does this mean to you? Do you know a saying about money in your language? Tell it to the class.

50 *Unit 4 Lesson 1*

	Expense/ Amount	Expense/ Amount	Expense Amount
Sunday			
Monday			
Tuesday			
Wednesday			
Thursday			
Friday			
Saturday			

Show them how to use the chart by filling in these examples:
lunch ($6.50)
gas ($20)
groceries ($89.76)

One Step Up

- Write the saying from the student book on the board.

- Ask learners what they think the saying means.
- If they have difficulty, offer an interpretation (e.g., "Be careful about spending small amounts of money. They can add up and become large savings.").

Use Unit Master 33 (Song: She'll Be Comin' 'Round the Mountain) to review contractions with *will* now or at any time during the rest of the unit.

Lesson 2: Saving More Money

- Read the title aloud. Then read the lesson objectives below it.
- Tell learners that in this lesson they will make a savings plan.

Attention Box

- Remind learners they saw a *flyer* on p. 27.
- Show your *photo ID* and ask volunteers to show theirs. Ask, "What information appears on your *photo ID?*"
- Explain that a check marked *for deposit only* cannot be cashed.

Question

Read the introductory question aloud and record learners' answers on the board or an overhead transparency. Try to elicit the following steps:

- Gather two pieces of identification. One should be a photo ID.
- Go to the bank and ask to talk to a bank officer.
- Answer the officer's questions and complete the forms.

Listening Tip

- Read the tip aloud with learners.
- Have learners describe what they see in the photo. Explain that looking carefully at the photo will help them understand the conversation.

🎧 Play the audio or read the listening script on p. 119. Follow the suggestions on p. 5 for listening comprehension.

Talk or Write

This exercise helps learners become skilled at using visual clues.

Answers

1. A bank clerk and Joseph.
2. Joseph has to fill out an application form and provide a photo ID.
3. 10 percent of his paycheck.
4. Because anyone can cash an endorsed check.

LESSON 2   Community

Saving More Money

- ◆ Learn about checking and savings accounts
- ◆ Ask and answer *Wh-* questions (Review)

How do you open a bank account?

flyer
photo ID
for deposit only

- ◆ Listening Tip 🎧 Look at the photo. Try to guess. Who is talking? What are they talking about? Listen to the conversation. Were you right? Answer the questions with a partner. You can read the words of the conversation on page 118.

How can I help you?

Joseph must learn about bank accounts. He will need a checking account to pay bills. He wants to open a savings account also. He needs to save for a deposit on an apartment. He knows that he will have other expenses too.

Talk or Write

1. Who is talking?
2. What does Joseph have to do to open an account?
3. How much does Joseph put into his savings account?
4. Why does the clerk tell Joseph not to endorse his check before he is in the bank?

Unit 4 Lesson 2 **51**

Extension

Ask these additional questions:

- What is the minimum deposit to open a savings account?
- What should you write on your check if you endorse it? Where do you write it?

One Step Up

Have partners role-play the conversation.

📄 Use Unit Masters 34 (Grammar: Find Your Match) and 35 (Life Skill: Complete a Check) now or at any time during the rest of the unit.

Master 35: Life Skill: Complete a Check

- Draw a personal check on the board or an overhead transparency.
- Discuss the parts of the check and how to write entries. Have volunteers fill in the parts with sample information.
- Give each pair two copies of the master.
- Have one partner use one copy to write a check to the other.
- Have the second partner endorse the check and write *for deposit only* on the back.
- Ask partners to switch roles and use the second copy.

Unit 4 *Lesson 2* **51**

Vocabulary

Follow the suggestions on p. 6 for introducing and reinforcing vocabulary.

Follow the suggestions on p. 6 for using vocabulary cards. Use the Vocabulary Card Masters for the words in the Vocabulary box.

Have learners add related words of their own (e.g., *withdraw, slip, amount, sign*).

Extension
Have learners copy the listening script conversation on p. 118 of the student book into their notebooks, underlining any vocabulary words.

One Step Up
Have learners as a group spell out each word as you write it on the board or an overhead transparency.

Partner Chat

Tell partners to first copy the five questions into their notebook, leaving space after each for the answers.

Grammar Talk

Follow the suggestions on p. 7 for introducing the grammar point.

Extension
Share this information with learners:
- *What* asks about *things* or *activities* but not *people.*
- *Where* asks about *location.*
- *When* asks about *time.*
- *Why* asks for a *reason.*
- *Who* asks about *people.*
- *How* asks about *manner* or *means.* Answers about *manner* often use adjectives and adverbs. Answers about *means,* such as the one in Grammar Talk, often use verbs.

Then do the following:
- Ask common questions of various learners (e.g., *Who are you? Where are we? When do we have class?*).

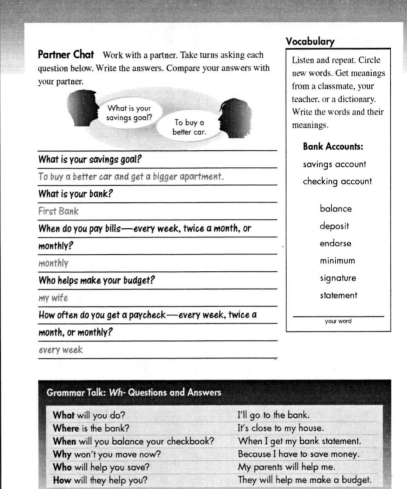

Partner Chat Work with a partner. Take turns asking each question below. Write the answers. Compare your answers with your partner.

What is your savings goal? To buy a better car.

What is your savings goal?
To buy a better car and get a bigger apartment.

What is your bank?
First Bank

When do you pay bills—every week, twice a month, or monthly?
monthly

Who helps make your budget?
my wife

How often do you get a paycheck—every week, twice a month, or monthly?
every week

Vocabulary

Listen and repeat. Circle new words. Get meanings from a classmate, your teacher, or a dictionary. Write the words and their meanings.

Bank Accounts:

savings account

checking account

balance

deposit

endorse

minimum

signature

statement

_____
your word

Grammar Talk: *Wh-* Questions and Answers

What will you do?	I'll go to the bank.
Where is the bank?	It's close to my house.
When will you balance your checkbook?	When I get my bank statement.
Why won't you move now?	Because I have to save money.
Who will help you save?	My parents will help me.
How will they help you?	They will help me make a budget.

The question words above ask for specific information. You cannot answer just yes *or* no.

52 *Unit 4 Lesson 2*

- Have learners form additional questions using all the question words.
- Write some of these questions on the board.
- Have partners ask and answer these new questions.

 Assign Workbook pp. 27–28.

Activity A

Extension

Ask learners to write a paragraph in their notebooks about their saving goals. Have them refer to the Writing Checklists on p. 126 of their books.

Attention Box

Read the word and its definition to learners, pointing or miming to convey meaning if possible. This word should be understood, but learners should not be expected to produce it at this point.

Activity B

- Show learners how to calculate 10 percent.
- Explain that they can find 10 percent simply by moving the decimal point one figure to the left.
- Draw arrows in the figures below to show how moving the decimal point produces the results:
  10% of 550 is 55.
  10% of 24 is 2.40.
  10% of 2,898 is 289.80.

Answers

Big City Taxi, amount saved per month: $185.32
Lawn Service, 10% of total: $12.00
Lawn Service, amount saved per month: $24.00
Total monthly savings: $209.32

Task 2

Provide this example on the board or an overhead transparency:

Income	10% of Total	Multiply by no. of paychecks per month
$277.50	$27.75	× 4 = $111.00

Have learners do this task independently. Their budget information is private, and they need not share it with other learners.

Circulate to assist learners having difficulty with the calculations.

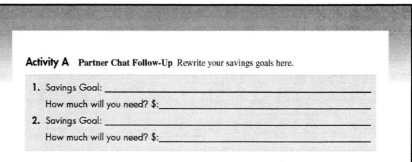

Activity A **Partner Chat Follow-Up** Rewrite your savings goals here.

1. Savings Goal: _____
   How much will you need? $:_____
2. Savings Goal: _____
   How much will you need? $:_____

Activity B Joseph knows that it is important to save monthly. He will put 10% of every paycheck into his savings account. How much will Joseph save every month?

per = for each

Joseph's Income	10% of total (move decimal point to the left)	Multiply by number of paychecks per month
Big City Taxi—$463.35	$46.33	x 4 =
Lawn Service—$120.00		x 2 =
	Total Monthly Savings:	

TASK 2 *Make a Savings Plan*

A good goal is to save 10% of your income every month. Some weeks you may save less, but try to save every month. It really adds up. Create your savings plan.

1. Add up your total household income.
2. Figure out 10%. This is how much to save each month.

Your Income	10% of total (move decimal point one number to the left)	Multiply by number of paychecks per month
$		
$		
$		
$		
	Total Monthly Savings:	

Technology Extra
Use a calculator.

Unit 4 Lesson 2 **53**

Technology Extra

Have learners use a calculator to check the figures in their savings plan.

Lesson 3: Spending Less, Saving More ✴www

- Follow the suggestions on p. 5 for talking about the title. Then read the lesson objectives listed below it.
- Explain to learners that in this lesson they will calculate what they spend and save each month. They will also learn about older children in the US who live away from their families.

Attention Box

- Write *thrift shop* and *garage sale* on the board.
- Discuss how these buying and selling environments differ from department stores.
- Ask learners if they have *thrift shops* and *garage sales* in their home countries.

This vocabulary should be understood, but learners should not be expected to produce the words at this point.

Question

Read the introductory question aloud. Brainstorm answers as a group. Draw an idea map on the board or an overhead transparency using learners' answers.

Reading Tip

- Read the tip aloud with learners.
- Since the idea here is to activate prior knowledge on the topic of saving money, ask learners to close their books as they brainstorm ideas.
- Write learners' ideas on the board or an overhead transparency. Organize them into an idea map.

Extension

Elicit these additional ideas for saving money:

- Don't go to restaurants. Eat at home.
- Don't go to the movies. Watch television or rent a movie for the whole family.
- Make presents instead of buying them.

LESSON 3   🏠 Home

Spending Less, Saving More

- ◆ Talk about saving money
- ◆ Learn about family life in the US

thrift shop
garage sale

How do you spend your income?

◆ Reading Tip Before you read something, think about the topic. Ask yourself, "What do I already know?" When you do this, you can remember many words that can help you understand what you read. Before you read Mrs. Delva's advice, think about what you already know about saving money. Brainstorm a list of saving tips with your class. Your teacher will write the tips on the board. Then read the advice that Joseph's mother gave him.

Mrs. Delva's Savings Advice

- When you find something you want, wait two weeks before buying. Sometimes you don't want it anymore.
- Make a list before you go shopping. Don't buy things that aren't on your list.
- Buy things on sale.
- Buy things at thrift shops and garage sales.
- Look many places for the same item. Compare prices.
- Rent an apartment with a friend. Share expenses.
- Buy a used car that doesn't use too much gas.
- Don't carry a lot of cash. You will spend it!
- Don't buy food out. Make your food at home.
- When you go out to eat, drink water.

I must be very careful with my money.

Talk or Write

1. What tips will save Joseph the most money? Write them in your notebook.
2. Did the class think of other tips?

What's Your Opinion? Some people say that you should save at least three months' expenses for an emergency. This is called an *emergency fund.* What do you think about this advice?

54 *Unit 4 Lesson 3*

- Compare prices. Look at many advertisements.
- Buy only things you really need.

Talk or Write

Have learners answer the questions alone or in pairs.

This exercise helps learners activate knowledge.

Answers

Answers will vary.

One Step Up

Ask learners to write in their notebooks their own lists of ways they will try to save. Tell them they need not share the list with anyone.

What's Your Opinion?

Answers will vary.

Extension

Ask these additional discussion questions:

- Do you have an emergency fund?
- Do you add money to it every month?
- If you do not have an emergency fund, what can you do in an emergency? (*Get help from other family members or friends; share a place to live with someone else.*)

Vocabulary

Follow the suggestions on p. 6 for introducing and reinforcing vocabulary.

Follow the suggestions on p. 6 for using vocabulary cards. Use the Vocabulary Card Masters for the words in the Vocabulary box.

Have learners add related words to the list (e.g., *price, contrast, house*).

In the US

Explain that young adults may move out of their family homes because they get a job or go to college or university.

Add that because many young people find it difficult to pay their own living expenses, they sometimes come back to the family home. Still, for young men and young women, the idea of living an independent life is more important in the US than in many other cultures.

Compare Cultures

After partners finish their discussions, have volunteers share their ideas with the class.

Pronunciation Target

🎧 Play the audio or read the listening script on p. 120. Stress the underlined syllable to model the pronunciation of long words.

- Ask learners to find other long vocabulary words in this unit.
- Have them dictate the words, emphasizing the stressed syllable. Write the words on the board or an overhead transparency, underlining the stressed syllable:

<u>bud</u>get	di<u>vide</u>
<u>bal</u>ance	ex<u>pen</u>ses
<u>pay</u>check	en<u>dorse</u>
<u>in</u>come	de<u>pos</u>it
<u>min</u>imum	e<u>lec</u>tric
ac<u>count</u>	<u>sig</u>nature
sub<u>tract</u>	<u>sav</u>ings
<u>state</u>ment	<u>check</u>ing

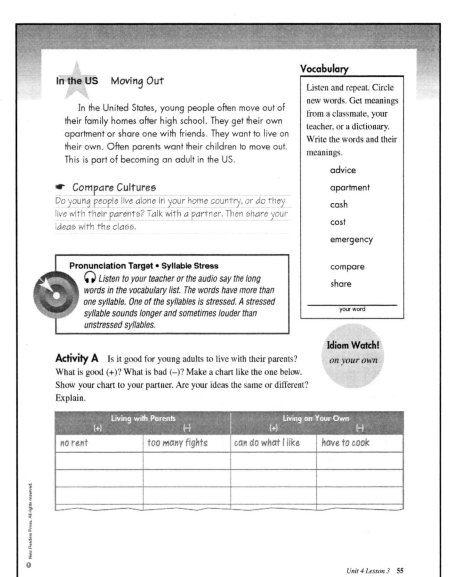

Unit 4 Lesson 3 55

📑 Use Unit Master 36 (Pronunciation/Listening: Dictation) now or at any time during the rest of the unit.

Activity A

Have learners complete their charts individually. Then have partners discuss what they wrote.

Extension

- Write the title *Living with Parents* at the top of a large sheet of paper. Title a similar sheet *Living on Your Own.*
- Divide each sheet into two columns. Place a plus sign above one column and a minus sign above the other.
- Post the pieces of paper on opposite sides of the classroom.
- Have learners go to the poster whose title they prefer. Ask them to write the reasons for their preference under the plus sign.
- Then ask learners to go to the other side of the room and write the reasons against this idea under the minus sign.
- When all learners have had a chance to write, discuss their opinions as a class.
- Tally the reasons. What seems to be the consensus of the class?

📖 Assign Workbook pp. 29–30.

Unit 4 *Lesson 3* **55**

Activity B

Have learners work in pairs. Ask one learner from each pair to report to the class the advice the pair wants to give Joseph.

Answer

If he saves $60 a month, it will take Joseph 20 months (or one year and eight months) to save $1,200.

Extension

Ask learners to talk about Joseph's income and expenses. Ask questions like these:

- Are they reasonable?
- Can you compare them to your own?
- Are they much higher or much lower?

Remind learners their own budget is private; they do not have to talk about specific amounts.

Attention Box

Pronounce and define *miscellaneous* for learners. One meaning might be *having many unrelated objects or ideas.*

This word should be understood, but learners should not be expected to produce it at this point.

Activity C

Have partners discuss the pie chart in the student book. Than have them write answers to the two questions.

Answers

- He spends 90% of his income, or approximately $1,884.
- He saves 10% of his income, or approximately $209.

One Step Up

Use Customizable Master 7 (Pie Chart). Follow the suggestions on p. 7 for customizing and duplicating the master. Make a copy for each learner.

- Show learners how to make calculations from dollar amounts to percentages (e.g., $200 *expense*

divided by $1000 *income* equals 20 *percent*).

- Ask learners to complete their pie charts with their own expenses and savings plan. Remind them to work independently because this information is private.

Task 3

Use Customizable Master 2 (2-Column Chart). Follow the suggestions on p. 7 for customizing and duplicating the master. Distribute a copy to each learner. Have learners work individually to complete their charts.

Review Unit Skills

See p. 8 for suggestions on games and activities to review the vocabulary and grammar in this unit.

Activity B Work with a partner. Look at Joseph's budget. What advice can you give him? How can he save more money? How long will it take Joseph to save $1200.00 if he saves $60.00 a month?

Monthly Income			Savings Goals		
Big City Taxi		$1853.40	1. Deposit on Apartment		$1200.00
Yard Service		$240.00	2. Emergency Fund		0
	Total	$2093.40		Total	$1200.00

Expenses that Stay the Same			Expenses that Change		
Rent		$600.00	Food		$200.00
Electric		$120.00	Clothing		$100.00
Car Insurance		$300.00	Telephone		$200.00
Renters Insurance		$50.00	Entertainment		$100.00
	Total A	$1070.00		Total B	$600.00

Total A + Total B = Total Expenses = $1670.00

Activity C Work with a partner. Read Joseph's budget as a pie chart. How much does Joseph spend monthly? How much does Joseph save?

misc. = miscellaneous

10% misc. expenses 10% savings 80% expenses

 TASK 3 Where Did the Money Go?

Look back at the spending journal you did for Task 1. Write the information you gathered in a chart like this one.

Expenses that Stay the Same		Expenses that Change	
		fast food	$25.00
		greeting card	$2.50

Unit 4 Project 🌐

Learners create a monthly budget.

Get Ready

Because everything about a budget is personal and private, learners should work independently in class.

📑 Use Unit Master 37 (Unit 4 Project: Make Your Budget). Distribute a copy to each learner.

Remind learners they have already collected the information they need:

- For Partner Chat in Lesson 2, they decided on savings goals.
- For Task 2, they listed all family income and made a savings plan.
- For Task 3, they used information gathered in Task 1 to chart their expenses.

Do the Work

Tell learners it is all right to share their budget and savings plan with their family members. Everyone in the family, and often everyone living in the same household, needs to understand a budget and savings plan and agree to help make it work.

Present Your Project

- Tell learners to explain to their families or other people they live with that they are making a budget plan in English class.
- Encourage learners to talk about how important it is for everyone to help in the planning. Everyone in the household needs to participate in any changes and feel good about the final plan.
- Suggest learners present the plan in a family or household meeting, perhaps after dinner or later in the evening. They should be sure everyone attends the meeting.
- Tell learners to use charts, if possible, to explain the plan and to encourage their family or household members to ask questions.

Writing Extension

Tell learners to use the Writing Checklists on p. 126 in their books as they edit and revise their writing.

UNIT 4 Project

Make Your Budget

Create a monthly budget. Look at it with your family.

Get Ready
1. Get a chart from your teacher.
2. Write your savings goals from page 53.
3. Write your income from Task 2, page 53.
4. Write your expenses from Task 3, page 56.

Do the Work

Monthly Income		Savings Goals	
1. 2.	Total	1. 2. 3. Emergency Fund	Total
Expenses that Stay the Same		**Expenses that Change**	
Rent Electric Car Insurance Renters Insurance	Total A	Food Clothing Telephone Entertainment	Total B
Total A + Total B = Total Expenses =			

Present Your Project

Show your budget to everyone who lives with you. Everyone must understand the budget. You have to work as a team to reach savings goals. Does anyone see how to save more money? What changes will you make to the plan? Remember, goals can change. If your savings goals change, you have to change the budget.

✏️ **Writing Extension** In your notebook, write about making a budget. What was difficult? How do you feel now that you have a plan?

Unit 4 Project 57

Assessment

📑 Use Generic Assessment Master 9 (Written Communication Rubric) to assess learner performance on the writing extension.

📖 Assign Workbook p. 31 (Check Your Progress).

📑 Use Unit Master 38 (Unit 4 Checkup/Review) whenever you complete this unit.

Unit 5: Bargain Shopping ✺www✺

Materials for the Unit

- Objects or pictures to illustrate bargains
- Newspaper, magazine, and catalog ads for clothing and other products, with a variety of ads for each type of item
- Scraps of cotton, denim, and leather (optional)
- Videotape of a television commercial (optional)
- Bag of clothing (varied types, styles, colors, and sizes), including items shown on p. 64
- Measuring tape
- Picture of a surfer riding a surfboard
- Printed copies of Internet shopping pages (optional)
- Customizable Masters 2–5
- Generic Assessment Master 12
- Unit Masters 39–44
- Vocabulary Card Masters for Unit 5

Bargain Shopping

- Read the title and unit goals. Then follow the suggestions on p. 5 for talking about titles.
- Introduce the word *bargain* by holding up an object or a picture of an object. Then write two prices on the board or an overhead transparency. Ask, "Which is a bargain?"
- Repeat with other objects or pictures until learners can answer correctly.

Discuss the word *bargain:*
- Put learners into small groups around two tables.
- On each table, place a few groups of newspaper ads. Each ad group should show the same kind of item (e.g., a particular appliance, an article of clothing, an over-the-counter medication).
- Tell the groups to look at the ads and select one item they would like to buy.
- Have them look at the ads for that item to find a *bargain.*

Bargain Shopping

Getting a Good Deal

Home 1   Work/School 2   Community 3

- **Vocabulary** Shopping ◦ Places to shop ◦ Clothing and electronics
- **Language** Comparative adjectives ◦ Compound sentences with *and . . . too* and with *or*
- **Pronunciation** Sounds of *th* ◦ Sounds of *s* and *st*
- **Culture** Shopping in the US

Can you find bargains?   Ann Judson takes her children shopping for things for school.

Think and Talk
1. Where are the Judsons going?
2. What will they do?
3. How do you think Ann feels?
4. How can they find bargains?

What's Your Opinion? What's good or bad about shopping?

58 *Unit 5*

Question
- Read the question below the arrow.
- Ask learners which items they wanted to buy in the previous activity. Why is each a *good buy?*

Photo
Follow the suggestions on p. 5 for talking about the photo. Then ask these questions:
- How many children do you see?
- Where are they?

Think and Talk
Have learners think individually about each question before answering.

Answers
1. The Judsons are going shopping.
2. They will shop for school.
3. Answers will vary.
4. Answers will vary.

What's Your Opinion?
Tell learners to consider time, transportation, convenience, money, and enjoyment as they discuss the question.

Picture Dictionary

Follow the suggestions on p. 6 for introducing and reinforcing vocabulary.

Follow the suggestions on p. 6 for using vocabulary cards. Use the Vocabulary Card Masters for the words in the Picture Dictionary.

Gather Your Thoughts

Draw the idea map shown in the student book on the board or an overhead transparency.
- Ask learners to supply the words as you complete the idea map.
- Have learners return to the small groups in which they discussed bargains.
- Ask them to cut from newspapers and magazines pictures of merchandise they buy and the names of places they shop.

Use Customizable Master 5 (Idea Map). Customize two maps, one with the head *Products* in the center circle, and the other with the head *Places*. Then follow the suggestions on p. 7 for duplicating the master. Make one copy of each of the maps for each learner.
- Have learners complete their idea maps with the pictures and text they cut out.
- Ask them to label each merchandise picture and add a reasonable price for the item.

What's the Problem?

Follow the suggestions on p. 5 for identifying and analyzing problems.
- Model the issue by telling learners what things can make *your* shopping difficult.
- Refer pairs of learners back to their responses in What's Your Opinion? as a starting point.

Setting Goals

Follow the suggestions on p. 5 for setting goals.

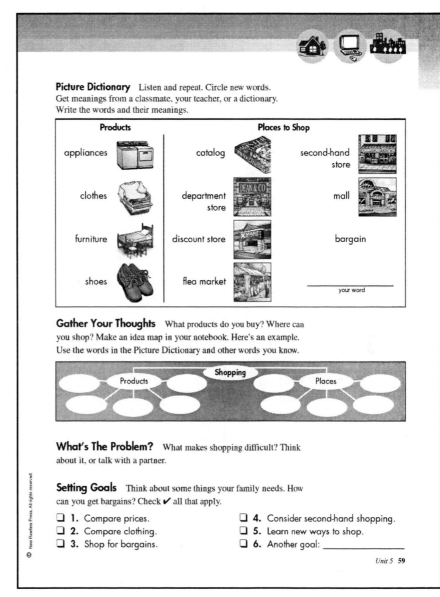

Picture Dictionary Listen and repeat. Circle new words. Get meanings from a classmate, your teacher, or a dictionary. Write the words and their meanings.

Products	Places to Shop	
appliances	catalog	second-hand store
clothes	department store	mall
furniture	discount store	bargain
shoes	flea market	_____ your word

Gather Your Thoughts What products do you buy? Where can you shop? Make an idea map in your notebook. Here's an example. Use the words in the Picture Dictionary and other words you know.

Products — Shopping — Places

What's The Problem? What makes shopping difficult? Think about it, or talk with a partner.

Setting Goals Think about some things your family needs. How can you get bargains? Check ✔ all that apply.

- ❑ 1. Compare prices.
- ❑ 2. Compare clothing.
- ❑ 3. Shop for bargains.
- ❑ 4. Consider second-hand shopping.
- ❑ 5. Learn new ways to shop.
- ❑ 6. Another goal: _____

Unit 5 **59**

Extension

Tell learners to think about which things on the goals list they can do to get the items they listed in Gather Your Thoughts.

One Step Up

Orally proficient learners can share their information with the class.

Lesson 1: Looking for School Clothes ☼www

- Follow the suggestions on p. 5 for talking about titles. Then point out the lesson objectives listed below it.
- In this lesson, learners will find out how to comparison shop.

Attention Box

- If possible, bring samples of *cotton, denim,* and *leather.* Point out items of learners' clothing made from these materials.
- Point out *pockets* in learners' own clothing.

This vocabulary should be understood, but learners should not be expected to produce the words at this point.

Question

Read the introductory question aloud and brainstorm answers with learners. Can learners look in the newspaper? On television? In magazines? On the Internet?

Reading Tip

Read the tip aloud. Then do the following:

- Point to the ad in the student book and ask learners to find the word or words that describe each picture (e.g., *sneakers*). Have learners circle the word or words as they say them.
- Ask learners to read the ad in their books.

Talk or Write

Have partners discuss the answers to the four questions.

This exercise helps learners become skilled at finding details in advertisements.

Answers

1. Jeans, sneakers, T-shirts, sandals, a dress, socks, briefs, and pants
2. $8.00 ($4.00 on each pair)
3. Small, Medium, Large, and Extra Large.
4. Briefs and pants

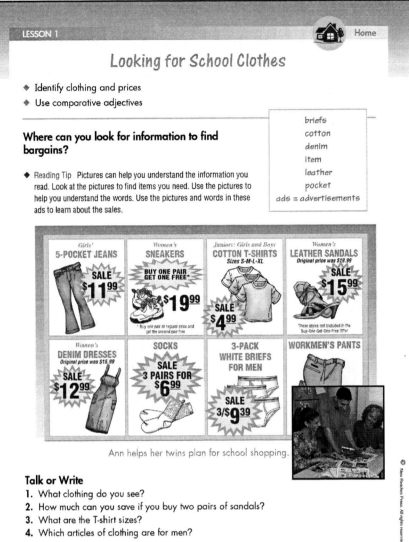

LESSON 1   🏠 Home

Looking for School Clothes

- ◆ Identify clothing and prices
- ◆ Use comparative adjectives

Where can you look for information to find bargains?

| briefs |
| cotton |
| denim |
| item |
| leather |
| pocket |
| ads = advertisements |

- ◆ Reading Tip Pictures can help you understand the information you read. Look at the pictures to find items you need. Use the pictures to help you understand the words. Use the pictures and words in these ads to learn about the sales.

Girls'
5-POCKET JEANS
SALE **$11⁹⁹**

Women's
SNEAKERS
BUY ONE PAIR GET ONE FREE*
$19⁹⁹
* Buy one pair at regular price and get the second pair free

Juniors: Girls and Boys
COTTON T-SHIRTS
Sizes S-M-L-XL
SALE **$4⁹⁹**

Women's
LEATHER SANDALS
Original price was $19.99
SALE **$15⁹⁹**
These styles not included in the Buy-One-Get-One-Free Offer

Women's
DENIM DRESSES
Original price was $15.99
SALE **$12⁹⁹**

SOCKS
SALE 3 PAIRS FOR **$6⁹⁹**

3-PACK WHITE BRIEFS FOR MEN
SALE **3/$9³⁹**

WORKMEN'S PANTS

Ann helps her twins plan for school shopping.

Talk or Write
1. What clothing do you see?
2. How much can you save if you buy two pairs of sandals?
3. What are the T-shirt sizes?
4. Which articles of clothing are for men?

60   *Unit 5 Lesson 1*

Extension
Ask these additional questions:
- What can you get for free? (*one pair of women's sneakers*)
- How many pairs of socks do you get for $6.99? (*three*)
- How much is one pair of briefs for men? (*$1.04*)
- What is the savings on a denim dress? (*$3.00*)

Picture Dictionary

Follow the suggestions on p. 6 for introducing and reinforcing vocabulary.

Follow the suggestions on p. 6 for using vocabulary cards. Use the Vocabulary Card Masters for the words in the Picture Dictionary.

To teach the clothing vocabulary, do one of the following:
- Point to a learner's clothing to illustrate each vocabulary word.
- Ask, "Who is wearing _____?"

Class Chat

Have learners copy the chart in their notebooks or use Customizable Master 3 (3-Column Chart). Follow the suggestions on p. 7 for customizing and duplicating the master. Make a copy for each learner.

One Step Up
- Have learners report back to the class on the places people buy their clothes.
- Model sentences for their reports (e.g., *"Eight people buy their clothes at Clothes 4 U."* *"A lot of people buy their clothes at department stores."*).
- Tell learners not to mention any learners' names when making their reports.

Grammar Talk

Follow the suggestions on p. 7 for introducing the grammar point.

Answers
These are the three ways to make comparisons:
- Use an adjective ending in *-er.*
- Use *more* + adjective.
- Use *better.*

Use *than* to compare one thing to another.

One Step Up
Explain the following grammar rules:
- To form the comparative of one-syllable adjectives, add *-er* (e.g.,

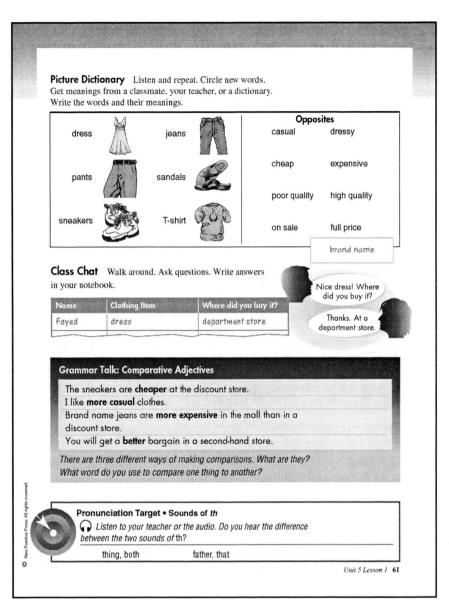

Unit 5 Lesson 1 **61**

small, smaller).
- To form the comparative of two-syllable adjectives that end in *y,* change the *y* to *i* and add *-er* (e.g., *pretty, prettier*).
- To form the comparative of most two- or three-syllable adjectives, use *more* before the adjective (e.g., *beautiful, more beautiful*)

Have learners copy these irregular adjectives into their notebooks:
good, better
bad, worse
many, more
much, more

Pronunciation Target

Play the audio or read the words in the student book.

Follow the suggestions on page 7 for teaching pronunciation and voiced and voiceless sounds.
- The *th* sound is voiced in the words *leather, mother, other,* and *that.* Have learners say these words, feeling the vibration in their throats.
- The *th* sound is voiceless in the words *thing, think, three,* and *both.* There is no vibration when saying the *th.*

Assign Workbook pp. 32–33.

Use Unit Master 39 (Grammar: Comparisons) now or at any time during the rest of the unit.

Unit 5 *Lesson 1* **61**

Activity A

As learners write their sentences, circulate to monitor their work.

Activity B

Ask volunteers to share their sentences with the class.

Activity C

- Provide newspaper and magazine clothing ads for learners to look at.
- Have learners make a chart like the one in the student book in their notebooks.

Extension

Assemble six large sheets of paper. Label each with one of these headings: *Department Stores, Discount Stores, Flea Markets, Second-Hand Stores, Catalogs,* and *Internet.* Then do the following:

- Post each sheet in a different area of the room.
- Tell learners to go to the poster that names their favorite place to shop.
- Ask them to write on the sheet the items they shop for in that place and the reasons they like to shop there.
- Ask learners with the same favorite shopping place to form a group and together write a paragraph about it.
- To edit their writing, have learners refer to the Writing Checklists on p. 126.

Task 1

Distribute clothing ads from magazines, newspapers, and catalogs to small groups of learners. Then do the following:

Use Customizable Master 4 (4-Column Chart). Follow the suggestions on p. 7 for customizing the master. Give one copy of the customized chart to each small group.

- Define *description* (e.g., *style, color, size*).

- Describe *quality* (e.g., *type of material, level of workmanship*).
- Draw a sample chart on the board or an overhead transparency. Write *Item: Dress* above the chart. Show learners a newspaper ad for a dress, and complete the *Newspaper* row of the chart with information from the ad. Under *Description,* include the style, color, and sizes available. Under *Quality,* include the material and level of workmanship. For example, if your ad features a denim jumper, you might complete the first row of the chart as shown below:

Price	Description	Quality
$59.99	Jumper, blue, SML	Denim, High quality

- Have learners work in groups to complete a chart together.

One Step Up

Tell partners to explain their Task 1 charts to each other. Then have them discuss which item they will buy.

Activity A **Class Chat Follow-Up** Look at your Class Chat notes. In your notebook, write sentences about your classmates' clothes.

Fayed bought her dress at a department store.

Activity B Talk to five different people. Ask them where they like to shop and why. Take notes in your notebook.

> I shop at a discount shoe store because it is cheaper.

> It's better to go to the mall. The shoes are nicer.

Write sentences. Share with the class.

Miriam likes to shop at the mall because she finds better quality clothes.

Activity C Work in a group. Look at newspaper and magazine ads for clothes. Make a chart like the one below. Write three items you want to buy, a place where you can buy each, and the prices.

Item	Shopping Place	Price
dress	department store	$59.99

TASK 1 **Compare As You Shop**
Choose one item you need to buy. Find the same item in different newspaper ads, magazine ads, and store catalogs. Compare the items. Use the chart.

One Step Up
With a partner, talk about your shopping choice. Which one will you buy?

	Price	Description	Quality
Newspaper			
Magazine			
Catalog			

62 Unit 5 Lesson 1

Lesson 2: A Shopping Spree ✳www

- Write this definition on the board or an overhead transparency: *Shopping spree = A shopping trip where you buy a lot*
- Explain that in this lesson learners will learn how to compare sizes in the US and their home countries. They will also compare shopping in their home countries with shopping in the US.

Question

Read the introductory question and tally learners' answers. Ask a learner to help you record on the board or a transparency the number of learners answering *yes* or *no*. Encourage learners to explain their answers.

Extension

After learners respond, follow up with these questions:
- Do you watch television commercials?
- Do you switch channels during commercials?
- Do you learn about bargains from television?

Tally learners' answers on the board or an overhead transparency.

Listening Tip

Read the tip aloud.

Tell learners that, while they are listening, they should try to imagine what they would be seeing if they were actually watching this commercial on television.

Extension

Before having learners listen to the script, use your VCR to record a television commercial at home and show it in class. Talk about it with learners.

🎧 Play the audio or read the listening script on p. 120. Follow the suggestions on p. 5 for listening comprehension.

Talk or Write

🎧 Read the questions aloud with learners. Then play the audio or read the script again.

LESSON 2 Work/School

A Shopping Spree

◆ Identify clothing
◆ Compare shopping issues in different cultures

Do you find out about bargains on television?

◆ Listening Tip 🎧 Close your eyes and pretend you are listening to a commercial. Write the items that are advertised. Listen again. You can read the words on page 119.

This shirt is on sale for only $22.95.

Ann works at Better Bargains Superstore. They are having a big sale. She is helping customers.

Talk or Write
1. Where are the bargains?
2. What items are advertised?
3. Listen for the comparative adjectives in the TV ad. Write them in your notebook. Write three sentences using the adjectives.

Unit 5 Lesson 2 **63**

This exercise helps learners become skilled at understanding commercials.

Answers
1. At the Better Bargains Superstore.
2. Brand-name clothes, sneakers and sandals, school supplies, appliances, furniture.
3. Better, easier, cheaper. (Sentences will vary.)

Extension
Have learners work in pairs to write a television commercial for one of the shopping places they selected in Task 1.

One Step Up
Have pairs of learners role-play commercials for a particular store. Then all learners can vote on whether they were persuaded to shop there.

Picture Dictionary

Follow the suggestions on p. 6 for introducing and reinforcing vocabulary.

Follow the suggestions on p. 6 for using vocabulary cards. Use the Vocabulary Card Masters for the words in the Picture Dictionary.

- Bring a bag of clothing to class. Include a variety of types, styles, colors, and sizes and as many as possible of the items in the Picture Dictionary on this page. (Use your judgment about bringing underwear.)
- Pull out each article of clothing and say the appropriate word.
- Have learners select clothing for an imaginary friend. Encourage them to have fun mixing and matching items.
- Have partners tell each other what their imaginary friend is wearing. Encourage them to use comparative adjectives in their descriptions.
- Ask learners to share their sentences with the class. Write selected sentences on the board or an overhead transparency.

Extension

As a review of clothing vocabulary, have learners call out all the clothing words they know. Write the words on the board or an overhead transparency and have learners copy the list into their notebooks.

One Step Down

For learners who have difficulty writing all the clothing words, make copies of the list.

In the US

Before learners read this section, use the text in the student book in a jigsaw activity:

- Write the sentence(s) for each bulleted topic on a large card, and put one card in each corner of the room. Number each corner (1–4).

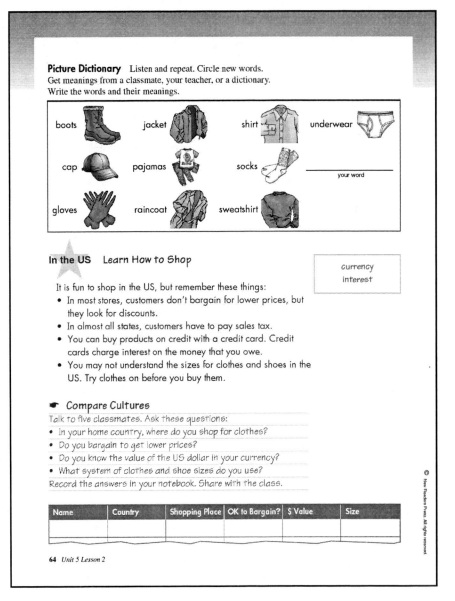

Picture Dictionary Listen and repeat. Circle new words. Get meanings from a classmate, your teacher, or a dictionary. Write the words and their meanings.

boots jacket shirt underwear
cap pajamas socks _____ your word
gloves raincoat sweatshirt

⭐ **In the US** Learn How to Shop

currency interest

It is fun to shop in the US, but remember these things:
- In most stores, customers don't bargain for lower prices, but they look for discounts.
- In almost all states, customers have to pay sales tax.
- You can buy products on credit with a credit card. Credit cards charge interest on the money that you owe.
- You may not understand the sizes for clothes and shoes in the US. Try clothes on before you buy them.

☛ **Compare Cultures**
Talk to five classmates. Ask these questions:
- In your home country, where do you shop for clothes?
- Do you bargain to get lower prices?
- Do you know the value of the US dollar in your currency?
- What system of clothes and shoe sizes do you use?
Record the answers in your notebook. Share with the class.

Name	Country	Shopping Place	OK to Bargain?	$ Value	Size

64 *Unit 5 Lesson 2*

- Put learners in small groups. Tell them they are going to learn how people in the US shop for good buys.
- Have learners number off from *one* to *four* and go to the corresponding corner.
- Tell learners to write in their notebooks the information they read in their corners. Then have them return to their home groups to share the information.
- Have each group write notes on the main things they learned about shopping in the US.

Compare Cultures

Use Customizable Master 3 (3-Column Chart). Customize the master by dividing each column in two to make a six-column chart.

Label the columns with these heads: *Name, Country, Shopping Place, OK to Bargain?, $ Value, and Size.*

Follow the suggestions on p. 7 for duplicating the master. Make a copy for each learner.

 Assign Workbook pp. 34–35.

Activity A

Get learners started with this activity:

- On the board or an overhead transparency, draw two columns with the heads *Centimeters* and *Inches*.
- Tell learners that to convert centimeters to inches, divide by 2.5. To convert inches to centimeters, multiply by 2.5. (These formulas give approximate conversions. For more exact conversions, use the table on p. 31.)
- Write these examples on the board:

	Cm.	In.
Waist	82.5	33
Height	190	76
Pants Length	86	34.4

- Ask a volunteer to measure your height with a tape measure.
- Write the measurement both in centimeters and in inches.
- Have additional volunteers measure one another's height.

Activity B

Use Customizable Master 4 (4-Column Chart). Label the columns with the heads *Item, Price, 6% Tax,* and *Subtotal.* Make a copy for each learner.

To show learners another way to calculate tax, write the following on the board or an overhead transparency:

Men's cotton sweater	$19.99
Women's wool gloves	$ 9.49
Ladies' satin pajamas	$24.99
Girls' sleep shirt	$16.99
Subtotal	$71.46
6% tax (71.46 × .06)	$ 4.29
Total	$75.75

Task 2

Make a copy of Customizable Master 3 (3-Column Chart) for this activity. Label the columns *Item, US Size,* and *Home Country*

Activity A   Work with a partner. Convert the metric sizes below to the US system.

> Divide the centimeters by 2.5 to get inches.

	Mr. Lafitte		Mrs. Lafitte	
	Metric	US	Metric	US
Height	175 cm	70 in.	155 cm	____
Waist	102 cm	____	85 cm	____
Pants Length	85 cm	____	75 cm	____

Activity B   Work with your partner. Write a list of clothing items Mr. and Mrs. Lafitte can buy. Write a price for each item. This state charges 6% tax. What is the total that the Lafittes will have to pay?

> To calculate the tax, you multiply the total times 0.06.

Item	Price	6% Tax	Subtotal
jacket	$79.99	$4.80	$84.79
_____	_____	_____	_____
_____	_____	_____	_____
_____	_____	_____	_____
		Total	_____

TASK 2 List Clothing Sizes

Work in groups. Do you buy clothes for another person? Complete a chart like this one.

Person's Name:		Relationship:
	US Size	Home Country Size
dress		
jacket		
pants		
shirt		
shoes		
other:		

Size. Then distribute a copy to each learner.

- Have learners write the list of clothes items on six rows in the first column.
- Tell learners to think of a child or a close family member whose sizes they can use to complete this chart.
- Remind learners that sizes can be numbers (e.g., shoes in US 7 or Home Country 36) or letters (e.g., T-shirts in US L or Home Country G).

Lesson 3: Surfing the Internet 🌐

- Write the expression *surfing the Internet* on the board. Illustrate it with a picture of a surfer riding the waves on a surfboard.
- Explain that the *Internet* is often called the *'Net*. The *World Wide Web* (or just the *Web*) is part of the Internet. Tell learners they can also say *surfing the 'Net* or *surfing the Web*.
- Read the lesson objectives aloud.
- Tell learners they will compare three ads for a product they want to buy—one from a newspaper, one from a catalog, and one from the Internet.

Question

- Write *Often, Sometimes,* and *Never* on the board.
- Read the question aloud and tally learners' responses.
- Ask learners who shop on the Internet to talk about what they have bought.

Then ask these questions:
- What are some pluses of shopping on the Internet? *(shopping at home, wide selection of goods, range of prices, product information online)*
- What are some minuses? *(cannot see quality, seller may be unknown, may have difficulty returning items)*

Reading Tip

- Read the tip aloud.
- Remind learners they discussed the word *scan* in Units 1 and 2. Ask them to provide a meaning (e.g., *looking quickly at a reading to see its major points*).
- Put learners in pairs for the word list activity. Circulate to help them.

Talk or Write

Have learners keep their previous partners to work on these questions.

This exercise helps learners become skilled at reading a web site.

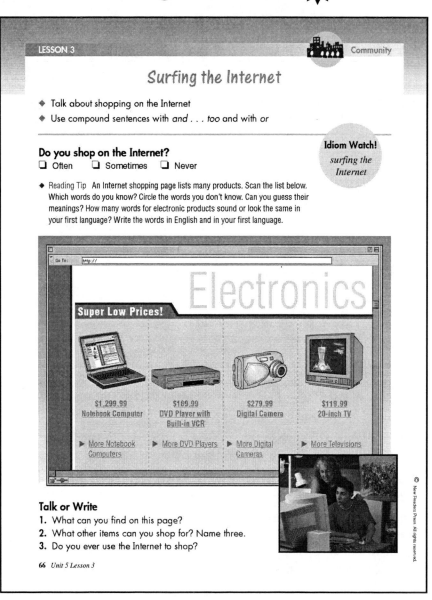

LESSON 3 Community

Surfing the Internet

◆ Talk about shopping on the Internet
◆ Use compound sentences with *and . . . too* and with *or*

Do you shop on the Internet?
Idiom Watch! *surfing the Internet*
☐ Often ☐ Sometimes ☐ Never

◆ Reading Tip An Internet shopping page lists many products. Scan the list below. Which words do you know? Circle the words you don't know. Can you guess their meanings? How many words for electronic products sound or look the same in your first language? Write the words in English and in your first language.

Go To: http://

Electronics

Super Low Prices!

$1,299.99 Notebook Computer | $169.99 DVD Player with Built-in VCR | $279.99 Digital Camera | $119.99 20-inch TV

▶ More Notebook Computers | ▶ More DVD Players | ▶ More Digital Cameras | ▶ More Televisions

Talk or Write
1. What can you find on this page?
2. What other items can you shop for? Name three.
3. Do you ever use the Internet to shop?

66 *Unit 5 Lesson 3*

Answers
1. Electronics (computer, DVD player, digital camera, TV).
2. Answers will vary.
3. Answers will vary.

Extension
Ask these additional questions:
- What costs $1,299.99? *(notebook computer)*
- What costs $279.99? *(digital camera)*
- How much does the TV cost? *($119.99)*
- How much does the DVD player cost? *($169.99)*

One Step Up
- Print out and make copies of Internet shopping pages. Ask learners with Internet access to bring some too.
- Put learners in groups. Give a copy of one of the web pages to each group. Have each group write questions about its page (e.g., *How much will shipping and handling cost?*)
- Tell each group to exchange copies of their web page with another group. Then have them ask the other group the questions they wrote.

Picture Dictionary

Follow the suggestions on p. 6 for introducing vocabulary.

Follow the suggestions on p. 6 for using vocabulary cards. Use the Vocabulary Card Masters for the words in the Picture Dictionary.

Extension

1. Distribute vocabulary cards for the words *camera, electronic game, fax,* and *wireless phone.* Ask volunteers to act out or mime the use of the device written on their cards. Have the class guess which item is being acted out.
2. Write these incomplete sentences on the board:
   Do you have a/an ____?
   ____ has/an ____ and a/an ____ too.
   Do you want to buy a/an ____ or a/an ____?
   Model asking the questions (e.g., "Do you have a camera?"). Write a sample answer. Then have volunteers ask other learners the questions.

Class Chat

 Use Customizable Master 2 (2-Column Chart). Follow the suggestions on p. 7 for customizing and duplicating the master and distributing the copies. Make one copy for each learner.

Ask two volunteers to model asking and answering the question.

Grammar Talk

Follow the suggestions on p. 7 for introducing the grammar point.

Tell learners that compound sentences are two sentences joined by a *conjunction (and, but,* or *or).*

Answers

And . . . too is used to say two different things.

Or is used to indicate a decision needs to be made between two different things.

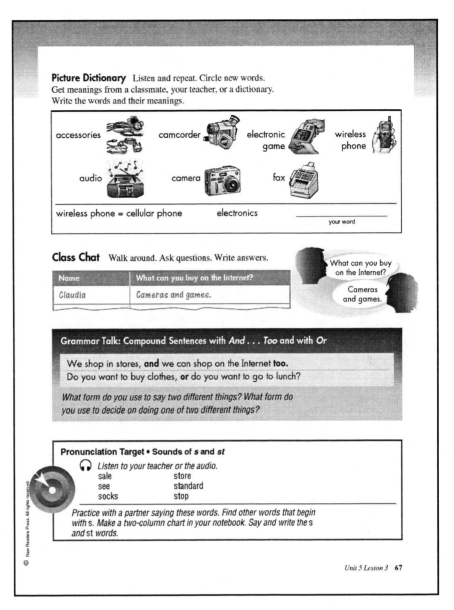

Picture Dictionary Listen and repeat. Circle new words.
Get meanings from a classmate, your teacher, or a dictionary.
Write the words and their meanings.

accessories   camcorder   electronic game   wireless phone
audio   camera   fax

wireless phone = cellular phone   electronics   _____ your word

Class Chat Walk around. Ask questions. Write answers.

Name	What can you buy on the Internet?
Claudia	Cameras and games.

What can you buy on the Internet? / Cameras and games.

Grammar Talk: Compound Sentences with *And . . . Too* and with *Or*

We shop in stores, **and** we can shop on the Internet **too.**
Do you want to buy clothes, **or** do you want to go to lunch?

What form do you use to say two different things? What form do you use to decide on doing one of two different things?

Pronunciation Target • Sounds of *s* and *st*
Listen to your teacher or the audio.

sale	store
see	standard
socks	stop

Practice with a partner saying these words. Find other words that begin with s. Make a two-column chart in your notebook. Say and write the s and st words.

Extension

- Ask learners to make sentences about their classmates using *and . . . too* and *or.*
- Review adverbs of frequency *(always, often, sometimes, never)* so learners can use them in their sentences.
- Have volunteers read some of their sentences. Write them on the board.

Pronunciation Target

Play the audio or read the words in the student book.
- Draw two columns on the board. Label one *S* and the other *ST.*
- Tell learners that *st* is a consonant blend. The two consonants make separate sounds but are pronounced quickly and smoothly together. Demonstrate its pronunciation.
- Read each word aloud and ask learners to repeat after you.
- Write each word in the appropriate column.
- Ask learners for other words beginning with *s* and *st.* Place each in the correct column.

Assign Workbook pp. 36–37.

Use Unit Masters 40 (Grammar: Order from a Catalog), 41 (Pronunciation: Tic-Tac-Toe Game), and 42 (Game: Bingo) now or at any time during the rest of the unit.

Activity A

- Tell partners to look through catalogs and flyers to select their items. If you have Internet access, have learners "shop" at an Internet shopping site.
- Have students write sentences following the models in their books.

Extensions

1. Have partners make a shared shopping list of everything they want to buy. Then have the pairs do the following:
   - Estimate the price of each.
   - Estimate sales tax and shipping charges.
   - Add the total amount they need for their "shopping spree."
2. Have each pair exchange lists with another pair. Then do the following:
   - Have partners select one or two items from the other pair's list to add to their own.
   - Tell partners to get back their original lists, add the new item(s), and write additional sentences.

Activity B

Put learners in small groups to discuss the pros and cons of shopping on the Internet.

Tell each group to write at least three compound sentences.

Extension

Have learners play a game of Give One, Get One.

- Tell each small group to send a representative to another group to exchange sentences.
- Tell the representatives to compare their sentences with those of the new group and ask questions about any new or confusing words, phrases or ideas.
- Have each representative select one sentence from the new group to add to his or her group's sentences.
- Continue until each representative has visited every group.

Activity A Talk with a partner. You have $80. Look at a shopping site on the Internet, or look at store catalogs and newspaper flyers.
- Find two things that you can buy. Write a sentence about them with *and*.
- Find two things that you like, but you can only afford to buy one of them. Write a sentence about them with *or*.

I can buy a pair of sneakers, and I can buy a pair of jeans too.

I can buy a CD player, or I can buy a computer game.

Activity B Work in a small group. Talk about the advantages and disadvantages of shopping on the Internet. Write compound sentences about shopping on the Internet, in stores, or through catalogs.

> advantage   +
> disadvantage −

Shopping on the Internet

Advantages (+)	Disadvantages (−)
bigger market	credit card fraud
stay home	shipping charges
more choices	cannot see merchandise

On the Internet, I have more choices, and I can stay home too.

In the stores, I can pay with cash, or I can use a credit card.

TASK 3 Compare Ads

Select an item you want to buy. Compare three ads: a newspaper ad, a catalog ad, and an Internet ad. Complete the chart.

	Newspaper	Catalog	Internet
Place to buy			
Description			
Cost			
Tax			
Shipping and handling			
Total			

Task 3

Use Customizable Master 4 (4-Column Chart). Follow the suggestions on p. 7 for customizing and duplicating the master. Make a copy for each learner.

Ongoing Assessment

When learners have completed this activity, walk around the room and look at their charts. Make notes on how well learners performed on the following features:

a. Completion of task
   0 = minimal content
   1 = most components of task
   2 = all components of task
b. Quality of content
   0 = poor, minimal content
   1 = average, some clear information
   2 = excellent, all information clear and complete
c. Quality of language
   0 = poor, many errors
   1 = average, some errors
   2 = excellent, very few errors

One Step Up

Ask learners to add other items to the first column. Allow them to generate the ideas. If they have difficulty, suggest *payment terms, quality, color,* and *brand*.

Review Unit Skills

See p. 8 for suggestions on games and activities to review the vocabulary and grammar in this unit.

Unit 5 Project

Learners work in groups to find and report on a bargain.

Get Ready

- Talk to learners about what they did in Tasks 1, 2, and 3. (In Tasks 1 and 3, learners comparison shopped. In Task 2, they listed US and home country clothing sizes for someone they know.)
- Help learners review any information gathered in the three tasks that might be used to generate ideas or gather ads for this project.

Do the Work

Use Unit Master 43 (Unit 5 Project: Find a Bargain). Make a copy for each learner.

- Encourage learners to be creative and artistic in designing their posters.
- Distribute poster paper, scissors, and other art supplies.

Present Your Project

Give each learner a copy of Generic Assessment Master 12 (Peer Assessment Form for Projects and Tasks).

- Follow the suggestions for peer assessment on p. 4.
- Ask each group to practice its presentation in front of another group.
- Learners complete and exchange the forms before doing their final presentations.
- When groups make their final presentations, encourage active listening by asking questions about other presentations.

Writing Extension

Tell learners to use the Writing Checklists on p. 126 to edit their statements.

Technology Extra

- Tell learners to use the Internet to find three shopping links.

Find a Bargain

Read ads, compare items, and find a bargain.

Get Ready

In a group, select an item that you need to buy:
- clothes for teenagers
- a computer
- a toy for small children
- a car
- furniture
- an appliance

Each person brings an ad from a different place. Look for special offers, coupons, or delivery charges. Compare the ads, and select one item.

Do the Work

Get an idea map from your teacher. Write information in it about the product. Create a poster with the following information:
- product selected
- brand
- shopping place
- size or color
- price
- total cost (including tax and shipping charge)
- reasons for selecting the product

Present Your Project

Select one person in the group to report to the class.

✏ **Writing Extension** Write about the item that your group selected. Explain why you chose that item.

💻 **Technology Extra**
Go to the Internet. Find three shopping links. List one product you find to buy in each of them. Calculate the total cost.

Unit 5 Project **69**

- Have each learner list a product and price found at each.
- Have each learner calculate the total cost of his or her three items.

Assign Workbook p. 38 (Check Your Progress).

Use Unit Master 44 (Unit 5 Checkup/Review) whenever you complete this unit.

Unit 6: Equal Rights 🌐

Materials for the Unit

- Child's jigsaw puzzle (approximately 24 pieces)
- Pamphlets from a job center (optional)
- Customizable Masters 3 and 5
- Generic Assessment Masters 10 and 11
- Unit Masters 45–51
- Vocabulary Card Masters for Unit 6

Equal Rights

Read the unit goals with learners. Tell them the themes of this unit are equality, discrimination, and equal rights.

Discuss the concepts *equality* and *difference*. How can we all be equal if we are all different?

- Use a child's jigsaw puzzle.
- Distribute one puzzle piece to each learner.
- Ask learners how the pieces are different (shape, size, color, and design).
- Have them bring their pieces to a table and put the puzzle together.
- Now ask how the pieces are equal (*Each has value and a reason to be, and each contributes to the whole.*).
- How are your learners different? How are they equal?

Question

Read the question below the arrow. Then do the following:

- After learners respond *yes* or *no*, elicit details by asking *wh*-questions.
- Ask respondents if this happens *often, sometimes,* or *never.* If needed, review these adverbs.
- Write some learners' responses on the board or an overhead transparency.

<u>One Step Up</u>

Ask learners why they think discrimination happens.

UNIT 6

Equal Rights

Protecting Your Legal Rights

Work/School 1   Home 2   Community 3

- ◆ **Vocabulary** Rights in the workplace • Equality and discrimination
- ◆ **Language** Modals: *may, should, could, would* • Present continuous (review) and past continuous
- ◆ **Pronunciation** Sounds of *a* • Reductions
- ◆ **Culture** Equal rights and the law in the US

machine repairperson

Do you ever feel discriminated against?

Amara is looking for a job as a machine repairperson. No one will hire her. Her aunt and uncle think she should look for an easier job. She feels discriminated against.

Think and Talk

1. What is Amara doing?
2. What is she looking for?
3. Do you think she will find the job she wants?

70   Unit 6

Attention Box

Read the phrase to learners, pointing or miming to convey meaning if possible. This vocabulary should be understood, but learners should not be expected to produce the phrase at this point.

Photo

Follow the suggestions on p. 5 for talking about the photo.

- Ask learners to describe what they see in the photo.
- Ask a learner to read the caption.

Then ask these questions:

- What are Amara's aunt and uncle doing?
- What do they think?
- How does Amara feel?

Think and Talk

- Have learners talk in pairs or small groups about the answers to the questions.
- Than have learners share their answers with the class.

<u>Answers</u>

1. Amara is looking at job applications and classified ads.
2. She is looking for a job as a machine repairperson.
3. Answers will vary.

Vocabulary

Follow the suggestions on p. 6 for introducing and reinforcing vocabulary.

Follow the suggestions on p. 6 for using vocabulary cards. Use the Vocabulary Card Masters for the words in the Vocabulary box.

- Have learners think of related words (e.g., *equal/unequal,* examples of ethnicities).
- Ask learners for synonyms, definitions, or illustrations of as many words as possible.
- Have learners spell out the words as you write them on the board or an overhead transparency.

Gather Your Thoughts

Have learners copy the idea map in their notebooks or use Customizable Master 5 (Idea Map). Follow the suggestions on p. 7 for customizing and duplicating the master. Make one copy for each learner.

Discuss the questions in the student book. Then do the following:

- Have learners draw pictures of jobs they would like to do.
- Put learners in groups to create a collage of the jobs they like.
- Draw the idea map from the student book on the board or an overhead transparency. Complete with some of the jobs learners illustrated.
- Help members of each group complete their own idea maps.

What's the Problem?

Follow the suggestions on p. 5 for identifying and analyzing problems.

- Model the issue by telling learners about your "wildest dream" job. Be imaginative.
- Ask learners if they think you could get that kind of job. Have them explain why or why not. If not, is there a possibility of discrimination? Is there a possible lack of qualifications?

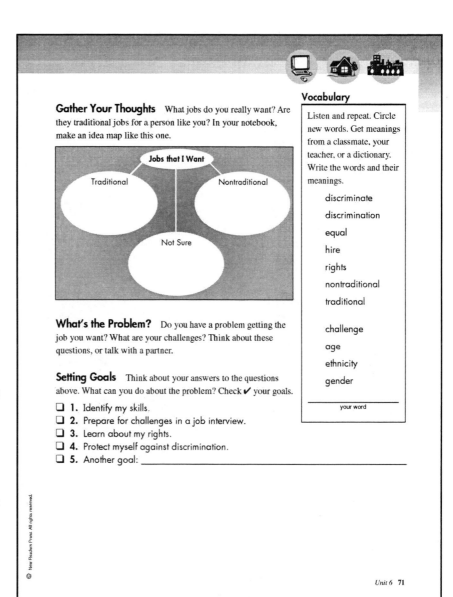

Gather Your Thoughts What jobs do you really want? Are they traditional jobs for a person like you? In your notebook, make an idea map like this one.

Jobs that I Want

Traditional

Nontraditional

Not Sure

What's the Problem? Do you have a problem getting the job you want? What are your challenges? Think about these questions, or talk with a partner.

Setting Goals Think about your answers to the questions above. What can you do about the problem? Check ✔ your goals.

- ❑ 1. Identify my skills.
- ❑ 2. Prepare for challenges in a job interview.
- ❑ 3. Learn about my rights.
- ❑ 4. Protect myself against discrimination.
- ❑ 5. Another goal: _____

Vocabulary

Listen and repeat. Circle new words. Get meanings from a classmate, your teacher, or a dictionary. Write the words and their meanings.

discriminate
discrimination
equal
hire
rights
nontraditional
traditional

challenge
age
ethnicity
gender

_____
your word

Unit 6 **71**

Write these incomplete sentences on the board:
_____ *would like to be* _____.
_____ *could* _____.
_____ *should* _____.
_____ *may/may not* _____.

- Write your name on the first line of each sentence and have learners complete the sentences about you.
- Have partners discuss the questions in the student book.
- Tell partners to write sentences about each other in their notebooks.
- Ask learners to tell about a more realistic job that they would like, and follow these steps again.

Setting Goals

Follow the suggestions on p. 5 for setting goals.

- Ask learners what they can do about the problem named in What's the Problem? above.
- Ask what they still need to learn to get a job they really want and how they can reach that goal.
- Have them review their goals for this unit and decide if they want to change any of them.

One Step Up

Orally proficient learners can share the information with the class.

Lesson 1: Getting the Job You Want

Read the title aloud with learners.

In this lesson, learners will find out how to write a thank-you letter.

Attention Box

- Read the words to learners.
- Write *plant* = *factory* on the board or an overhead transparency. Ask if anyone works or has worked in a factory.
- Ask those who say *yes* to tell you what jobs they did. Write those jobs on the board.
- Write *position* = *job* on the board.
- Then ask learners who have a job if they think they could get a good recommendation from their boss for the new job they want.

This vocabulary should be understood, but learners should not be expected to produce the words at this point.

Question

Read the introductory question aloud with learners. Discuss possible reasons for having trouble getting a job.

Listening Tip

- Tell learners that when they listen to a conversation, looking closely at the speakers and their expressions makes the conversation easier to understand.
- Read the tip aloud. Then tell learners it can help them if they look at the photo in their books while listening to this conversation.

Play the audio or read the listening script on p. 120. Follow the suggestions on p. 5 for listening comprehension.

Photo

Ask learners what they see in the picture. Then ask these questions:
- Where is Amara?
- Why is she there?

LESSON 1   Work/School

Getting the Job You Want

- Talk about qualifications and challenges
- Use the modals *may, should, could, would*

Did you ever have trouble getting the job you wanted?

- Listening Tip 🎧 A picture can give you some information about the topic. Look at the photo and then listen to the job interview. You can read the words on page 119. Listen again and try to follow along with the conversation.

machine repair
operator
position
recommendation
textile plant

Ben Sanders interviews Amara.

Talk or Write
1. Where is Amara?
2. What job is she applying for?
3. What job does the interviewer think she should apply for?
4. Do you think she'll get the job she wants?

72 Unit 6 Lesson 1

- Can you describe the interviewer?
- Is she acting correctly?

Extension
To answer the last question, refer learners back to In the US for Unit 1.

Talk or Write

This exercise helps learners understand a conversation.

Answers
1. Amara is in the office of a textile plant.
2. She is applying for the machine repair position.
3. The interviewer thinks she should start as an operator.
4. Answers will vary.

One Step Up
Dictate the conversation while learners write it.

Extension
Have pairs read the conversation.
- Encourage them to act hurried and unfriendly when playing the part of the interviewer.
- Remind them the applicant needs to remain calm and polite.

Vocabulary

Follow the suggestions on p. 6 for introducing and reinforcing vocabulary.

Follow the suggestions on p. 6 for using vocabulary cards. Use the Vocabulary Card Masters for the words in the Vocabulary box.

Have learners add related words of their own (e.g., *job, application, interview, education, work*).

Class Chat

Use Customizable Master 3 (3-Column Chart). Follow the suggestions on p. 7 for customizing and duplicating the master. Make a copy for each learner.
- Tell learners to share only what they feel comfortable talking about.
- If privacy is an issue or if learners have not been rejected for a job, have them invent plausible answers.
- Ask two volunteers to model asking and answering the questions.

Grammar Talk

Follow the suggestions on p. 7 for introducing the grammar point.

Answers
Modals need to be used with the base form of another verb to make a complete verb and a complete sentence. They do not have an *s* in the third person singular.

Ask learners for additional sentences with *may, should, could,* and *would.*

Extension
Give learners the following information, depending upon their prior knowledge of grammar and academic background.

Use *may* to express:
- A polite request (e.g., *May I use the bathroom?*)
- Permission (e.g., *You may go to the party.*)

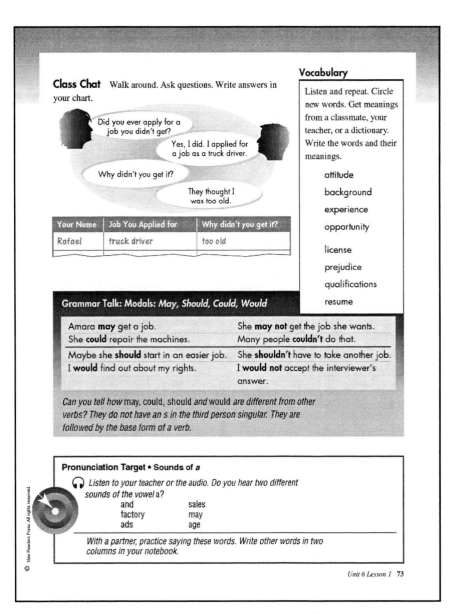

Unit 6 Lesson 1 73

- Less than 50 percent certainty (e.g., *It may snow tonight.*)

Use *should* to express:
- Advisability (e.g., *He should get a new job.*)
- More than 90 percent certainty (e.g., *Everything should be OK.*)

Use *could* to express:
- Past ability (e.g., *When I was 12, I could run faster than my older brothers.*)
- A request that implies ability (e.g., *Could you help me?*)

Use *would* to express:
- A request (e.g., *Would you study with me?*)
- A repeated action in the past (e.g., *Every night Tina and Jack would walk to the little store to buy something.*)
- A polite way of expressing desire (e.g., *I would like very much to see you again.*)
- An unfulfilled wish (e.g., *It would be wonderful, wouldn't it?*)

Pronunciation Target

 Play the audio or read the words in the book, emphasizing the short and long *a* sounds.

Assign Workbook pp. 39–40.

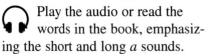 Use Unit Master 45 (Game: Tic-Tac-Toe) now or at any time during the rest of the unit.

Activity A

Put learners in pairs. Tell them to practice the conversation two or three times before writing any additional sentences.

Extension

After they have finished the activity, ask partners to write and practice an interview of their own.

Activity B

After groups complete question 3, have them revise their letters. Then tell each group to choose one learner to read the revised note aloud for the whole class.

Answers

1. She begins the letter *Dear Mr. Sanders.* She ends the letter *Sincerely, Amara Mirembe.*
2. 2, 1, 3, 4
3. Answers will vary.

Task 1

- Ask learners which jobs they would like to apply for and write them on the board or an overhead transparency. Remind them that in Unit 1 they already talked about jobs they would like to have.
- Make a tally of any jobs wanted by more than one learner.
- Put learners who want the same job in the same group so they can help each other complete the task.
- Encourage volunteers to tell about their choices and to read their thank-you notes to the class.

One Step Up

Ask learners to write sentences about the task using modals (e.g., I *may* try to learn more about a carpenter job.)

Activity A With a partner, role-play the conversation between Amara and the interviewer. You can read the words on page 119. Practice saying the words with *a*. Add your own sentences to the conversation. What would you say?

Activity B Work with a group. Read the thank-you note Amara sent to Ben Sanders. Write answers to the questions.

August 4, 2004

Dear Mr. Sanders:

I would like to thank you for interviewing me for the position of machine repairperson. I am very interested in that position. I have two years of experience working with the same kind of equipment you use in your factory. I could be good for your company. Please contact me if you should require more information.

I hope that you may consider my application favorably.

Sincerely,
Amara Mirembe
Amara Mirembe

1. How does Amara begin and end the letter?
2. In which order does she do the following? Number the items.

_____ a. mention her previous work as a machine repairperson

_____ b. thank Mr. Sanders for seeing her

_____ c. offer to give him more information

_____ d. hope to get the job

3. What would you change in the letter?

TASK 1 Write a Thank-You Letter
Choose a job you would like to apply for. Answer the questions.

Job: _____

1. Why did you choose this job?
2. What are your qualifications?
3. What are the challenges in getting this job?
Now write a thank-you note in your notebook. Follow Amara's model.

Lesson 2: It's Everyone's World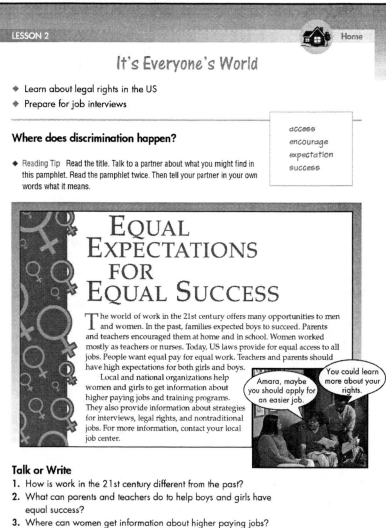

- Follow the suggestions on p. 5 for talking about titles. Explain the link between the title and the idea of *equal opportunity*.
- In this lesson, learners will find out about legal rights in the US and prepare for job interviews.

Attention Box

- Write each word on the board or an overhead transparency.
- Encourage learners to provide definitions, synonyms, and related words to show meaning.

This vocabulary should be understood, but learners should not be expected to produce the words at this point.

Question

Record learners' responses on an idea map on the board or an overhead transparency:

- Write *Discrimination* in the center circle. Label three surrounding circles *On the Job, In the Community, At Home*.
- Read the introductory question aloud and brainstorm answers with learners. Write the answers in the appropriate circle on the idea map.
- Refer learners back to the unit theme question on p. 70 (*Do you ever feel discriminated against?*). Encourage them to incorporate their ideas from that question into this discussion.

Reading Tip

Extension

After learners have told their partners what they learned from the reading, ask them if the information is also true for their home countries.

Talk or Write

This exercise helps learners become skilled at retelling information.

Answers
1. Work in the 21st century offers many opportunities to men and to women. US laws provide for equal access to all jobs.
2. Parents and teachers should have high expectations for both girls and boys.
3. Women can get information about higher paying jobs from local and national organizations.
4. Amara can go to her local job center.

Extension
Use the Internet or a local phone book to locate your nearest employment center.

- Bring in pamphlets from a job center.
- Put learners in groups of four and give each group a pamphlet.

Have groups select roles of reader, leader, recorder, and reporter:

- The reader reads the pamphlet aloud to the group.
- The leader asks questions (e.g., "What services can you get at a job center?") and leads a discussion about the pamphlet.
- The recorder takes notes.
- The reporter uses the notes to report the group's findings to the class.

Vocabulary

Follow the suggestions on p. 6 for introducing and reinforcing vocabulary.

Follow the suggestions on p. 6 for using vocabulary cards. Use the Vocabulary Card Masters for the words in the Vocabulary box.

In the US

Have learners work in groups:
- Assign one of the first four laws to each group.
- Ask each group to think of a specific example of job discrimination forbidden by the law assigned to them.
- The reporter from each group shares the group's example with the class while learners in other groups try to identify the law.
- The first group to identify the law correctly tells its example next.

Compare Cultures

Learners may not know of specific laws against discrimination in their countries.
- Take learners to the media center, computer lab, or library and help them research this topic.
- Lead a discussion about US laws as compared to those in their countries. Be sensitive to your own possible cultural biases and present both countries in a positive light. Focus on what might improve and what individuals could do to make improvement happen.
- Ask if learners sometimes feel discriminated against because they do not speak English fluently. What can they or someone else do to change that situation?
- Have partners write sentences comparing the discrimination laws in their home countries with those in the US.

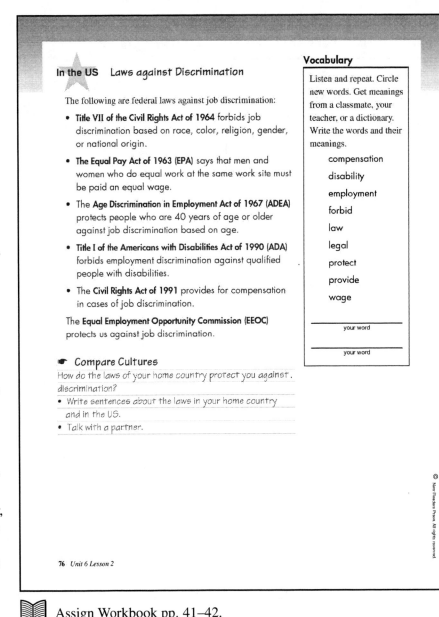

In the US   *Laws against Discrimination*

The following are federal laws against job discrimination:

- **Title VII of the Civil Rights Act of 1964** forbids job discrimination based on race, color, religion, gender, or national origin.
- **The Equal Pay Act of 1963 (EPA)** says that men and women who do equal work at the same work site must be paid an equal wage.
- The **Age Discrimination in Employment Act of 1967 (ADEA)** protects people who are 40 years of age or older against job discrimination based on age.
- **Title I of the Americans with Disabilities Act of 1990 (ADA)** forbids employment discrimination against qualified people with disabilities.
- The **Civil Rights Act of 1991** provides for compensation in cases of job discrimination.

The **Equal Employment Opportunity Commission (EEOC)** protects us against job discrimination.

☛ **Compare Cultures**

How do the laws of your home country protect you against discrimination?
- Write sentences about the laws in your home country and in the US.
- Talk with a partner.

Vocabulary

Listen and repeat. Circle new words. Get meanings from a classmate, your teacher, or a dictionary. Write the words and their meanings.

compensation

disability

employment

forbid

law

legal

protect

provide

wage

_____
your word

_____
your word

Assign Workbook pp. 41–42.

Activity A

Use Customizable Master 3 (3-Column Chart). Follow the suggestions on p. 7 for customizing the master. Make a copy for each learner.

Encourage learners to think of examples of discrimination due to gender, race or ethnicity, age, and disabilities.

<u>Extension</u>

Ask learners to write at least four sentences in their notebooks describing why people may be discriminated against and what the community can or should do about it.

Activity B

<u>Extension</u>

Ask learners, "Is it always wrong to treat boys and girls differently? Why or why not?" Have them give examples of when or where different treatment may be OK.

One Step Up

Ask volunteers to share their thoughts with the class.

Attention Box

Read the word and its definition aloud. Be sure of comprehension before moving to Activity C.

Activity C

Explain to learners that interview questions that can be asked of only one gender are often inappropriate and may be illegal. Review the examples in the book and add these examples of illegal or inappropriate questions:

- Are you married?
- Would you stay home if your husband or child were sick?
- Would you be able to work alone at night with me?

Draw a two-column chart on the board or an overhead transparency and do the following:

- Ask learners to think of questions that might be inappropriate if asked in a job interview. Write these questions in one column.
- Ask learners how they would answer these questions. Write their answers in the second column.
- When all the questions and answers have been recorded, have volunteers role-play each question and answer.

Task 2

Tell learners to review the personal challenges they listed in What's the Problem? on p. 71. Then have them complete the task in their notebooks.

<u>Ongoing Assessment</u>

Use the following rubric to evaluate this task:

a. Content: challenges in a job interview; possible questions and answers
   0 = very minimal
   1 = adequate
   2 = comprehensive
b. Grammar, spelling and punctuation
   0 = many errors that interfere with comprehension
   1 = some errors that do not interfere with comprehension
   2 = very few, if any, errors

Activity A

Tell learners to write their sentences using the information from their Class Chat charts.

Activity B

- Using your own work experience, write a sample answer on the board or an overhead transparency (e.g., *Before teaching English, I was studying to be a teacher, and I was working at night as a waitress.*).
- After learners complete the activity in their books, ask volunteers to dictate sentences to you about their previous *(past continuous)* and current *(present continuous)* work experience.
- Write some of their sentences on the board or an overhead transparency.

Task 3

- Put learners in pairs.
- Tell partners to take notes as they talk.
- After partners have finished their discussions, ask volunteers to use their notes and report their conversations to the class.

Extension

Ask learners to think of other stories about discrimination. Have volunteers dictate their stories as you write them on the board or an overhead transparency.

One Step Up

Ask learners to write a story about a personal experience with discrimination.

When they finish, have them check their writing against the Writing Checklists on p. 126.

Use Unit Master 48 (Grammar: What Could You Do?) now or at any time during the rest of the unit.

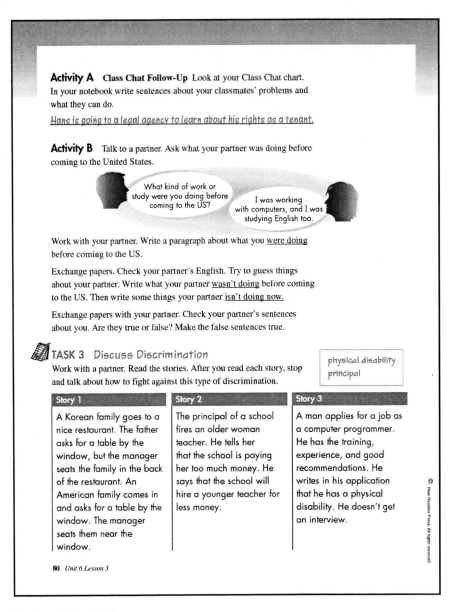

Activity A Class Chat Follow-Up Look at your Class Chat chart. In your notebook write sentences about your classmates' problems and what they can do.

Hans is going to a legal agency to learn about his rights as a tenant.

Activity B Talk to a partner. Ask what your partner was doing before coming to the United States.

> What kind of work or study were you doing before coming to the US?

> I was working with computers, and I was studying English too.

Work with your partner. Write a paragraph about what you were doing before coming to the US.

Exchange papers. Check your partner's English. Try to guess things about your partner. Write what your partner wasn't doing before coming to the US. Then write some things your partner isn't doing now.

Exchange papers with your partner. Check your partner's sentences about you. Are they true or false? Make the false sentences true.

TASK 3 Discuss Discrimination

Work with a partner. Read the stories. After you read each story, stop and talk about how to fight against this type of discrimination.

> physical disability
> principal

Story 1	Story 2	Story 3
A Korean family goes to a nice restaurant. The father asks for a table by the window, but the manager seats the family in the back of the restaurant. An American family comes in and asks for a table by the window. The manager seats them near the window.	The principal of a school fires an older woman teacher. He tells her that the school is paying her too much money. He says that the school will hire a younger teacher for less money.	A man applies for a job as a computer programmer. He has the training, experience, and good recommendations. He writes in his application that he has a physical disability. He doesn't get an interview.

80 *Unit 6 Lesson 3*

Review Unit Skills

See p. 8 for suggestions on games and activities to review the vocabulary and grammar in this unit.

Unit 6 Project

Learners complete a discrimination complaint form.

Get Ready

Discuss with learners what they did in Tasks 1, 2, and 3. (In Task 1, learners wrote a thank-you letter as a follow-up to an interview. In Task 2, they prepared for a job interview. In Task 3, they discussed discrimination in a restaurant, a school, and a workplace.)

Do the Work

Use Unit Master 49 (Unit 6 Project: Make a Complaint). Make a copy for each learner.

- Have each learner complete a Discrimination Complaint Form. They may choose to write about their own experience or that of someone they know. Alternatively, they may use Amara's experience or one of the stories from Task 3 (p. 80).
- Circulate; ask questions to assist learners in providing the information.
- Help learners compile any additional information they need to complete their forms.

Assessment

Use Unit Master 50 (Project Assessment Form) to assess each learner's finished complaint form. Make a copy of the master for each learner, and place the completed form in the learner's portfolio.

Present Your Project

Model the presentation. Use an experience from your own life, if possible, or one of the three stories in Task 3.

Do not correct errors as learners present. Instead, list common errors and talk about them in a future class.

UNIT 6 Project

Make a Complaint

Complete a discrimination complaint form.

Get Ready

Think of a case of discrimination that you know about. You may use Amara Mirembe's story or one of the stories in Task 3.

complaint cover letter

Do the Work

Complete the complaint form. Your teacher will give you a copy.

DISCRIMINATION COMPLAINT FORM

1. Name: _____ Address: _____
   Phone (home): _____ (work): _____

2. Basis of the discrimination
   ☐ race ☐ color ☐ religion ☐ national origin ☐ retaliation
   ☐ age ☐ gender ☐ disability ☐ marital status ☐ sexual orientation
   ☐ other (specify): _____

3. Dates of the discrimination: from _____ to _____

4. Name of person(s) who you believe discriminated against you
   Name: _____ Job title: _____
   Name: _____ Job title: _____

5. Because of the discrimination I was
   ☐ fired ☐ not hired ☐ not promoted ☐ not given benefits ☐ paid less
   ☐ other: _____

6. Details of complaint _____

Signature _____ Date _____

Present Your Project

Tell the class about the discrimination and your complaint. Read the form you completed.

✎ **Writing Extension** Write a short cover letter to send with the complaint form.

🖥 **Technology Extra**

Find the Internet address for the Equal Employment Opportunity Commission of the US government. Go there and find a page that interests you. Share it with the class.

© New Readers Press. All rights reserved.

Unit 6 Project **81**

Writing Extension

Refer learners to Amara's follow-up letter on p. 74 to review letter style.

Technology Extra

Assist learners in navigating the government site.

Self-Assessment

Give each learner a copy of the Speaking and Listening Self-Check and the Writing and Reading Self-Check (Generic Assessment Masters 10 and 11). Go over the items together. The completed forms will become part of each learner's portfolio.

 Assign Workbook p. 45 (Check Your Progress).

Use Unit Master 51 (Unit 6 Checkup/Review) whenever you complete this unit.

Unit 7: Paying Taxes 🔳

Materials for the Unit

- Copies of paychecks and stubs with personal information covered or deleted
- Blank yearly calendar
- Calculators
- Variety of blank forms (e.g., job applications, school registration forms, surveys, health forms)
- Tax forms (W-2, W-4, W-5, and 1040)
- Customizable Masters 2–4, 6
- Generic Assessment Master 9
- Unit Masters 52–58
- Vocabulary Card Masters for Unit 7

Paying Taxes

Read the title and unit goals with learners.

This unit focuses on understanding paychecks and taxes. Discuss the meanings of *income* and *taxation*. Then ask these questions:

- How do people use the money they earn? *(to pay for goods [e.g., food, clothing, housing] and services [e.g., telephone, heat, water])*
- What are some things that everyone in the community pays for? *(fire department, police, roads, schools, etc.)*
- How do people pay for community services? *(through taxes on sales, property, and income)*

Draw a pie chart on the board or an overhead transparency. Mark off sections to show how local, state, and federal governments take a slice of each taxpayer's "pie" to pay for community, state, and national services.

Question

Read the question below the arrow. Ask learners who receive paychecks if they understand why some of the money is missing from their checks.

Paying Taxes

Understanding Paychecks and Taxes

Work/School 1   Home 2   Community 3

- Vocabulary Paychecks • Taxes
- Language Verbs followed by infinitives • Order of adjectives
- Pronunciation Sounds of *e* • Sounds of *t* and *d*
- Culture Taxation in the US

celebrate
confused
missing

Do you know what to expect when you are paid?

Puri gets his first paycheck in the US. He wants to celebrate, but some of his money is missing. He is confused.

Think and Talk
1. What is Puri thinking?
2. Who can help him?
3. Did you ever feel like this?

What's Your Opinion? What should Puri say to his employer?

82 *Unit 7*

Attention Box

Read the words to learners, miming to convey meaning. This vocabulary should be understood, but learners should not be expected to produce the words at this point.

Photos

Ask learners to describe each photo. Ask questions like these:
- Where is Puri?
- What is he doing?

Caption

- Read the caption with learners.
- Review the meaning of *missing* (*gone, not there*).

Think and Talk

Answers
1. Puri thinks the amount in his paycheck is wrong.
2. His boss can help him.
3. Answers will vary.

What's Your Opinion?

Answers will vary, but they should include the idea that Puri should ask his boss why some of the money Puri earned is not in his paycheck.

Picture Dictionary

Follow the suggestions on p. 6 for introducing and reinforcing vocabulary.

Follow the suggestions on p. 6 for using vocabulary cards. Use the Vocabulary Card Masters for the words in the Picture Dictionary.

Gather Your Thoughts

Ask learners to bring copies of their old paychecks and pay stubs. Tell them that the information on their paychecks and stubs is private and they will not have to share it. For learners not in the workforce, provide copies of paychecks and stubs with personal information covered or deleted.

• Draw the idea map from the student book on the board or an overhead transparency.
• Copy the words in the center circle and the first two of the five surrounding circles.
• Ask learners where else they can get information about paychecks and taxes.
• Write learners' suggestions (e.g., ask the boss, ask the human resources department, go to the Internet, find an accountant) in the blank circles.

Tell learners to look at their paychecks and stubs and write one or two questions about their pay.

• Ask volunteers to share their questions.
• Write the questions on a large sheet of paper and post it for future reference.

What's the Problem?

Follow the suggestions on p. 5 for identifying and analyzing problems.
• Draw a two-column chart on a large sheet of paper.
• Ask learners why they have to pay taxes. List their reasons in the first column.

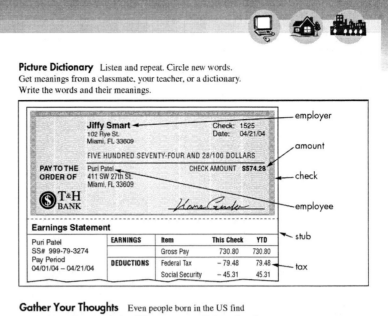

Picture Dictionary Listen and repeat. Circle new words. Get meanings from a classmate, your teacher, or a dictionary. Write the words and their meanings.

Gather Your Thoughts Even people born in the US find paychecks and taxes confusing. Where can you get information about paychecks and taxes? Talk about ideas with your teacher. Make a chart like this in your notebook. Write the answers on your chart.

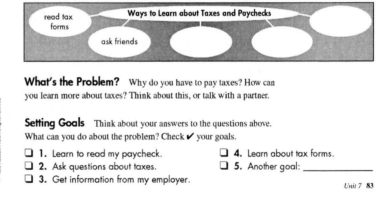

What's the Problem? Why do you have to pay taxes? How can you learn more about taxes? Think about this, or talk with a partner.

Setting Goals Think about your answers to the questions above. What can you do about the problem? Check ✔ your goals.

❑ 1. Learn to read my paycheck. ❑ 4. Learn about tax forms.
❑ 2. Ask questions about taxes.   ❑ 5. Another goal: _____
❑ 3. Get information from my employer.

• Ask learners how they can learn more about taxes. List their responses in the second column.
• Post the paper for future reference.

Setting Goals

Follow the suggestions on p. 5 for setting goals.

<u>One Step Up</u>
Have orally proficient learners share their information with the class.

Lesson 1: Where Does All the Money Go? 🔲www

Read the title aloud for learners.
- Follow the suggestions on p. 5 for talking about titles.
- In this lesson, learners will find out about their paychecks and pay stubs.

Question

Read the introductory question aloud.
- Elicit more information by asking *wh-* questions (e.g., "What don't you understand?").
- Refer to the list of questions about paychecks you posted in Gather Your Thoughts (p. 83). Elicit answers from learners.

Reading Tip

Read the tip aloud with learners.
- Make an overhead transparency of the Vocabulary Card Master for the paycheck and stub in the Picture Dictionary on p. 83.
- Point to each part of the check and the stub and ask volunteers to read the explanation that applies to that part.
- Understanding some terms will help learners understand other terms. Use a calendar to explain *year-to-date* and *pay period*.

Put learners in pairs. Then do the following:
- Assign different terms to each pair of learners.
- Ask the pairs to rewrite the explanations in their own words.
- Have volunteers share their new explanations.
- Write the terms and the learners' explanations on the board or an overhead transparency.

Talk or Write

This exercise helps learners become skilled at reading diagrams.

Answers
1. Gross income is larger than net income.

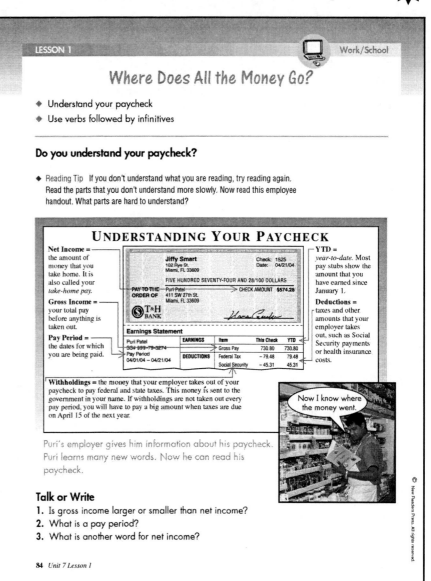

LESSON 1 — Work/School

Where Does All the Money Go?

◆ Understand your paycheck
◆ Use verbs followed by infinitives

Do you understand your paycheck?

◆ Reading Tip If you don't understand what you are reading, try reading again. Read the parts that you don't understand more slowly. Now read this employee handout. What parts are hard to understand?

UNDERSTANDING YOUR PAYCHECK

Net Income = the amount of money that you take home. It is also called your *take-home pay.*

Gross Income = your total pay before anything is taken out.

Pay Period = the dates for which you are being paid.

YTD = *year-to-date.* Most pay stubs show the amount that you have earned since January 1.

Deductions = taxes and other amounts that your employer takes out, such as Social Security payments or health insurance costs.

Jiffy Smart
102 Rye St.
Miami, FL 33609
Check: 1525
Date: 04/21/04
FIVE HUNDRED SEVENTY-FOUR AND 28/100 DOLLARS
PAY TO THE ORDER OF Puri Patel
411 SW 27th St.
Miami, FL 33609
CHECK AMOUNT $574.28
T+H BANK

Earnings Statement

Puri Patel	EARNINGS	Item	This Check	YTD
334-999-79-3274		Gross Pay	730.80	730.80
Pay Period 04/01/04 – 04/21/04	DEDUCTIONS	Federal Tax	– 79.48	79.48
		Social Security	– 45.31	45.31

Withholdings = the money that your employer takes out of your paycheck to pay federal and state taxes. This money is sent to the government in your name. If withholdings are not taken out every pay period, you will have to pay a big amount when taxes are due on April 15 of the next year.

Now I know where the money went.

Puri's employer gives him information about his paycheck. Puri learns many new words. Now he can read his paycheck.

Talk or Write
1. Is gross income larger or smaller than net income?
2. What is a pay period?
3. What is another word for net income?

2. A pay period is the dates for which you are being paid.
3. *Take-home pay* is another word for *net income.*

You may prefer to have learners do Activities B and C at this point. Then review these activities quickly after Activity A.

Extension

Use Unit Master 52 (Life Skill: Complete a Paycheck and Stub). Distribute one copy to each learner.
- Have partners complete the paycheck and stub with income figures for a fictional person. Tell

them to be as realistic as possible.
- If possible, have them use calculators for this activity. Provide this example:

Gross Pay	$2,741.50
Taxes	$754.80
Deductions	$396.33
Net Pay	$1,590.37

- Ask volunteers to share their figures.

Vocabulary

Follow the suggestions on p. 6 for introducing and reinforcing vocabulary.

Follow the suggestions on p. 6 for using vocabulary cards. Use the Vocabulary Card Masters for the words in the Vocabulary box.

Partner Chat

 Use Customizable Master 3 (3-Column Chart). Follow the suggestions on p. 7 for customizing and duplicating the master. Make a copy for each learner.
- Put learners in pairs.
- Ask volunteers to share their answers with the class.

Grammar Talk

Follow the suggestions on p. 7 for introducing the grammar point.

Answers
The helping verb changes.

The original verb always stays the same (i.e., in the base form).

Extension
Explain to learners that certain verbs can be followed by an *infinitive,* which is the word *to* plus the base form of the verb (e.g., *to know, to learn*). Verbs that are followed by an *infinitive* are *want, need, have, begin, decide, hope, try, plan, learn, promise,* and *ask.*
- List some or all of these verbs on the board or an overhead transparency.
- Refer to the questions generated in Gather Your Thoughts and the reasons for paying taxes suggested in What's the Problem? (p. 83).
- Have learners create sentences orally using the verbs on the board followed by infinitives.
- Write their sentences on the board or an overhead transparency.

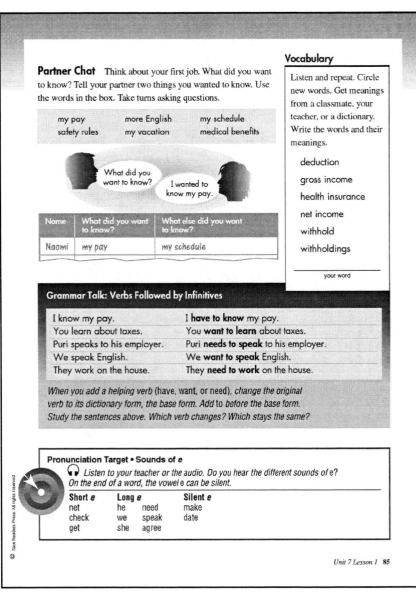

Partner Chat Think about your first job. What did you want to know? Tell your partner two things you wanted to know. Use the words in the box. Take turns asking questions.

| my pay | more English | my schedule |
| safety rules | my vacation | medical benefits |

What did you want to know?
I wanted to know my pay.

Name	What did you want to know?	What else did you want to know?
Naomi	my pay	my schedule

Vocabulary

Listen and repeat. Circle new words. Get meanings from a classmate, your teacher, or a dictionary. Write the words and their meanings.

deduction

gross income

health insurance

net income

withhold

withholdings

your word

Grammar Talk: Verbs Followed by Infinitives

I know my pay.	I **have to know** my pay.
You learn about taxes.	You **want to learn** about taxes.
Puri speaks to his employer.	Puri **needs to speak** to his employer.
We speak English.	We **want to speak** English.
They work on the house.	They **need to work** on the house.

When you add a helping verb (have, want, or need), *change the original verb to its dictionary form, the base form. Add* to *before the base form. Study the sentences above. Which verb changes? Which stays the same?*

Pronunciation Target • Sounds of *e*

🎧 *Listen to your teacher or the audio. Do you hear the different sounds of* e*? On the end of a word, the vowel* e *can be silent.*

Short *e*	Long *e*		Silent *e*
net	he	need	make
check	we	speak	date
get	she	agree	

Unit 7 Lesson 1 **85**

Pronunciation Target

🎧 Play the audio or read the words in the student book. If you read the words, emphasize the sounds of long and short *e*.

Extension
- Draw three columns on the board or an overhead transparency. Head the columns *Short e, Long e,* and *Silent e*.
- Ask one or several volunteers to write the words in the correct column as other learners randomly call them out.

One Step Up
- When learners have called out all the words, have them dictate additional words with the sounds of *e*.
- As an alternative, ask volunteers to compete in this higher-level activity.
- Provide a small prize to the volunteer who writes the most words in the correct columns.

📖 Assign Workbook pp. 46–47.

📑 Use Unit Master 53 (Grammar: Bingo Game) now or at any time during the rest of the unit.

Activity A

Have learners write sentences in their notebooks using the verbs *have* and *need*. Tell them to use the information in their Partner Chat charts.

Attention Box

This vocabulary and the relationships between the terms should be understood, but learners should not be expected to produce the words at this point.

Activity B

Put learners in pairs to answer the questions about Puri's paycheck. Explain to learners that the pay stub on p. 83 is incomplete. In order to calculate Puri's total deductions, they must subtract his net income from his gross income.

Answers
1. $730.80
2. 04/01/04–04/21/04
3. 999-79-3274
4. $574.28
5. $156.52

Activity C

After learners have completed the activity and checked their work, ask volunteers to read the sentences aloud.

Answers
2. amount
3. withheld
4. deductions
5. taxes
6. net income

Task 1

- Put learners in small groups.
- Give each group copies of several paychecks and stubs with the personal information covered or deleted.
- Have each group find on their paycheck all the items asked for in the student book. Then have them compare the checks to see how they are the same and how they are different.

Activity A Partner Chat Follow-Up Look at your Partner Chat chart. In your notebook, write sentences using *have* and *need*.

Naomi has to know her schedule. Naomi needs to know her pay.

Activity B With a partner, find the following items on Puri's paycheck, page 83. Answer the questions.

1. What is Puri's gross income? _____
2. What is the pay period? _____
3. What is Puri's Social Security number? _____
4. What is Puri's take-home pay? _____
5. What is the total of Puri's deductions? _____

gross income
– deductions
net income

Activity C Use the words in the box to fill in the blanks.

| amount | deductions | ✓employer | net income | taxes | withheld |

Puri was very happy. His _____employer_____ gave him his first US paycheck! At first, Puri thought the _____ on the check was too low. Now he knows that some money is _____ from each paycheck. The stub shows his gross income and all the _____. His employer withholds money for _____ and Social Security. The amount that is left after deductions is called his _____.

TASK 1 Read Paychecks
Your teacher will give you copies of paychecks and stubs with personal information covered. In a small group, look at the checks. Can your group find the gross pay, net pay, pay rate, pay period, federal tax, and other deductions? How are the paychecks the same? How are they different? With the class, make a list of all the deductions.

- Ask one member from each group to visit another group to compare their findings.
- Have those learners rotate until all groups are visited.
- Then tell the rotating learners to return to their home groups and report by comparing their own group's answers to those of other groups.
- With the class, list on the board or an overhead transparency all of the deductions learners found.

Use Unit Master 54 (Thinking Skill: A Pie Chart) now or at any time during the rest of the unit.

Lesson 2: Taxes—How Much Can You Control?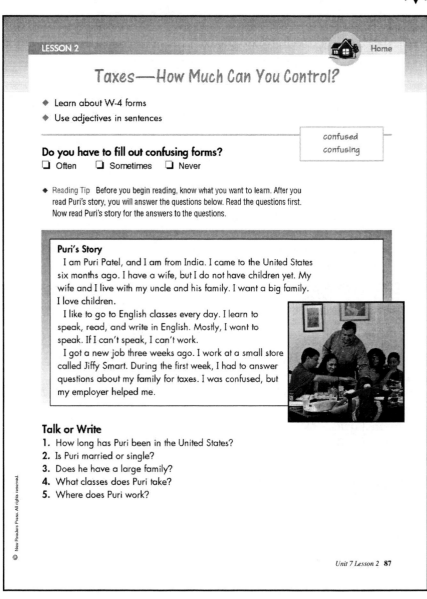

- Read the title and lesson objectives with learners.
- In this lesson, learners will find out how to complete a W-4 form.

Attention Box

Read the words to learners, pointing or miming to convey meaning when possible. This vocabulary should be understood, but learners should not be expected to produce the words at this point.

Question

Read the introductory question aloud.

- Elicit more information by asking *wh-* questions (e.g., "When do you have to fill out confusing forms?").
- Show learners a variety of blank forms (e.g., job applications, school registration, surveys).
- Talk about some common elements (e.g., name, address) that are easy to understand.
- Then discuss other elements—concepts, language structures, vocabulary (e.g., *race*)—that might be confusing.

Reading Tip

Read the tip aloud with learners.

Reinforce the tip by telling learners it is always a good idea to read the questions first. Doing this will tell them what information they need to look for as they read.

Extension

After learners read the story and answer the questions, they can read the story again to learn more about Puri.

Talk or Write

This exercise helps learners read for specific information.

Answers

1. Puri has been in the US six months.
2. Puri is married.

3. No, he has only his wife.
4. Puri takes English classes.
5. Puri works at a small store called Jiffy Smart.

Extension
Ask these additional questions:
- Does Puri have any children? *(no)*
- Who does he live with? *(his uncle and his uncle's family)*
- What does he want? Why? *(He wants a big family because he loves children.)*
- Why does he need to speak English? *(He needs to speak English so he can work.)*
- Who helped him? *(his employer)*

One Step Up
- Ask learners to write their own story in their notebooks. Tell them to closely follow Puri's story as a model.
- Tell them to refer to the Writing Checklists on p. 126 to help them revise their writing.

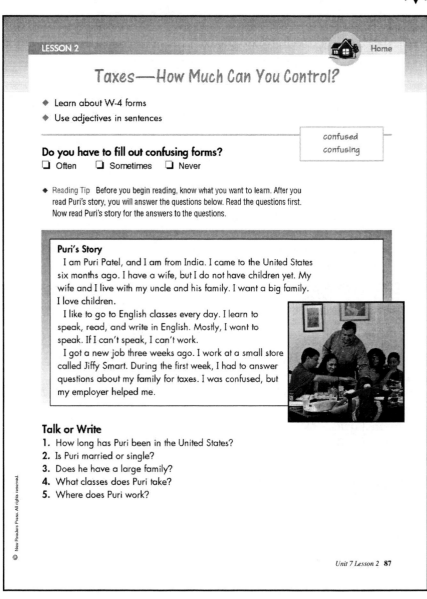

LESSON 2   Home

Taxes—How Much Can You Control?

- ◆ Learn about W-4 forms
- ◆ Use adjectives in sentences

Do you have to fill out confusing forms?
❏ Often   ❏ Sometimes   ❏ Never

> confused
> confusing

◆ Reading Tip   Before you begin reading, know what you want to learn. After you read Puri's story, you will answer the questions below. Read the questions first. Now read Puri's story for the answers to the questions.

Puri's Story
    I am Puri Patel, and I am from India. I came to the United States six months ago. I have a wife, but I do not have children yet. My wife and I live with my uncle and his family. I want a big family. I love children.
    I like to go to English classes every day. I learn to speak, read, and write in English. Mostly, I want to speak. If I can't speak, I can't work.
    I got a new job three weeks ago. I work at a small store called Jiffy Smart. During the first week, I had to answer questions about my family for taxes. I was confused, but my employer helped me.

Talk or Write
1. How long has Puri been in the United States?
2. Is Puri married or single?
3. Does he have a large family?
4. What classes does Puri take?
5. Where does Puri work?

Unit 7 Lesson 2 87

© New Readers Press. All rights reserved.

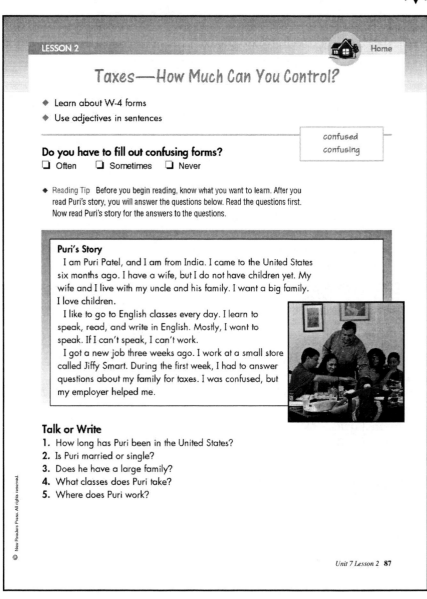

Unit 7 *Lesson 2* **87**

Vocabulary

Follow the suggestions on p. 6 for introducing vocabulary.

Follow the suggestions on p. 6 for using vocabulary cards. Use the Vocabulary Card Masters for the words in the Vocabulary box.

- Ask volunteers to call out sentences about themselves using the words in the first cluster (e.g., "I am not *married.*").
- Write the sentences on the board or an overhead transparency.
- Create a follow-up sentence for each, using the words in the second cluster (e.g., Sonali is *single.* She can *claim* only one *dependent.*).

Partner Chat

Extension

- After discussing learners' responses, ask them to suggest additional questions.
- Write some of these on the board or an overhead transparency.
- Have learners tell you which are polite and which are impolite.

Grammar Talk

Follow the suggestions on p. 7 for introducing the grammar point.

Remind learners that adjectives do not change from singular to plural.

Answers

Adjectives usually come before nouns or after the verb *be*.

When you have more than one adjective, you put a comma between the adjectives.

One Step Up

- Ask learners to look at the stories they wrote about themselves in the previous One Step Up. Have them underline the adjectives.
- Ask volunteers to read you a sentence from their stories containing an adjective.
- Write selected sentences on the board, underlining the adjectives.

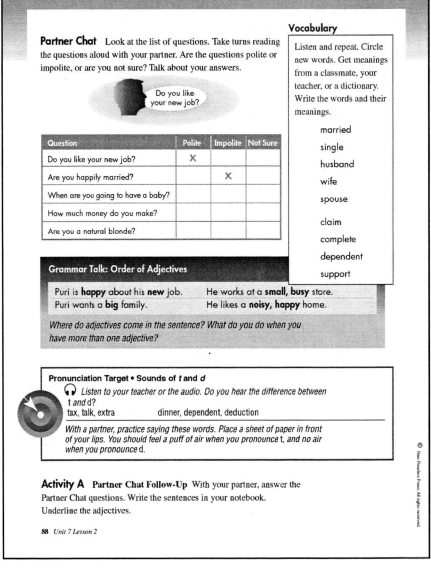

Partner Chat Look at the list of questions. Take turns reading the questions aloud with your partner. Are the questions polite or impolite, or are you not sure? Talk about your answers.

Do you like your new job?

Question	Polite	Impolite	Not Sure
Do you like your new job?	X		
Are you happily married?		X	
When are you going to have a baby?			
How much money do you make?			
Are you a natural blonde?			

Vocabulary

Listen and repeat. Circle new words. Get meanings from a classmate, your teacher, or a dictionary. Write the words and their meanings.

married
single
husband
wife
spouse
claim
complete
dependent
support

Grammar Talk: Order of Adjectives

Puri is **happy** about his **new** job.   He works at a **small, busy** store.
Puri wants a **big** family.   He likes a **noisy, happy** home.

Where do adjectives come in the sentence? What do you do when you have more than one adjective?

Pronunciation Target • Sounds of *t* and *d*

🎧 *Listen to your teacher or the audio. Do you hear the difference between t and d?*
tax, talk, extra   dinner, dependent, deduction

With a partner, practice saying these words. Place a sheet of paper in front of your lips. You should feel a puff of air when you pronounce t, and no air when you pronounce d.

Activity A **Partner Chat Follow-Up** With your partner, answer the Partner Chat questions. Write the sentences in your notebook. Underline the adjectives.

88 *Unit 7 Lesson 2*

Pronunciation Target

 Play the audio or read the words in the student book, emphasizing the sounds of *t* and *d*.

Extension
Draw two columns on the board or an overhead transparency, labeling them with the letters *t* and *d*. Then do the following:

- Have learners read the words in random order as one or more volunteers write the words in the correct column.
- Have learners dictate additional words with the sounds of *t* and *d* while a volunteer writes them.

Activity A

After partners answer the chat questions, have them write sentences and underline the adjectives.

📖 Assign Workbook pp. 48–49.

📑 Use Unit Master 55 (Pronunciation: Tic-Tac-Toe Game) now or at any time during the rest of the unit.

Activity B

🎧 Play the audio or read the listening script below twice. The first time, tell learners to listen as they follow the text in their books. The second time, tell learners to fill in the blanks.

Listening Script
Listen. Complete the explanation of a W-4 form with the words in the box.
Form W-4 tells how much money to <u>withhold</u> from your paycheck for taxes. You write how many allowances you want to claim. If no one else can <u>claim</u> you as a dependent, you enter *one* for yourself. If you are married, you may want to claim your <u>spouse</u> too. You can claim any children you support as <u>dependents</u>. When you claim more dependents, you take home more <u>net</u> pay. However, you may have to pay more <u>taxes</u> to the IRS in April.

Answers
1. withhold
2. claim
3. spouse
4. dependents
5. net
6. taxes

Activity C

- Have learners find a classmate they do not know well to interview.
- As a model, interview a learner that has accelerated oral skills.
- After learners have interviewed a partner and written the partner's story, have partners introduce one another to the rest of the class.

Task 2

Make copies of a W-4 form and give one to each learner. (This form can be found on the IRS web site.)
- Have learners complete the form for themselves or for Puri.

Activity B 🎧 When you get a new job, you need to complete a W-4 form. Listen to the audio. Complete the explanation of a W-4 form with the words in the box.

Internal Revenue Service (IRS)
W-4

claim	dependents	net	spouse	taxes	withhold

Form W-4 tells how much money to _____ from your paycheck for
                                    1
taxes. You write how many allowances you want to claim. If no one else can

_____ you as a dependent, you enter 1 for yourself. If you are married,
       2
you may want to claim your _____ too. You can claim any children you
                                  3
support as _____. When you claim more dependents, you take home
              4
more _____ pay. However, you may have to pay more
        5
_____ to the IRS in April.
     6

Activity C Interview a classmate that you don't know well. Use the answers to write a story. Rewrite the story in your notebook. Share the story with the class.

1. What is your full name?   4. Are you married or single?
2. Where are you from?   5. Do you have children?
3. When did you come to the US?   6. What do you like to do?

_____ 's Story

This is _____. He/she is from _____. He/she came

to the US _____ (number) (months/years) ago. _____ is (single/married)

and has _____ (number) children. He/she likes to _____.

📝 **TASK 2** Fill Out a W-4 Form
Get a copy of a W-4 form from your teacher. Fill it out for yourself or for Puri. You can find information for Puri on his paycheck on page 83 and in his story on page 87.

Unit 7 Lesson 2 **89**

- Tell learners who fill the form out for themselves to use the information on their own paycheck and stub.

One Step Up
Explain that *Earned Income Credit* is a tax benefit for workers with low income who have children.
- The IRS web site contains information about and qualification for the *Earned Income Credit.*
- Those who qualify owe less in taxes and may even get cash back.
- Those who fill out a *W-5 Earned Income Credit Advance Payment Certificate* can get the money added to their paychecks.

- Tell learners they can get the W-5 form from their employers.

Extension
Bring a W-5 form and help learners complete it. (This form can be found on the IRS web site.)

Lesson 3: Getting a Refund www

- Follow the suggestions on p. 5 for talking about titles. Then read the lesson objectives with learners.
- In this lesson, learners will learn about different tax forms and some reasons for taxation.

Attention Box

- Write each word or term on the board or a transparency.
- Ask learners for definitions, synonyms, related words, and illustrations to show the meaning of *accountant* and *system*.
- For *1040 form* and *W-2 form*, show samples of the forms. (These forms can be found on the IRS web site.)

This vocabulary should be understood, but learners should not be expected to produce the words at this point.

Question

- Read the question aloud with learners. Then ask the questions below. Tell learners to raise their hands to indicate a *yes* answer.
  Do you feel confused?
  Do you feel angry?
  Do you feel happy?
  Do you feel that you understand?
- After each question, have a volunteer tally the number of people raising their hands.
- Have a recorder write the adjectives on the board or an overhead transparency and under each adjective the number of people who feel that way.

<u>Extension</u>
Continue the discussion by asking, "What do you think your tax money pays for?"

Refer to the list of reasons for paying taxes that the class generated and posted in What's the Problem? on p. 83.

Listening Tip

Read the tip aloud with learners. Reinforce it by telling learners it is

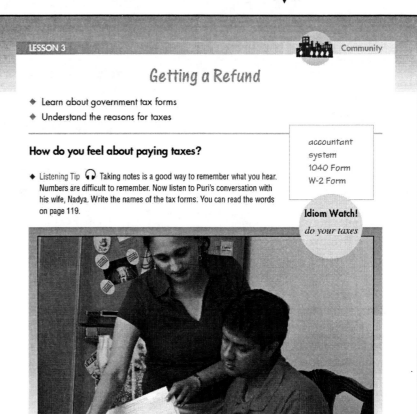

LESSON 3   Community

Getting a Refund

◆ Learn about government tax forms
◆ Understand the reasons for taxes

How do you feel about paying taxes?

accountant
system
1040 Form
W-2 Form

Idiom Watch!
do your taxes

◆ Listening Tip 🎧 Taking notes is a good way to remember what you hear. Numbers are difficult to remember. Now listen to Puri's conversation with his wife, Nadya. Write the names of the tax forms. You can read the words on page 119.

Puri and Nadya are doing their tax forms.

Talk or Write
1. What are Puri and Nadya talking about?
2. Why does she think that he can learn about the tax system?
3. What tax form did Puri get from his job?

90   *Unit 7 Lesson 3*

always a good idea to take notes; they can help you remember what you hear.

🎧 Play the audio or read the listening script on p. 121. Follow the suggestions on p. 5 for listening comprehension.

Talk or Write

This exercise helps learners become skilled at listening to conversations.

<u>Answers</u>
1. Puri and Nadya are talking about completing the tax forms.
2. She thinks he can learn about the tax system because he is an accountant.

3. Puri got a W-2 Form from his job.

<u>Extension</u>
Ask these additional questions:
- What does Nadya offer to her husband? *(mint tea)*
- What is Puri trying to do? *(understand the tax system)*
- What does he need to complete? *(1040 form)*
- Is Nadya happy that they do not owe money? Why? *(yes, because they need extra money)*

Vocabulary

Follow the suggestions on p. 6 for introducing and reinforcing vocabulary.

Follow the suggestions on p. 6 for using vocabulary cards. Use the Vocabulary Card Masters for the words in the Vocabulary box.

Extension

• Have pairs use the vocabulary words to make sentences with adjectives. Tell them to underline the adjectives (e.g., *The federal government owes me a nice, big refund.*)

• Have one learner in each pair write one sentence on the board and underline the adjectives.

In the US

Read this section aloud to learners. Then do the following:

• Draw an idea map on the board or an overhead transparency. Label the center circle with the question *What are taxes for?*

• Ask learners to tell you what taxes pay for. In the smaller circles write their ideas (e.g., *schools, libraries, courthouses, roads, parks, sanitation, police, firefighters, defense*).

• Label one large sheet of paper with the words *We agree with taxation because . . . .* Label another large sheet with the words *We disagree with taxation because . . . .* Post the sheets on opposite sides of the room.

• Tell learners to go to the side of the room whose poster best matches their opinion and write the reasons why they agree or disagree with taxation.

• Ask one volunteer from each opinion group to read the group's reasons.

• Summarize learners' opinions on the board or an overhead transparency. Use as many adjectives as possible in your sentences.

• Ask learners to copy the summary sentences in their

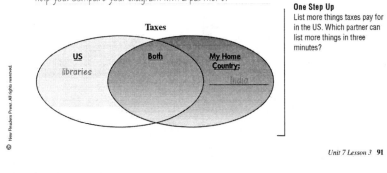

In the US   Why Do People Pay Taxes?

The Internal Revenue Service (IRS) is the federal agency that collects taxes on income. States may also collect income taxes. Income taxes pay for schools and teachers, libraries and courthouses, roads and parks, police and firefighters, the military, and much more. Some people do not like taxes. They think the government takes too much money. Others want the government to pay for more services such as health care, child care, and welfare programs. This would mean more taxes. There will always be people who disagree on taxes.

Whether you agree with taxes or not, you must remember to fill out a federal income tax form at the end of each year. This form and the money you owe are due on April 15th. Your employer will give you a W-2 form. The W-2 tells how much money you earned last year and how much money the government withheld for taxes. If your taxes are simple, you can use a 1040EZ. You use this form to calculate the money that you need to pay or get back. When you get money back, it is called a *refund*.

Compare Cultures

Make a diagram like the one below to compare how countries use taxes. Use the words in the vocabulary box to help you. Compare your diagram with a partner's.

Taxes

US — libraries | Both | My Home Country: India

Vocabulary

Listen and repeat. Circle new words. Get meanings from a classmate, your teacher, or a dictionary. Write the words and their meanings.

calculate

collect

owe

refund

federal

state

courthouse

fire fighter

military

police

welfare

your word

One Step Up
List more things taxes pay for in the US. Which partner can list more things in three minutes?

notebooks. Have them underline the adjectives.

• Help learners create a time line with events like those below showing the responsibilities of workers and employers regarding taxation.

New Job	Worker files W-4 form with employer
January	Employer sends worker W-2 form
April 15	Worker files 1040 form with IRS; worker pays more taxes or gets refund

Compare Cultures

 Use Customizable Master 6 (Venn Diagram). Follow the

suggestions on p. 7 for customizing and duplicating the master. Make a copy for each learner.

Have partners compare their completed diagrams.

One Step Up

• Set a time limit of three minutes.

• Have partners compete to see who can list more things taxes pay for in the US.

 Assign Workbook pp. 50–51.

Use Unit Master 56 (Grammar: Find Your Match) now or at any time during the rest of the unit.

Activity A

Use Customizable Master 2 (2-Column Chart). Label the chart *Taxes in My Community.* Label the two columns *Yes* and *No.* Make one copy for each group.

Alternatively, draw the chart on the board or an overhead transparency.

Then do the following:

- Have learners work in groups.
- If you distribute the chart, tell each group to select a recorder to write their responses on the group's copy. Otherwise, have the recorder in each group copy the chart into his or her notebook.
- Tell learners to list things they pay taxes on in the *Yes* column and things they do not have to pay taxes on in the *No* column.
- After groups complete their lists, ask a reporter in each group to read the group's lists to the class.
- Ask learners from other groups if they agree with those lists.

Attention Box

Read the definitions aloud. (More information on filing status can be found on the IRS web site.)

This vocabulary should be understood, but learners should not be expected to produce the words at this point.

Activity B

Some learners may think reading tables is not an academic skill. Tell them that being able to read tables well is important, not only to understand taxes but also to succeed on tests for school and work.

- To check comprehension, ask learners one or two questions about the tax table.
- Point out that the terms *filing jointly* and *head of household* are defined in the Attention Box.
- Ask learners what they think *filing separately* means.

Activity A Work with your group. Find out about your community. Do you have to pay sales taxes? Make a list of things you pay taxes on. Make a list of things you don't have to pay taxes on. Talk to the class about your lists.

Activity B Look at the tax table. How much federal tax do you have to pay if you earn . . .

$41,210 a year and you are single? ____________

$41,425 a year and you are the head of your household? ____________

$41,150 a year and you are married filing jointly? ____________

$41,530 a year and you are married filing separately? ____________

Tax Table

If line 39 (taxable income) is—		And you are—			
At least	But less than	Single	Married filing jointly	Married filing separately	Head of a household
41,000		Your tax is —			
41,000	**41,050**	7,901	6,154	8,457	6,751
41,050	**41,100**	7,914	6,161	8,471	6,764
41,100	**41,150**	7,928	6,169	8,484	6,778
41,150	**41,200**	7,942	6,176	8,498	6,792
41,200	**41,250**	7,956	6,184	8,512	6,806
41,250	**41,300**	7,969	6,191	8,526	6,819
41,300	**41,350**	7,983	6,199	8,539	6,833
41,350	**41,400**	7,997	6,206	8,553	6,847
41,400	**41,450**	8,011	6,214	8,567	6,861
41,450	**41,500**	8,024	6,221	8,581	6,874
41,500	**41,550**	8,038	6,229	8,594	6,888

filing jointly = filling out the form together
head of household = a single person who works to support the family

TASK 3 *Make a List of Tax Forms*

Get a large envelope. Label it with the word "taxes" and write the year on the outside. With a small group, list all the tax forms and receipts you want to collect in the envelope. Copy the list onto the envelope. Think of a safe place to keep your envelope.

92 *Unit 7 Lesson 3*

© New Readers Press. All rights reserved.

- Ask learners why they think the tax amount varies according to category.
- Have learners work in groups complete the activity.

Answers
$7,956; $6,861; $6,169; $8,594

Extension
Ask learners to do the following:

- Calculate their income
- Find their filing status and the appropriate tax table on the IRS web site
- Decide how much federal tax they need to pay
- Complete a mini-form like this one:

Name:
Income:
You are: (check one)
❑ Single
❑ Married filing jointly
❑ Married filing separately
❑ Head of household
Federal Tax:

Task 3

Brainstorm with learners the forms and receipts they might need to file their taxes. Needed forms and receipts might include the following.
Forms: W-2; 1040
Receipts: medical expenses, business expenses, job-hunting expenses, mortgage information

Unit 7 Project

Learners complete a tax form and calculate taxes.

Get Ready

 Distribute a copy of Unit Master 57 (Unit 7 Project: Calculate Taxes), a copy of the 1040EZ, to each group.

- Talk about what learners did in Tasks 1, 2, and 3. (In Task 1, learners read paychecks and pay stubs. In Task 2, they completed a W-4 form. In Task 3, they made a list of the tax forms and receipts they needed to file taxes.)
- Encourage learners to recall these tasks, which built skills for the unit project.

Do the Work

Have small groups complete the tax form together using the tax table on p. 92 in their books.

Present Your Project

Have groups compare the results of their calculations.

Extension

Invite a tax accountant as a guest speaker to discuss the unit topics. If possible, choose someone who understands the language challenges of non-native speakers and is willing to adapt his or her presentation to their level of English proficiency.

Writing Extension

Tell learners to use the information from their completed forms to write their letters. Remind them that they wrote letters in Unit 6.

Assessment

 Use Generic Assessment Master 9 (Written Communication Rubric) to evaluate each learner's letter. Follow the instructions on p. 4 for using this master.

Technology Extra

Assist learners in finding the needed forms on the IRS web site.

Calculate Taxes

Practice completing a 1040EZ Form for Puri Patel. Calculate how much federal income tax Puri has to pay or how much of a refund he will get.

Get Ready

Work in small groups. Get a copy of Form 1040EZ from your teacher. Look back at Puri's employment information. Puri Patel is a 33-year-old married man. His W-2 form stated that he earned $41,513 in wages. The income tax withheld was $8,162. His wife earned no income this year.

Do the Work

Complete the 1040EZ Form for Puri. Use the Tax Table on page 92 to calculate how much federal income tax he has to pay. Puri and Nadya want to file jointly. Will he receive a refund? Will he have to pay more taxes? What can he do next year?

Present Your Project

Compare your answers with another group. Are they the same?

Writing Extension Write a short letter to Puri from the IRS. Will he get good news or bad news? Share your letter with the class.

Technology Extra
Go to the IRS web site. Look for the latest tax forms and information. Practice completing the forms about your income.

 Assign Workbook p. 52 (Check Your Progress).

 Use Unit Master 58 (Unit 7 Checkup/Review) whenever you complete this unit.

Unit 8: Understanding Yourself

Materials for the Unit

- Candy hearts and chocolate kisses
- Candles, flowers, greeting cards
- Magazine pictures of couples in romantic settings and of friends sharing special times
- Chart showing divorce rates in other countries (optional)
- Copies of a skills inventory from the Internet
- Customizable Masters 3 and 6
- Generic Assessment Master 9
- Unit Masters 59–64
- Vocabulary Card Masters for Unit 8

Understanding Yourself

Read the title and unit goals with learners. Then read the question below the arrow.

This unit focuses on understanding more about yourself and your relationships. Discuss the concepts of *self* and *relationships* by using candy hearts and chocolate kisses.

- Hand out candy for learners to enjoy.
- Tell learners that the heart represents love and emotion. Tell them that to understand your heart is to understand yourself and your emotions.
- Explain that one way to show love is kissing. Demonstrate how children "throw kisses."
- Write on the board or an overhead transparency these two expressions of love:
  I ♥ U
  OOOXXX = hugs (O) and kisses (X)
- Bring a variety of greeting cards, candles, flowers, and magazine pictures of couples in romantic settings and friends sharing special times. Invite learners to bring pictures of special celebrations.
- Discuss special moments shared with spouses and/or friends and family (e.g., anniversaries and birthdays).

- Ask learners which loving gestures they most remember (e.g., flowers, a romantic evening, a special gift).

Photo

Follow the suggestions on p. 5 for talking about the photo.

Ask learners to describe what is happening in the photo. Then ask these questions:

- What does Carlos's boss want him to do? Why?
- Why does Donna think a promotion will help?
- Why are they holding hands?

Think and Talk

- Ask learners to think individually about each question. Be sensitive to their privacy regarding question 5.
- As learners respond, write their answers on the board or an overhead transparency.
- Use idea maps to talk about questions 3, 4, and 5. For each, put the question in the center.

Possible Answers

1. Carlos and his girlfriend are in a restaurant.
2. They are talking about his promotion.
3. Carlos is excited because he may be getting a promotion.
4. Donna feels happy and excited.
5. Answers will vary.

Picture Dictionary

Follow the suggestions on p. 6 for introducing and reinforcing vocabulary.

Follow the suggestions on p. 6 for using vocabulary cards. Use the Vocabulary Card Masters for the words in the Picture Dictionary.

Extension

Brainstorm names of famous people who fit the descriptive adjectives (e.g., Picasso was *artistic*. Michael Jordan is *athletic*.).

Gather Your Thoughts

Have learners use words from the vocabulary list to describe themselves.

Extension

Have learners bring in pictures or drawings of themselves doing the things that best show who they are. Then do the following:

- Display the pictures or drawings. Title the display *"Who I Am."*
- Together, create captions for learners' pictures (e.g., *Anwar is outgoing.*).
- Ask volunteers to use words to describe themselves. Tell them they should use at least two descriptive words from this Picture Dictionary.

What's the Problem?

Follow the suggestions on p. 5 for identifying and analyzing problems. Then do the following:

- Explain to learners that to find the right job, it is important to understand who you are, what you like and do not like to do, and what you are good at and bad at.
- Acknowledge that there may be things they do well but do not like doing. There also may be things they do not do well but like doing.

Model the issue with a class chart:

- Tell learners some of the things you do well and like doing.

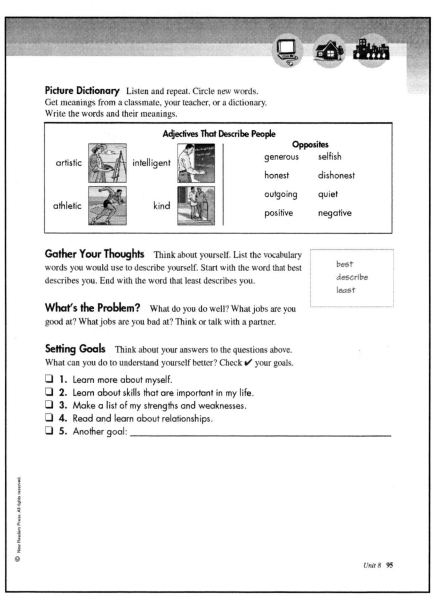

Picture Dictionary Listen and repeat. Circle new words. Get meanings from a classmate, your teacher, or a dictionary. Write the words and their meanings.

Adjectives That Describe People

		Opposites	
artistic	intelligent	generous	selfish
		honest	dishonest
athletic	kind	outgoing	quiet
		positive	negative

Gather Your Thoughts Think about yourself. List the vocabulary words you would use to describe yourself. Start with the word that best describes you. End with the word that least describes you.

best
describe
least

What's the Problem? What do you do well? What jobs are you good at? What jobs are you bad at? Think or talk with a partner.

Setting Goals Think about your answers to the questions above. What can you do to understand yourself better? Check ✔ your goals.

- ❏ **1.** Learn more about myself.
- ❏ **2.** Learn about skills that are important in my life.
- ❏ **3.** Make a list of my strengths and weaknesses.
- ❏ **4.** Read and learn about relationships.
- ❏ **5.** Another goal: _____

Unit 8 **95**

- Tell learners some of the things you do not do well and do not like doing.
- Draw a two-column chart on the board or an overhead transparency. Write the head *Things I Do Well and Like Doing* above the first column. Write the head *Things I Don't Do Well and Don't Like Doing* above the second column.
- Fill in a few examples about yourself.

Have learners work individually to complete a similar chart in their notebooks.

- Tell them to write three to five things in each column.

- Have each learner choose one item from each column to write in the class chart.
- Ask learners to write their names after their entries.

Setting Goals

Follow the suggestions on p. 5 for setting goals.

Ask learners to think about other things they can do to understand themselves better. Have partners talk about personal goals for this unit.

One Step Up

Orally proficient learners can share their information with the class.

Unit 8 95

Lesson 1: Strengths and Weaknesses ✳

- Follow the suggestions on p. 5 for talking about titles. Then read the lesson objectives with learners.
- Tell learners that in this lesson they will find out more about their strengths and weaknesses. They will also evaluate job possibilities by thinking about those strengths and weaknesses and things they like and do not like to do.

Attention Box

Write each word on the board or an overhead transparency.

Encourage learners to help provide definitions, synonyms, related words, and illustrations to show meaning.

This vocabulary should be understood, but learners should not be expected to produce the words at this point.

Questions

Read the questions aloud and brainstorm answers with learners.

- Record learners' answers on the board or an overhead transparency.
- If learners have difficulty, remind them they answered a similar question in What's the Problem? on p. 95.

Reading Tip

Read the tip aloud with learners.

- Explain that the skills listed in the inventory are ones that people in government, schools, and companies think are important for adults to have.
- Read the skills inventory with learners.
- Discuss each skill with learners. Be sure each is understood before moving on to the next.

Talk or Write

This exercise helps learners become skilled at reading surveys.

Work/School

Strengths and Weaknesses

◆ Find out about your strengths and weaknesses
◆ Use reflexive pronouns

career
negotiate

What do you do best? What do you need to improve?

◆ Reading Tip One way to understand what you read is to think about how it relates to your own life. Think about *your* skills. Now study Carlos's skills inventory. Put a star next to two skills you do best. Circle two skills you need to improve.

Career Skills Inventory

This test will evaluate your skills and weaknesses in the workplace. Check whether each statement is true always, sometimes, or never.

	Always True	Sometimes	Never True
Communication			
I am a good listener.	☐	☑	☐
I am a good speaker.	☐	☑	☐
I can write my ideas well.	☐	☑	☐
Working with Others			
I enjoy working with other people.	☐	☑	☐
I am a good leader.	☑	☐	☐
I like to help others.	☑	☐	☐
Decision Making & Problem Solving			
I can use math to solve problems.	☐	☐	☑
I make decisions easily.	☐	☑	☐
I can negotiate to resolve conflicts.	☐	☐	☑
Learning			
I read to learn new things.	☐		
I enjoy doing research on the computer.	☑		
I like taking classes.	☐		

The inventory shows that I work well with other people.

Talk or Write

1. With a partner, talk about the meaning of each skill in the inventory. In your notebook, explain each skill in your own words.
2. Which skills do you need most in your job or family life?

96 *Unit 8 Lesson 1*

Answers
1. Answers will vary.
2. Answers will vary.

Extension
Refer learners to the "I" statements listed in the skills inventory. Then ask these questions about the four skill categories:
- Which of these do you do well when you communicate with others?
- Which of these do you do well when you work with others?
- Which of these do you do well when you have to solve problems?
- Which of these do you do well when you need to learn something?

One Step Up
Have volunteers present orally the explanations they wrote in their notebooks for each skill in question 1. Discuss the explanations until the best definition for each skill is identified. Then have learners write the definitions on the board or an overhead transparency.

Prepare a handout listing the skills and their definitions. Make a copy for each learner.

Vocabulary

Follow the suggestions on p. 6 for introducing and reinforcing vocabulary.

Follow the suggestions on p. 6 for using vocabulary cards. Use the Vocabulary Card Masters for the words in the Vocabulary box.

- Assist learners in adding related words of their own (e.g., *decision/decide, leader/lead, good/better/best or best/worst*).
- In an exaggerated fashion, act out meanings for *strongest* and *weakest*.

Class Chat

Use Customizable Master 3 (3-Column Chart). Follow the suggestions on p. 7 for customizing and duplicating the master. Make a copy for each learner.

- Draw the chart on the board or an overhead transparency.
- Model the chat by having learners volunteer information about themselves.
- Then have learners walk around, ask questions, and record responses in their charts.

Grammar Talk

Follow the suggestions on p. 7 for introducing the grammar point.

Write the reflexive pronouns on the board or an overhead transparency:

myself	*ourselves*
yourself	*yourselves*
herself/himself/itself	*themselves*

Have learners copy the pronouns into their notebooks. Then do the following:

- Ask learners to say the subject pronoun for each reflexive pronoun.
- Then ask them to create one sentence with each reflexive pronoun.
- Write the sentences on the board. To check them, ask learners for feedback and make corrections as needed.

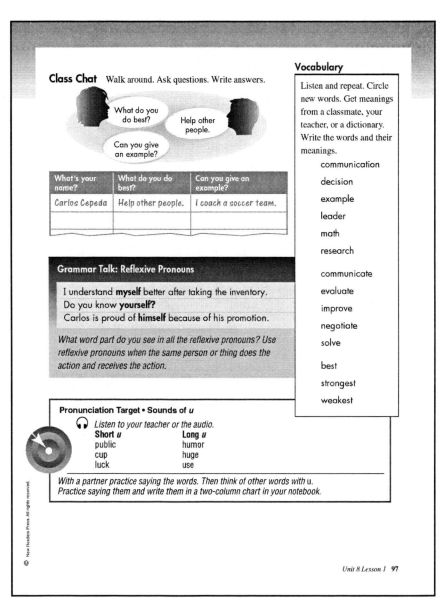

- Ask learners to copy the revised sentences into their notebooks.
- Have them work with a partner to create other sentences with reflexive pronouns.
- Ask volunteers to read the new sentences.

Answer
The word part in all the reflexive pronouns is *-self.*

Pronunciation Target

Demonstrate the short and long sounds of *u*, exaggerating the position of the mouth for each.

Play the audio or read the words in the student book, emphasizing the long and short *u*.

- Have learners call out other words with the sound of short or long *u*.
- Write the words on the board (e.g., *music, but, under, stub, trust, university, husband*).
- Have partners practice the words together: one points to a word, and the other pronounces it.
- Circulate to listen for correct pronunciation and answer any questions.

Assign Workbook pp. 53–54.

Unit 8 *Lesson 1* **97**

Activity A

<u>Extension</u>

Draw a two-column chart on a large piece of paper. Label one column *Strengths* and the other *Weaknesses*. Then do the following:

- Model the activity by writing your own strengths and weaknesses.
- Ask volunteers to tell you their strengths and weaknesses.
- Compile a class list of strengths and weaknesses.
- Tell learners that sometimes in a group strengths and weaknesses can balance each other, which is why it can be good to work as a team.

Activity B

Using information from the Class Chat, have learners write sentences in their notebooks about their class-mates.

Activity C

If learners have difficulty generating sentences, remind them they have already written about people's strengths for other activities in this unit.

<u>One Step Up</u>

The quotation below comes from Shakespeare's *Hamlet*. Learners may not completely understand it at this level, but the power of the English language comes through:

> *This above all: to thine own self be true,*
> *And it must follow, as the night the day,*
> *Thou canst not then be false to any man.*

Relate the quote (which means *be an honest and authentic person; do not act like something you are not*) to the unit theme of understanding yourself—who you are, how you relate to others, etc.

Task 1

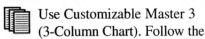 Use Customizable Master 3 (3-Column Chart). Follow the

suggestions on p. 7 for customizing and duplicating the master and distributing a copy to each learner.

Refer learners back to the skills inventory on p. 96. Designate each corner of the room as one of the skills categories. Then do the following:

- Tell learners to go to the corner designated for their strongest type of skill.
- Have them talk with other learners who have the same strength. Discuss how they know they are strong in this area.
- Ask learners to create a list of jobs that could be good for people like them. Explain that not every

job they list has to be one all of them would like to have or would be good at, but it should make good use of the skills in that section of the survey.

- After completing their charts, tell learners to choose one job from the list to talk about.

Use Unit Master 59 (Thinking Skill: What Are My Strengths?) now or at any time during the rest of the unit.

Activity A Tell a partner about yourself. Tell one strength and one weakness.

What do you know about yourself?

I am good at solving problems, but I am not very good at working with people.

Activity B Class Chat Follow-Up Write sentences in your notebook about your classmates.

Carlos knows himself better now. He is good at helping other people.

Activity C In your notebook, write sentences about people you know. What did they accomplish by themselves using their strengths?

by yourself

Andrea took care of the problem at work by herself. She spoke to her boss.

Now write sentences about yourself in your notebook. What can you do by yourself?

TASK 1 Evaluate Jobs for Your Skills

Look at the skills inventory on page 96. Write your strongest skill: communication, decision making, etc. Find other people in your class with the same strength. Discuss jobs that are good for you. Evaluate each job. Complete a chart like the one below.

Jobs	Positive	Negative
1. Manager	more money	more stress
2.		
3.		

Select one job. Make a presentation to the class. Tell why the job is good for you. Tell why it could be bad for you.

Lesson 2: Coming Together

- Follow the suggestions on p. 5 for talking about titles.
- In this lesson, learners will talk about relationships and think about things that are important in a good personal relationship.

Attention Box

- Read the words to learners, pointing or miming to convey meaning when possible.
- Create idea maps using word families (e.g., *self-confidence/self-confident/confidence/confident*) or feelings (e.g., *self-confidence, worry, etc.*).

This vocabulary should be understood, but learners should not be expected to produce the words at this point.

Question

Read the introductory question aloud to learners.

- Brainstorm reasons couples may get angry or argue (e.g., *money, stress, different political or religious ideas, different views on rearing children, problems with in-laws*). If necessary, explain the word *in-laws*.
- Write learners' reasons on a large piece of paper and post it.

Listening Tip

Read the tip aloud with learners. Explain that sometimes people do not tell their feelings with words. They show them in their faces and body language. Give the examples below and have volunteers use their bodies and faces to show feelings:

- You have just won a new car. *(excitement)*
- You have a phone message from your child's school. *(worry)*
- A car cuts in front of you on the road. *(anger)*
- Your boss tells you that your work is good. *(self-confidence)*

 Play the audio or read the listening script on p. 121.

Talk or Write

This exercise helps learners become skilled at listening to conversations.

Possible Answers

1. Carlos was worried that he would not be the best person for the new position. His skills inventory showed that his strength was working with other people, and in the new job he would work alone.
2. Donna thinks Carlos needs more self-confidence and that he is negative and worries too much.
3. They are angry because they both had a hard day at work. Carlos feels Donna is not listening to him.
4. Answers will vary.

Extension

Ask these additional questions:

- Where is the new position? *(in the research department)*
- Why do you think Carlos tells Donna that she is not listening to him? *(Answers will vary.)*

One Step Up

Ask partners to write two more lines to the conversation. Have volunteers act out their conversations.

Coming Together

- Discuss relationships
- Learn about marriage and divorce in the US

feeling
self-confidence
worry/worried

Why do couples get angry?

- Listening Tip 🎧 Listening for feelings can help you understand what you hear. Now listen to the conversation between Carlos and Donna. Try to imagine what they are feeling. You can read the words on page 119.

Carlos and Donna need to be more sensitive with each other.

Talk or Write
1. What was Carlos worried about? Why?
2. What does Donna think?
3. Why are they angry?
4. How can they communicate better?

Unit 8 Lesson 2 **99**

Vocabulary

Follow the suggestions on p. 6 for introducing and reinforcing vocabulary.

Follow the suggestions on p. 6 for using vocabulary cards. Use the Vocabulary Card Masters for the words in the Vocabulary box.

In the US

- What does the reading say can cause conflict in a marriage? (stress)
- What does it say are two things that people can do? (understand themselves and each other)
- Draw an idea map on the board with the word Divorce in the center circle.
- Ask learners why they think the divorce rate in the US is so high. Write their reasons in the outer circles.

To practice reading the bar graph, ask these questions:

- For every 100 marriages that occurred in ____(name of country) in 1999, how many divorces occurred?
- Which country has the lowest divorce rate? (Turkey)
- Which country has the highest divorce rate? (Belarus)
- List the countries in order from the lowest rate of divorce to the highest. (Turkey, Croatia, Spain, Israel, France, Canada, US, Russia, Belarus)

Compare Cultures

- If possible, bring in a chart that shows the divorce rates in other countries. Try to find one that shows the number of divorces per 100 marriages that year so that it can be easily compared with the graph in the student book. (Look for this information on the Internet.)
- Encourage learners to discuss divorce rates as well as engage-

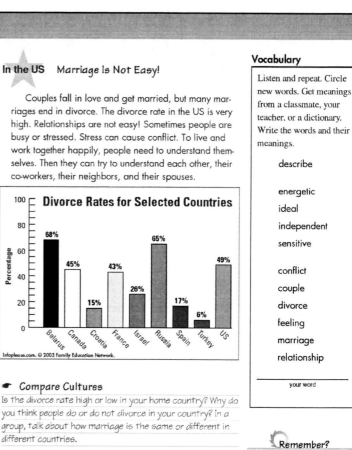

In the US Marriage Is Not Easy!

Couples fall in love and get married, but many marriages end in divorce. The divorce rate in the US is very high. Relationships are not easy! Sometimes people are busy or stressed. Stress can cause conflict. To live and work together happily, people need to understand themselves. Then they can try to understand each other, their co-workers, their neighbors, and their spouses.

Divorce Rates for Selected Countries

Belarus 68%, Canada 45%, Croatia 15%, France 43%, Israel 26%, Russia 65%, Spain 17%, Turkey 6%, US 49%

Infoplease.com. © 2003 Family Education Network.

Compare Cultures

Is the divorce rate high or low in your home country? Why do you think people do or do not divorce in your country? In a group, talk about how marriage is the same or different in different countries.

Activity A Work in a group of three. Students A and B talk. Student C listens to them. Student A talks about an imaginary or a real problem. Imagine a problem with your spouse, a co-worker, your boss, a neighbor, a friend, or a family member. Student B gives advice. Student C listens and then gives advice. Then exchange roles. Repeat until each group member has played all three roles.

100 Unit 8 Lesson 2

Vocabulary

Listen and repeat. Circle new words. Get meanings from a classmate, your teacher, or a dictionary. Write the words and their meanings.

describe

energetic

ideal

independent

sensitive

conflict

couple

divorce

feeling

marriage

relationship

_____

your word

Remember?

stress

stressed

ment and marriage customs in their home countries.

Extension
Write these group discussion questions on the board or an overhead transparency:

- Are there any customs from your home countries that could help people in the US have better marriages?
- Are there any US customs that could help people in your home countries have better marriages?

One Step Up
Ask volunteers to tell the class what they learned about marriage or divorce customs in another learner's country.

Activity A

- Put learners in groups of three.
- Assign the roles of person with a problem, person who gives advice, and observer (a person who listens and gives advice).
- Have learners choose three "problems" to discuss, changing roles for each so that each learner has the opportunity to play all three roles.

Use Unit Master 60 (Study Skill: Create a Bar Graph) now or at any time during the rest of the unit.

Assign Workbook pp. 55–56.

Activity B

Have partners discuss the list of options together. Then have them write examples for each in their notebooks.

Activity C

Explain any adjectives that learners do not understand.

One Step Up

Have each group create the ideal partner for their ideal person.

- Tell the groups to look at each characteristic of their ideal person and decide what kind of person would be able to cooperate well with that person and influence him or her positively.
- Write the adjectives from the unit opener, Lesson 1, and Lesson 2 on the board or an overhead transparency as a reference for learners.
- Tell groups that in the US, people often say, "Opposites attract." However, many people really want a partner who is similar to them. Groups need to think about these ideas when creating the partner for their ideal person.
- Have one learner from each group describe the ideal person to the class. Have another group member describe the ideal partner.

Attention Box

Read the words to learners, pointing or miming to convey meaning when possible. This vocabulary should be understood, but learners should not be expected to produce the words at this point.

Task 2

Put learners in small groups.

- Tell group members to read the list of behaviors in their books and check *Yes* or *No*. Then have learners discuss why people should or should not engage in the behaviors listed.

Activity B What are some ways you can improve your relationships? Work with a partner. Check ✔ all that apply. Give examples.

- ❏ Talk about your feelings.
- ❏ Listen carefully.
- ❏ Join discussion groups.
- ❏ Go to counseling.
- ❏ Spend more time with others.
- ❏ Talk about problems with parents or friends.
- ❏ Talk with a spiritual leader.
- ❏ Watch self-help videos or read self-help books.
- ❏ Reduce the stress in your life.
- ❏ Other: _____

Activity C Work in a small group. Read about Carlos and Donna.

Carlos Cepeda is ambitious, hard-working, and intelligent. He is also kind and generous. At times, he can be selfish.

Donna Sullivan is energetic and independent. She is athletic and outgoing.

With your group, create an imaginary, ideal person. What characteristics would your ideal person have? Make a list.

Our ideal person is _____ , _____ , _____

_____ , _____ , _____ .

TASK 2 Describe Good Relationships

In small groups, look at the chart below. Check *Yes* for things that are important in a relationship. Check *No* for things that are not good for a relationship. Talk about why. Complete the chart. Share with your class.

accept
criticize
respect

Yes	No		Yes	No	
____	____	Good listening	____	____	Understanding yourself
____	____	Showing anger	____	____	Accepting differences
____	____	Hiding feelings	____	____	Never apologizing
____	____	Communicating openly	____	____	Criticizing
____	____	Showing feelings	____	____	Cooperating
____	____	Respecting other's opinions	____	____	Other: _____

Unit 8 Lesson 2 **101**

- Have learners write in their notebooks the reasons people should or should not do each behavior.
- Ask a volunteer from each group to share with the class the things they *should do* and the reasons why. Encourage learners to express varying opinions.
- Tell learners that there may be two or more good opinions about some actions. For example, sometimes there may be good reasons for not showing anger, while at other times there may be good reasons for showing it.

- Ask volunteers to share the things people *should not do* and the reasons why they should not. Again, encourage debate.

Lesson 3: Neighbors Helping Neighbors

Read the title with learners. Then read the lesson objectives listed below it.

- Follow the suggestions on p. 5 for talking about titles.
- In this lesson, learners will learn to talk about helping in their neighborhood. They will also learn to solve a neighborhood problem that they select.

Attention Box

- Write the words on the board.
- Encourage learners to provide definitions, synonyms, and related words (e.g., *association/group/meeting*). Write their suggestions on the board or an overhead transparency.
- Add the verb forms *associate* and *maintain* to the list on the board.

This vocabulary should be understood, but learners should not be expected to produce the words at this point.

Question

Read the introductory question aloud. Brainstorm answers by drawing an idea map on a large piece of paper.

Write the words *Neighborhood Issues* in the middle circle. Write learners' responses in the smaller circles.

Reading Tip

Tell learners that to get specific information from something you read, you need to focus on the details.

Ask them what information they need to learn from an e-mail message announcing a meeting. Suggest these *wh-* questions as prompts:

What? (What is the meeting about?)

When? (When is the meeting?)

Where? (Where is the meeting?)

Why? (Why are we meeting?)

Who? (Who is invited?)

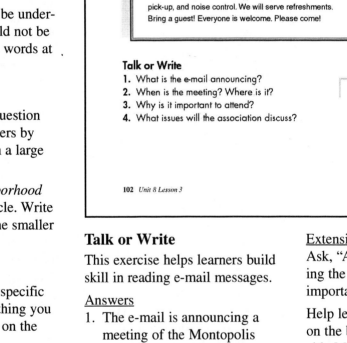

Talk or Write

This exercise helps learners build skill in reading e-mail messages.

Answers

1. The e-mail is announcing a meeting of the Montopolis Neighborhood Association.
2. The meeting is on Wednesday, September 10, at 8:00 P.M. at the Town Hall.
3. Answers will vary but should include discussing important issues or needing help.
4. The association will discuss crime watch, children's safety, lawn maintenance, trash pick-up, and noise control.

Extension

Ask, "Are the issues for the meeting the same issues you listed as important in your neighborhood?"

Help learners draw a Venn diagram on the board. (Refer to Customizable Master 6 for help with this diagram.) Above one circle, write *Issues for Us*. Above the other circle, write *Issues for Montopolis*. Write *Both* where the circles overlap. Fill in the circles together.

Vocabulary

Follow the suggestions on p. 6 for introducing and reinforcing vocabulary.

Follow the suggestions on p. 6 for using vocabulary cards. Use the Vocabulary Card Masters for the words in the Vocabulary box.

Class Chat

Use Customizable Master 3 (3-Column Chart). Follow the suggestions on p. 7 for customizing and duplicating the master. Distribute a copy to each learner.

Grammar Talk

Follow the suggestions on p. 7 for introducing the grammar point.

- Write a model sentence using the future tense (e.g., *I will take a vacation next summer.*). Then write the same sentence with *be going to* instead of *will*.
- Introduce negative sentences with *will* by writing another model sentence about yourself (e.g., *I will not see my son for a month.*).
- Have learners tell you some of their plans. Ask, "What will you do next summer?"
- Use their responses to write pairs of sentences on the board; use *will* and *be going to*. Try to use different subject pronouns *(he, she, they, we)* to show that *will* does not change its form but *be going to* does.
- Follow up by asking questions to elicit a negative response. Let learners see that the negative form of *will* is *will not*. Do not use the contraction *won't* at this point.
- Record learners' responses on the board using both *will* and *be going to* forms.

Answer
Will and *be going to* are the two ways of talking about the future.

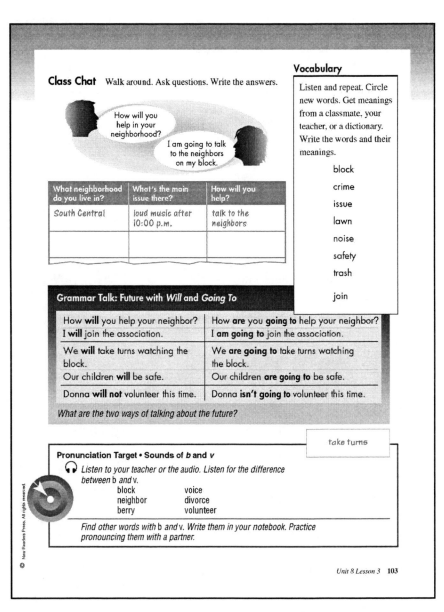

Pronunciation Target

Play the audio or read the words in the student book, emphasizing the sounds of *b* and *v*.

- Explain that *b* is pronounced with the lips touching and then opening; *v* is pronounced with the top front teeth touching the bottom lip. Demonstrate with exaggerated pronunciation of the two sounds.
- Draw two columns on the board with the headings *b* and *v*. Write each word in the correct column as learners listen.

Have learners copy the columns from the board into their notebooks. Then tell pairs to practice the words.

- Write these additional words with *b* and *v* on the board or an overhead transparency: *benefits, bilingual, interview, bored, busy, government, neighborhood, serve, drive, boots, save.*
- Have one partner dictate the words from the board in random order while the second partner writes them in the correct column. Then have partners switch roles.

Assign Workbook pp. 57–58.

 Use Unit Master 61 (Pronunciation: Dictation) now or at any time during the rest of the unit.

Activity A

First have learners compose their sentences. Then have partners compare their sentences to complete the diagram.

 Use Customizable Master 6 (Venn Diagram), distributing a copy to each learner. Follow these steps:

- Tell learners to label their diagrams, following the model in the student book.
- Have partners work together to complete their diagrams.
- Ask volunteers to share their diagrams by copying them on the board or an overhead transparency.

One Step Up

Tell learners to write a paragraph about what they are going to do to make their relationships with their neighbors better. Refer them to the Writing Checklists on p. 126 to revise their writing.

Attention Box

Read the phrase to learners, pointing or miming to convey meaning. This phrase should be understood, but learners should not be expected to produce it at this point.

Task 3

Have learners work in small groups to choose one of the problems and write a plan for solving it.

 Use Generic Assessment Master 9 (Written Communication Rubric) to evaluate each group's report.

Extensions

1. Copy this model chart on the board or an overhead transparency:

Tasks	Name	Days and Times
Crime watch	Aaron Avela	Monday. 7:00 to 10:00 P.M.

 Use Customizable Master 3 (3-Column Chart). Follow the suggestions on p. 7

for customizing and duplicating the master. Write the heads *Tasks, Name,* and *Days and Times* at the top of the chart. Give a copy to each learner.

Have learners walk around and ask each other what they can volunteer for. Tell them to complete their charts as they go.

2. Have partners talk about things they can do to make their relationships better.

 Use Customizable Master 3 (3-Column Chart). Follow the suggestions on p. 7 for customizing and duplicating the master. Write the heads *Work, Personal Life,* and *Neighborhood*

at the top of the chart. Give a copy to each learner.

Copy this model on the board or an overhead transparency:

Work	Personal Life	Neighborhood
Listen better	Tell our children we love them	Attend association meetings

Tell partners to complete their charts as they talk. Explain that their ideas do not have to be the same because their situations may not be the same.

 Use Unit Master 62 (Grammar: What Will You Do?) now or at any time during the rest of the unit.

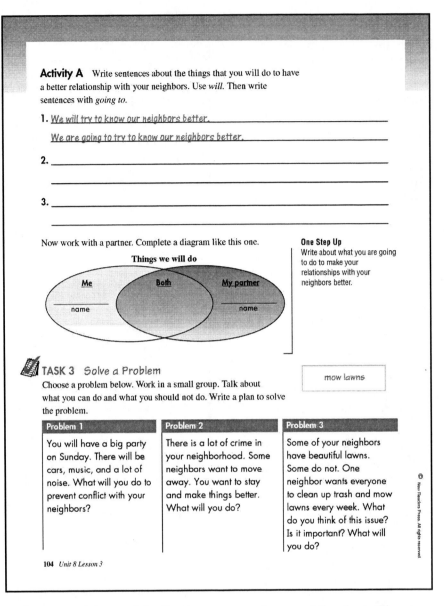

Unit 8 Project

Learners find their strengths and weaknesses on a skills inventory.

Get Ready

Tell learners to look back at Task 1 (p. 98). Help them decide which areas were their strongest. Review their reasons for their choices.

Do the Work

📑 Use Unit Master 63 (Unit 8 Project: Describe Yourself). Distribute a copy to each learner.

- Demonstrate the directions by making an overhead transparency of Master 63.
- Talk learners through the inventory as you fill in a few rows of the chart. Use the examples in the student book or provide some of your own.
- Tell learners to complete their own inventories.
- Have learners use the inventory to write personal improvement plans in their notebooks.

Present Your Project

Put learners in small groups to talk about the information in their inventories.

Ongoing Assessment

While learners are completing this activity, walk around the room and listen to their conversations. Try to listen to at least five different conversations. Make notes on how well learners perform on the following features:

a. Quality of inventory
   - 0 = not completed or completed with errors that interfere with meaning
   - 1 = some information, some errors
   - 2 = completed with no errors or few minor errors

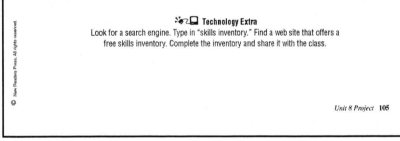

UNIT 8 Project

Describe Yourself

Find your strengths and weaknesses on a skills inventory.

Get Ready
Look back at your work for Task 1. What did you decide was your strongest area? Why?

Do the Work
Get a copy of the skills inventory from your teacher. Find the skills you are strongest in. Make a list of jobs or tasks that would make good use of your skills. Find the skills you are weakest in. Make a list of things you can do to improve these skills. How will you improve your weakest skills? Use a chart like this one. Write a plan in your notebook.

My Strongest Skills	Jobs I Can Do Well
1. leadership	1. team leader or supervisor
2. helpful/friendly	2. customer service
3. computer research	3. information technology
My Weakest Skills	What I Can Do to Improve
1. listening	1. Be more patient and attentive.
2. math	2. Take a math class.
3. negotiating	3. Read about negotiation skills.

Present Your Project
Show your skills inventory to your group. Talk about your strengths. Give an example of two or three of your strongest skills.

🖥 **Technology Extra**
Look for a search engine. Type in "skills inventory." Find a web site that offers a free skills inventory. Complete the inventory and share it with the class.

Unit 8 Project 105

b. Fluency and communicative ability
   - 0 = very poor
   - 1 = communicates haltingly
   - 2 = communicates clearly and with confidence

Technology Extra

Bring copies of a skills inventory for learners who do not have Internet access.

📖 Assign Workbook p. 59 (Check Your Progress).

📑 Use Unit Master 64 (Unit 8 Checkup/Review) whenever you complete this unit.

Unit 9: It Takes a Team 🔲

Materials for the Unit

- Party favors and decorations
- Ads for food, drinks; catalogs for party decorations and facilities
- Sample grocery or store coupons and gift certificates
- Sample tickets (optional)
- Objects to illustrate your own success story
- Customizable Masters 3 and 5
- Generic Assessment Masters 9–12
- Unit Masters 65–71
- Vocabulary Card Masters for Unit 9

It Takes a Team

- Read the title and unit goals with learners. Then follow the suggestions on p. 5 for talking about titles.
- Tell learners this unit focuses on celebrating and recognizing success.

Discuss the concept of *celebration:*
- Bring a variety of party favors and decorations (e.g., hats, streamers, horns, confetti).
- Ask learners to tell you what they represent.

Attention Box

Read the words to learners, pointing or miming to convey meaning. This vocabulary should be understood, but learners should not be expected to produce the words at this point.

Question

Read the question below the arrow. Then do the following:
- Draw an idea map on a large piece of paper. Write the words *What We Celebrate* in the center circle.
- Ask learners what people in the US celebrate (e.g., birthdays, weddings, graduations, births, anniversaries, promotions, successes at work). Write their responses in the other circles.

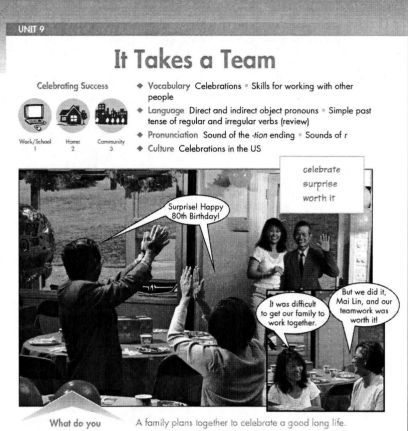

Photos

Follow the suggestions on p. 5 for talking about the photos.

Ask learners what they see in the photos. Then ask these questions:
- What does the party room look like?
- What do you think they will do at the party? Eat? Talk? Sing "Happy Birthday"? Present gifts?

Think and Talk

Ask learners to think about each question. Then do the following:
- Have learners discuss their ideas in pairs or small groups.
- Ask one group to report their answer for each of the first three questions and the other groups tell whether they agree or disagree.
- Have individual learners explain their answers to question 4.

Answers

1. Mai Lin is at a restaurant or party room. There is a surprise party for her father's 80th birthday.
2. Her father looks happy and surprised because the family is celebrating his birthday.
3. It was difficult to get the family to work together.
4. Answers will vary.

Vocabulary

Follow the suggestions on p. 6 for introducing and reinforcing vocabulary.

Follow the suggestions on p. 6 for using vocabulary cards. Use the Vocabulary Card Masters for the words in the Vocabulary box.

Have learners add to the list related words of their own.

Provide sample sentences for the word pairs (e.g., I *celebrate* my birthday in December. My birthday is always a big *celebration*.).

Gather Your Thoughts

Distribute copies of Customizable Master 5 (Idea Map). Have learners complete their maps with their own ideas before discussing them with a partner. Encourage them to use vocabulary words as they complete their maps.

Create a display about celebrations:
- Have learners bring pictures of their celebrations.
- Make photocopies of the pictures to create the display. Title it *Our Celebrations*.
- Together, create captions for each picture (e.g., *Ira's family celebrates Hanukkah.*).

What's the Problem?

Follow the suggestions on p. 5 for identifying and analyzing problems.

Model the issue by telling learners about a time you disagreed with other people while planning an event.
- Tell learners what event you were planning and what the problem was.
- Describe how you and the other person or people resolved the problem (e.g., by using parts of both ideas; by choosing or voting; by finding a completely different solution).
- Outline the new plan you made together.

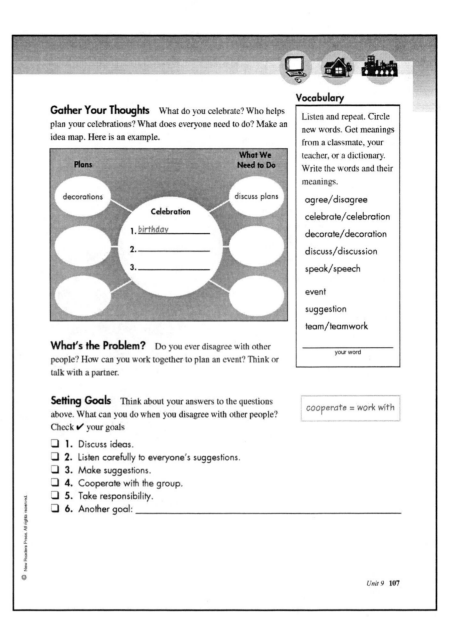

Gather Your Thoughts What do you celebrate? Who helps plan your celebrations? What does everyone need to do? Make an idea map. Here is an example.

Plans

decorations

Celebration

1. *birthday*

2. _____

3. _____

What We Need to Do

discuss plans

Vocabulary

Listen and repeat. Circle new words. Get meanings from a classmate, your teacher, or a dictionary. Write the words and their meanings.

agree/disagree
celebrate/celebration
decorate/decoration
discuss/discussion
speak/speech

event
suggestion
team/teamwork

_____
your word

What's the Problem? Do you ever disagree with other people? How can you work together to plan an event? Think or talk with a partner.

Setting Goals Think about your answers to the questions above. What can you do when you disagree with other people? Check ✔ your goals

❑ 1. Discuss ideas.
❑ 2. Listen carefully to everyone's suggestions.
❑ 3. Make suggestions.
❑ 4. Cooperate with the group.
❑ 5. Take responsibility.
❑ 6. Another goal: _____

cooperate = work with

Unit 9 107

Then do the following:
- Ask learners to write a few sentences in their notebooks about a time they disagreed with a person or a group. Tell them to describe the same three things that you modeled—the event and problem, how the problem was resolved, and the new plan.
- Have learners share their sentences with a partner.

Attention Box

Read the word and its definition to learners, pointing or miming to convey meaning if possible. This word should be understood, but learners should not be expected to produce it at this point.

Setting Goals

Follow the suggestions on p. 5 for setting goals.

<u>One Step Up</u>
Have orally proficient learners share their information with the class.

Lesson 1: Working Together

- Follow the suggestions on p. 5 for talking about titles.
- Read the lesson objectives aloud with learners.
- In this lesson, learners will focus on strategies for success at work. They will also think about what is needed for successful teamwork.

Attention Box

- Write the words on the board or an overhead transparency.
- Encourage learners to provide definitions, synonyms, and other words in the same word families (*confident, product*).

This vocabulary should be understood, but learners should not be expected to produce the words at this point.

Question

Read the introductory question and brainstorm answers with learners. List their strategies for success on the board or an overhead transparency.

Caption

Read the caption aloud. Tell learners about a time you were told that you did something well. Describe how you felt.

Listening Tip

Read the tip aloud.

Play the audio or read the listening script on p. 121 twice. Follow the suggestions on p. 5 for listening comprehension.

Talk or Write

This exercise helps learners become skilled at understanding conversations.

Answers
1. The boss is congratulating Mai Lin because her team had the highest sales total this month.
2. Mai Lin is a team leader in the factory store.

LESSON 1   Work/School

Working Together

◆ Talk about strategies for success
◆ Use direct and indirect object pronouns

What are your main strategies for success?

◆ Listening Tip 🎧 When you listen, think about your own life. This will help you understand what you hear. Now listen to the conversation between Mai Lin and her boss. What would you say if your boss asked you to speak to other employees? You can read the words on page 119.

confidence
factory
production

Mai Lin's boss congratulates her for her good work.

Talk or Write
1. What is the boss talking about?
2. What is Mai Lin's position in the factory store?
3. Why should she be proud of herself?
4. What does her boss ask her to do?
5. Did something like this ever happen to you?

108 *Unit 9 Lesson 1*

---

3. She should be proud of herself because her strategies for success helped her team have the highest sales total.
4. Her boss asks her to speak about her strategies for success at the next employees' meeting.
5. Answers will vary.

Extensions
1. Add these additional questions: Why is Mai Lin worried? (*She is worried the other employees won't understand her English.*) What does her boss tell her? (*to have more confidence in herself*) What will Mai Lin try to do for him? (*speak at the employees' meeting, share her ideas*)

2. Try these activities with learners:
- Have learners role-play the conversation.
- Compliment various learners in the class (e.g., Maria has good handwriting. Eric asks good questions.).
- Ask learners to walk around and compliment each other.
- Have learners work in pairs to create a natural conversation in which they compliment each other.

Vocabulary

Follow the suggestions on p. 6 for introducing and reinforcing vocabulary.

Follow the suggestions on p. 6 for using vocabulary cards. Use the Vocabulary Card Masters for the words in the Vocabulary box.

Help learners form additional family word pairs (e.g., *gift/give, strategy/strategize*).

Class Chat

Use Customizable Master 3 (3-Column Chart). Follow the suggestions on p. 7 for customizing and duplicating the master. Give a copy to each learner. Then ask two volunteers to model asking and answering the questions in the chart.

Grammar Talk

Follow the suggestions on p. 7 for introducing the grammar point.

Remind learners that they have already learned both direct and indirect object pronouns. Give them examples by writing sentences with each type of pronoun used alone. Use the model sentences, transforming them like this:

My family planned the party for him.
My family planned it.

Extensions

1. Depending on the level of your learners, tell them the following: The direct and indirect object pronouns *me, you, him, her, it, us, you,* and *them* replace an object noun.

   When a sentence has a direct and an indirect object pronoun, the direct object goes before the indirect object pronoun.

   Indirect object pronouns often follow prepositions like *to* or *for.*

2. Have learners turn to p. 119 of their books and look at the listening script for this lesson.

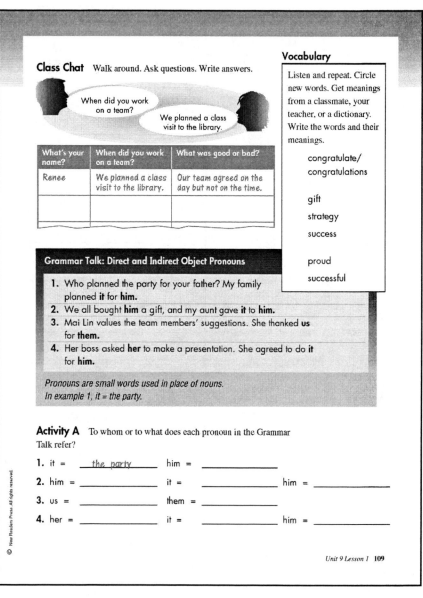

Read each sentence and ask learners to tell you the direct and indirect object. Remind them that some sentences will have no object pronouns.

Ask learners to tell you to which word each pronoun refers.

Answers

You could tell them about your strategies for success. *(them = employees)*

I am worried they won't understand me. *(me = Mai Lin)*

I will try to do it for you, Mr. Cohen. *(it = share her ideas, make a speech; you = Mr. Cohen)*

Activity A

Tell learners to look at the sentences in the Grammar Talk to complete this activity.

Answers

1. it = the party, him = the father
2. him = the father, it = a gift, him = the father
3. us = the team members, them = suggestions
4. her = Mai Lin, it = a presentation, him = the boss

Assign Workbook pp. 60–61.

Pronunciation Target

🎧 Play the audio or read the words in the student book.

- On the board or an overhead transparency, write these additional words with the *-tion* ending:

  application   congratulations
  immigration   invitation
  solution   tradition

- Have partners practice pronouncing the words and dictating them to each other.

Activity B

Have learners write sentences about their classmates in their notebooks. Tell them to use the information from their Class Chat charts.

Activity C

- Have partners talk about events they helped plan.
- Ask them to write sentences about these events in their notebooks.
- Then have them list any pronouns they used in their sentences and tell to what or whom the pronouns refer.

Task 1

Use Customizable Master 3 (3-Column Chart). Follow the suggestions on p. 7 for customizing and duplicating the master. Make a copy for each learner.

Create a model chart on the board. Enter information from your personal experience or that of volunteers.

Use Unit Master 65 (Grammar: What Are They Celebrating?) now or at any time during the rest of the unit.

Pronunciation Target • Sound of *-tion* ending
🎧 *Listen to your teacher or the audio.*
celebration   decoration   suggestion

Repeat the words. Find more words that end in -tion. Write them in your notebook. Practice saying the words with a partner.

Activity B **Class Chat Follow-Up** Write sentences about your classmates.

1. *Renee helped plan a visit to the library. Everyone wanted to go on Friday, but they did not agree on the time.*

2. _____

   _____

3. _____

   _____

Activity C Work with a partner. Talk about a successful event that you helped plan. Tell why you did it. In your notebook, write about your event and your partner's event.

I planned a celebration for my teacher. I did it for her.

Write the pronouns and to what or whom they refer.

it = a celebration, her = my teacher

TASK 1 *Describe Successful Team Planning*
Work with a small group. Think of two examples of successful teamwork in your life. Tell about one example in your personal life and one in your school or work life. Write details in a chart like this one.

	Personal Event	School or Work Event
What		
Who		
When		
Where		
Why		

110 *Unit 9 Lesson 1*

Lesson 2: Sharing Success

Read the title and lesson objectives with learners.
- Follow the suggestions on p. 5 for talking about titles.
- In this lesson, learners will focus on teamwork. In groups, they will also write and deliver a speech about teamwork.

Idiom Watch!

Help learners understand the idiom *show respect.*
- Discuss with learners why it is important to *show respect.*
- Ask learners why they should *show respect* to their friends, boss, co-workers, teachers, family, children, and, especially, themselves.
- While some learners may see respect as having to do with hierarchy and authority, the focus here should be on the need for *all* people to treat one another with respect.

Question

Read the introductory question aloud. Brainstorm answers with learners:
- Draw an idea map on the board or an overhead transparency.
- Label the center circle *Things to share with family or friends.*
- In the outer circles, write learners' suggestions (e.g., a problem, a sickness, a funny event, a surprise, a happy event).

Reading Tip

Read the tip aloud with learners.

Tell learners to think about their own experiences. Ask volunteers what they have learned from experience that helps them in life.
- Read Mai Lin's speech aloud, using appropriate expression.
- Ask a volunteer to read Mai Lin's speech as he or she thinks Mai Lin might have read it.

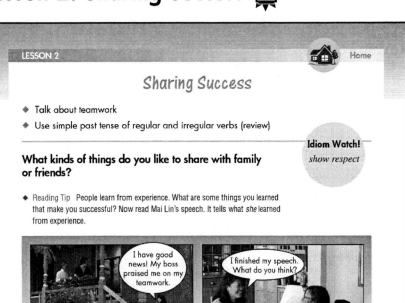

LESSON 2   Home

Sharing Success

- ◆ Talk about teamwork
- ◆ Use simple past tense of regular and irregular verbs (review)

Idiom Watch!
show respect

What kinds of things do you like to share with family or friends?

◆ Reading Tip People learn from experience. What are some things you learned that make you successful? Now read Mai Lin's speech. It tells what *she* learned from experience.

> I have good news! My boss praised me on my teamwork.

> I finished my speech. What do you think?

Sharing success makes it better.

When my family and I came to this country, we were very scared. We were also sad because we left behind people we loved. We found new friends in the US. We learned that we were not alone.

I understood at that time how important it was to work as a team. We always showed respect to members of our family, especially the older people. If we listen to them, we can learn from them.

As a team leader at work, I did the things that I learned from my family. I listened to other people, and I respected their opinions. I tried to be honest. I expected them to act the same way with me. We all were proud of our work, and we wanted to earn the respect of others. Those are the secrets of our success!

Talk or Write
1. What did Mai Lin learn from her family?
2. What are her ideas for successful teamwork?
3. What did you learn in your home country that helped you in the US?

Unit 9 Lesson 2 **111**

Talk or Write

This exercise helps learners read to understand cause and effect.

<u>Answers</u>
1. From her family, Mai Lin learned to listen to other people and to respect their opinions.
2. At work Mai Lin did the things she learned from her family, and these things gave her ideas for successful teamwork:
   Listen to teammates and respect their opinions.
   Be honest with them.
   Expect them to be honest.
   Be proud of our work.
   Earn the respect of other people.
3. Answers will vary.

Vocabulary

Follow the suggestions on p. 6 for introducing and reinforcing vocabulary.

Follow the suggestions on p. 6 for using vocabulary cards. Use the Vocabulary Card Masters for the words in the Vocabulary box.

Ask learners to suggest synonyms, definitions, or illustrations for each of the words.

Extension

Point out that the words *praise, respect,* and *trust* are nouns as well as verbs. On the board or an overhead transparency, write model sentences using each of these words as a noun and as a verb.

Class Chat

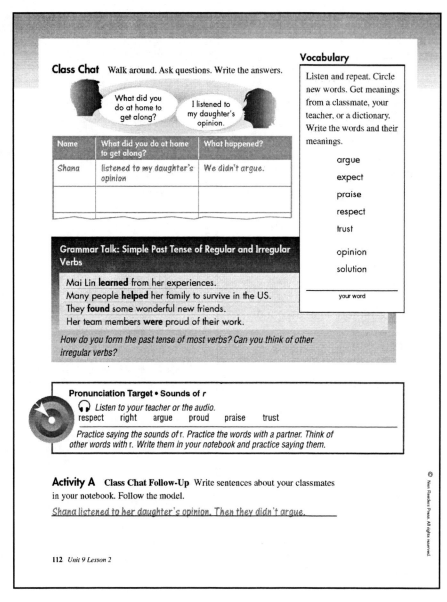

Use Customizable Master 3 (3-Column Chart). Follow the suggestions on p. 7 for customizing and duplicating the master. Make one copy for each learner.

Review Mai Lin's story on p. 111. Identify points about her family life as models for this chart. Ask questions like these:

- What did Mai Lin do at home to get along? *(She showed respect for everyone.)*
- What happened? *(She learned to work as a team member.)*

Ask two volunteers to model asking and answering the questions in the chart.

Grammar Talk

Follow the suggestions on p. 7 for introducing the grammar point.

Answers

To form the past tense of most verbs, add *-ed* to the base form.

Irregular verbs have different forms. Tell learners to refer to p. 125 for a list of irregular verbs. These verbs have irregular simple past forms.

Extensions

1. Remind learners of other things

112 Unit 9 *Lesson 2*

they have learned about verbs in the past tense:

- To form the negative in the simple past, use *did not* or *didn't* and the base form of the verb.
- To ask a simple past *yes/no* question, place *did* at the beginning of the question. Then add a subject and the base form of the verb (e.g., *Did he go?*).

2. Ask learners to tell what they or their families and friends did during the past week. Then ask them to tell some things they did not do. Have them use the regular verbs they know and the list of irregular verbs on p. 125.

One Step Up

Ask learners to write a short paragraph about the things they or their families and friends did and did not do in the past week.

Tell learners to use the Writing Checklists on p. 126 for help in revising their paragraph.

Pronunciation Target

Play the audio or read the words in the student book.

Activity A

Have learners use the information in their Class Chat charts to write sentences about their classmates.

Assign Workbook pp. 62–63.

Activity B

- Have learners copy the idea maps in their books into their notebooks.
- Tell partners to discuss their projects with one another.
- Then have them organize their ideas using the idea maps.

Extension
Ask learners what things a team leader can do to create or build positive team spirit (e.g., make sure team members share the same goals).

Then ask what things a leader might do that would create negative feelings among team members (e.g., talk negatively about some members of the group to other members).

One Step Up
- On a large sheet of paper, write the "good team leader" points listed in the student book. Post it for learners to see.
- Ask learners how many of these points are true for team members as well. Have a volunteer check the points as you discuss them.

Activity C

Bring some ads for food and drinks and some catalogs for party decorations and facilities.

Ask learners if they can think of other party expenses Mai Lin and her family might have had (e.g., party favors; paper dishes, plastic utensils, and paper napkins; entertainment).

- Have learners work in small groups to look at the resources, find items, and complete their list of supplies and cost estimates.
- Ask a recorder in each group to write the list.
- Then have a reporter from each group share the group's list and cost estimates with the class.

Attention Box

Read the word to learners, pointing or miming to convey meaning. This

---

Activity B Here are Mai Lin's notes on being a good team leader.

A good team leader. . .	
• listens with understanding	• is open to new ideas
• discusses problems	• trusts the group
• communicates honestly	• makes good decisions
• expects cooperation	• finds solutions

Work with a partner. Think of a time you had a family, work, or community team project. Write some things people did to cooperate. Then write some things they did not do.

Cooperation: discussed problems

Conflict: argued

Activity C Work in your group. How much do you think it cost to have Mai Lin's father's surprise party? Estimate the cost and sales tax for a party in your area.

Number of people: _____   Decorations: _____

Food: _____   Location: _____

Drinks: _____

TASK 2 Write a Group Speech about Teamwork

Work in a small group. Write a speech about teamwork. One person visits a different group and reads the speech. The new group makes positive comments and gives some suggestions for improvement. Return to your group. Revise your group's speech.

revise

Positive Comments	Suggestions for Improvement
meaningful	more details
emotional	speak louder
well organized	speak slower
interesting	practice pronunciation

One Step Up
One person from each group reads the revised speech to the class.

---

word should be understood, but learners should not be expected to produce it at this point.

Task 2
Tell learners to review the list they made in Activity B describing ways to create a good team.

Give a copy of Generic Assessment Master 12 (Peer Assessment Form for Projects and Tasks) to each learner.
- Follow the suggestions for peer assessment on p. 4.
- Have one member from each group practice the group's speech in front of another group.

- Tell learners to complete and exchange the forms before revising their speeches.
- Ask group reporters to read their group's speech to the class. Encourage active listening by asking learners questions about other speeches.

One Step Up

Have one member of each group read the revised speech to the class.

Use Unit Masters 66 (Pronunciation: Dictation) and 67 (Game: Bingo) now or at any time during the rest of the unit.

Lesson 3: Enjoying Success 🔳

Read the title and lesson objectives with learners.

- Follow the suggestions on p. 5 for talking about titles.
- Tell learners that in this lesson, they will discuss ways to celebrate different occasions. They will also write a speech about a success they have had.

Attention Box

Write each word on the board or an overhead transparency. Then do the following:

- Show a variety of grocery or store coupons to convey the meaning of *coupon*.
- Show a *gift certificate*.
- Brainstorm examples of *rewards* (e.g., a gift given to a child who has a good report card).

This vocabulary should be understood, but learners should not be expected to produce the words at this point.

Caption

Read the caption aloud with learners. Point out that in this sentence *reward* is a verb.

Question

Read the question aloud. Provide a personal example to help generate learners' responses.

Reading Tip

Read the tip aloud. Ask learners if they remember the meaning of the word *scan*.

Extension

- Have learners work in small groups. Distribute various tickets, certificates, and coupons.
- Have groups scan their items to find the main information for these categories:

  place _____
  price _____
  savings _____
  restrictions _____
  other information _____

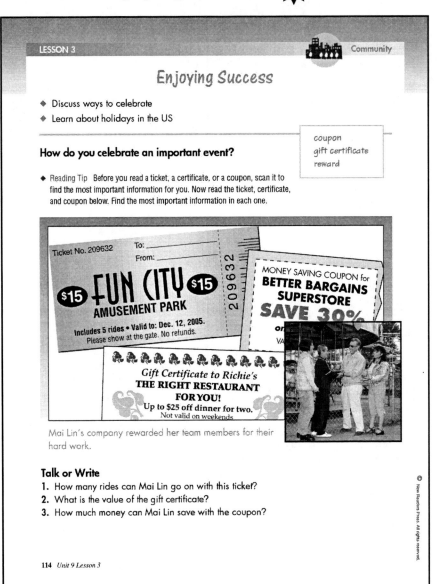

LESSON 3   Community

Enjoying Success

- ◆ Discuss ways to celebrate
- ◆ Learn about holidays in the US

coupon
gift certificate
reward

How do you celebrate an important event?

- ◆ Reading Tip   Before you read a ticket, a certificate, or a coupon, scan it to find the most important information for you. Now read the ticket, certificate, and coupon below. Find the most important information in each one.

Ticket No. 209632   To: _____   From: _____

$15 **FUN CITY** $15
AMUSEMENT PARK

209632

Includes 5 rides • Valid to: Dec. 12, 2005.
Please show at the gate. No refunds.

MONEY SAVING COUPON for
BETTER BARGAINS SUPERSTORE
SAVE 30%

Gift Certificate to Richie's
**THE RIGHT RESTAURANT
FOR YOU!**
Up to $25 off dinner for two.
Not valid on weekends

Mai Lin's company rewarded her team members for their hard work.

Talk or Write
1. How many rides can Mai Lin go on with this ticket?
2. What is the value of the gift certificate?
3. How much money can Mai Lin save with the coupon?

114   *Unit 9 Lesson 3*

Tell learners not all the items will have information for every category.

- Tell learners that *restrictions* means limits (e.g., times or places the item cannot be used.).
- Encourage learners to ask questions if they do not understand other vocabulary on their items.
- Ask learners to report back to the large group on some or all of their tickets, certificates, or coupons.

Talk or Write

This exercise helps learners become skilled at scanning for information.

Answers
1. Five rides
2. $25.00
3. 30%

Extension

Ask these additional questions:

- What are the *restrictions* of the Fun City Amusement Park ticket? (*Valid to: Dec. 12, 2005*)
- Where does this ticket have to be shown? (*at the gate*)
- What is "The Right Restaurant for You"? (*Richie's*)

Vocabulary

Follow the suggestions on p. 6 for introducing and reinforcing vocabulary.

Follow the suggestions on p. 6 for using vocabulary cards. Use the Vocabulary Card Masters for the words in the Vocabulary box.

Attention Box

Read the words to learners, pointing or miming to convey meaning when possible. This vocabulary should be understood, but learners should not be expected to produce the words at this point.

In the US

Read the passage aloud while learners follow silently. Then ask learners if any of these special days are celebrated in their home countries. How?

Extensions

1. Write the names of each celebration day on a separate card (*Independence Day, Thanksgiving, Halloween,* and *Birthdays*).

   • Ask a volunteer to read the names of the four celebrations.

   • Put learners into four groups and give each group a different card.

   • Ask each group to show how they would celebrate the day on their card. Encourage learners to be creative and use their imaginations.

   • Tell them they can role-play, act out, and include props.

2. Discuss other celebrations in the US. List them on the board or an overhead transparency and brainstorm about each of them. Tell learners about these holidays:

New Year's Eve is celebrated on December 31 to welcome the new year. People wear party hats. At midnight they throw

---

In the US   What Do We Celebrate?

The 4th of July, or Independence Day, celebrates the signing of the Declaration of Independence in 1776. It celebrates the *birth* of the United States. Many people join friends, family, and neighbors in a picnic because the holiday is in the summer. Everyone enjoys fireworks at night!

Thanksgiving is another US holiday. It is a day to share a big meal and give thanks. Many people eat roast turkey. This holiday celebrates the first settlers to North America. Native Americans helped them. In the fall, the settlers had a feast and invited the Native Americans to join them.

On Halloween, children in the US dress in costumes. They go to neighbors' homes and ask for candy. People decorate with pumpkins and witches.

Americans also celebrate birthdays. Children often have big birthday parties. There is a cake with candles. Guests bring gifts. Everyone sings "Happy Birthday to You."

☞ Compare Cultures

What is one traditional celebration in your country?
• Take notes. When did you celebrate? Where? What did you do? Was there special food? Music? Decorations?
• Then talk with a partner.
• Tell your partner how you celebrated the last time.

Vocabulary

Listen and repeat. Circle new words. Get meanings from a classmate, your teacher, or a dictionary. Write the words and their meanings.

birth

birthday

feast

guest

holiday

invite

invitation

occasion

_____
your word

candy
costume
fireworks
Native American
pumpkin
roast
settler
turkey
witch

One Step Up
Tell the class about your country's celebration.

Unit 9 Lesson 3 **115**

---

paper streamers, celebrate with champagne, and hug and kiss one another. They say, "Happy New Year!"

Valentine's Day is celebrated on February 14. In the past it was a day to honor Saint Valentine. Now it is a romantic day for people in love and for all people who love one another. People give cards, candy, and flowers. Hearts symbolize this day.

Memorial Day is a day to remember men and women who served the country in the Armed Forces. Many communities have patriotic parades and ceremonies.

Labor Day honors all workers. It is a day to relax.

Compare Cultures

Ask learners to make notes in their notebooks about a traditional celebration in their home countries. Then have partners share their celebrations with one another.

One Step Up

Have learners share their celebrations with the whole class.

 Assign Workbook pp. 64–65.

Activity A

- Have learners copy the two-column chart into their notebooks.
- Put learners in pairs. Tell learners to list a few of their favorite US holiday celebrations in the first column. In the second column, ask them to write a brief description of how they celebrate each occasion.
- Have partners tell each other about their favorite holidays by reading what they wrote.

<u>Extension</u>
Have the partners write their favorite holidays in their home countries and describe their activities on that day. Then have them share their descriptions with their partners.

<u>One Step Up</u>
Ask volunteers to share one of their descriptions with the class.

Activity B

Have learners copy the chart into their notebooks. Then put learners in groups of four.

Review regular and irregular simple past before the groups complete their charts.

One Step Up

Ask volunteers to tell the class what they did last weekend.

Task 3

Have learners work independently to write their speeches and then pair up for peer reviews.

Then tell learners to rewrite their speeches, incorporating their partners' suggestions.

<u>Assessment</u>
 Use Generic Assessment Master 9 (Written Communication Rubric) to evaluate each learner's speech.

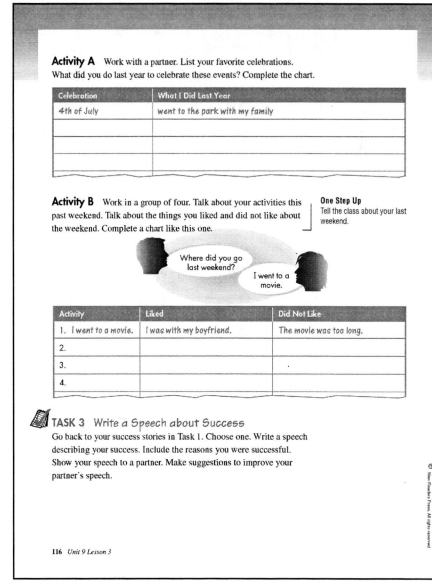

Activity A Work with a partner. List your favorite celebrations. What did you do last year to celebrate these events? Complete the chart.

Celebration	What I Did Last Year
4th of July	went to the park with my family

Activity B Work in a group of four. Talk about your activities this past weekend. Talk about the things you liked and did not like about the weekend. Complete a chart like this one.

One Step Up
Tell the class about your last weekend.

Where did you go last weekend?

I went to a movie.

Activity	Liked	Did Not Like
1. I went to a movie.	I was with my boyfriend.	The movie was too long.
2.		
3.		.
4.		

TASK 3 Write a Speech about Success
Go back to your success stories in Task 1. Choose one. Write a speech describing your success. Include the reasons you were successful. Show your speech to a partner. Make suggestions to improve your partner's speech.

116 *Unit 9 Lesson 3*

 Use Unit Master 68 (Grammar: How Do You Celebrate?) now or at any time during the rest of the unit.

<u>Review Unit Skills</u>
See p. 8 for suggestions on games and activities to review the vocabulary and grammar in this unit.

Unit 9 Project

Learners present a personal success story to the class.

Get Ready

Discuss with learners what they did in Tasks 1, 2, and 3. (In Task 1, they described successful team planning. In Task 2, learners wrote a group speech about teamwork. In Task 3, they wrote a speech about a personal success.)

Then do the following:
- Help learners to use the information from Task 3 or to pick a different story so that they can write their presentations.
- Model the assignment using an example from your own life. Bring some of the items listed in the student book to illustrate your success story.

Do the Work

Make a copy of Unit Master 69 (Unit 9 Project: Present a Success Story) for each learner. Tell learners to use them to make notes for their speeches.

Make sure that the objects learners have collected attest to their success. Then have them begin work on their posters. Objects can be attached to their posters or displayed and explained during their presentations.

To make their presentation posters interesting and attractive, provide learners with art supplies, scissors, and magazines with pictures they can cut out.

Present Your Project

Have learners deliver their speeches in front of the class, with their posters and any collected objects beside them.

Assessment

Use Unit Master 70 (Project Assessment Form). Make a copy of the master for each learner, and place the completed form in the learner's portfolio.

UNIT 9 Project

Present a Success Story

Present a success story to the class.

Get Ready
Think of a success story in your life. It could be the one that you selected for Task 3 or a different one. Collect things related to your success:
- photos
- objects
- tickets, flyers
- cards, invitations
- other: _____

Do the Work
1. Revise the speech you wrote for Task 3 or write a new speech. Use the cards from your teacher. Tell about what you and others did to cause the success. Tell how you celebrated.
2. Make a poster. Use pictures. Use other things that help make your speech interesting.

When and Where You Celebrated

We all went to Fun City last weekend. We had a great time!

I took my parents to Richie's for dinner on Thursday night. I wanted to share my success with them.

Present Your Project
Give your speech to the class.

Writing Extension Write sentences about each of the speeches presented. Write the name of the speaker. Say something positive. Then say something to help improve the speech.

 Technology Extra
Create a presentation on the computer, or write the speech on your word processor. Try to include color, pictures, and different types of letters.

© New Readers Press. All rights reserved.

Unit 9 Project 117

Writing Extension

Use Generic Assessment Master 12 (Peer Assessment Form for Projects and Tasks). Give each learner as many copies as there are people in the class.

Have learners fill out one copy of the form for each speaker, writing one positive comment and one suggestion for improvement. Be sure they understand this form is meant to be helpful; it is not the place for negative criticism.

After all speakers have presented, collect the forms, review them, and distribute them to the speakers.

Assign Workbook p. 66 (Check Your Progress).

Use Unit Master 71 (Unit 9 Checkup/Review) whenever you complete this unit.

Self-Assessment

Give each learner a copy of the Speaking and Listening Self-Check and the Writing and Reading Self-Check (Generic Assessment Masters 10 and 11). Go over the items together. The completed forms will become part of each learner's portfolio.

Listening Scripts

This section contains scripts for the content of the audiotape and audio CD for *English—No Problem!* level 2. Pronunciation cues are indicated in square brackets.

Unit 1
Time for a Change

Lesson 1, Page 13
Pronunciation Target: Sentence Stress
Listen to the sentences from Grammar Talk. Do you hear the stress?
Nicholas talks to his wife.
Nicholas can talk to his wife.

I help my husband think of new ideas.
I can help my husband think of new ideas.

I quit my job.
I can<u>not</u> quit my job.
I <u>can't</u> quit my job.

Nicholas stays at his job.
Nicholas can<u>not</u> stay at his job.
Nicholas <u>can't</u> stay at his job.

Lesson 2, Page 16
Pronunciation Target: Intonation in Statements and Questions
Listen. Notice when the voice goes up and when it goes down.
Where does Nicholas go for information? ↑
He goes to the Employment Center. ↓
Can you fix things? ↑
Yes, I can. ↓

Lesson 3, Page 18
Good News!
Nicholas is at a job interview. Listen to the conversation.
Interviewer: Good morning, Mr. Gorovoy *[Gor-uh-voy]*.
Nicholas: Good morning, sir.
Interviewer: I see from your application that you work in the auto industry.
Nicholas: Yes, sir, but I'm interested in becoming an electrician.
Interviewer: You're in the right place. Our com pany is growing. We need ambitious workers who want to learn. Why do you think you can be a good electrician?

Nicholas: Well, I helped my wife's uncle wire his house. I learn quickly, and I can read technical directions.
Interviewer: There are many places to work. Why are you interested in our company?
Nicholas: I know that you have a job-training program.
Interviewer: Yes, we have an 18-month electrician's-helper program.
Nicholas: I want to work and go to school at the same time.
Interviewer: Our program pays you during your training. And we have an opening. Are you interested?
Nicholas: Yes, I am! How much does it pay?
Interviewer: This job pays seven hundred dollars a week. We also have excellent benefits. When can you start?
Nicholas: I can start in two weeks.
Interviewer: Good. Welcome to the team!
Nicholas: Thank you very much.

Unit 2
New Beginnings

Lesson 1, Page 24
Adjusting to a New Country
Listen to the phone message.
Hi Mom and Grandma, this is Raisa *[Ray-suh]*. Sorry we missed you. Luisa and I stayed at school for swimming practice. Our coach ordered pizza. We want to stay and eat with the team. Call the school if we need to come home for dinner, 555-3333 *[five-five-five, three-three-three-three]*. Love ya. Bye.

Lesson 1, Page 25
Pronunciation Target: Sounds of Simple Past-Tense Endings
Listen. Do you hear the difference between the sounds of *-ed [E-D]?*
called
cleaned

wanted
added

cooked
talked

Lesson 1, Page 26
Activity C
Listen to Fotini *[Foe-tee-nee]* and her daughter

Ritza *[Reet-zuh]* talk.

Ritza: Mom, are you sorry that you came to the United States?

Fotini: Oh, no. But sometimes I'm not sure that I can help.

Ritza: You help us so much! The girls and I are very happy that you are here.

Lesson 2, Page 29

Pronunciation Target: Sounds of *o* [O]

Listen for the different sounds of *o*. *[O]*

shop, got

phone, broke

road, coach

low, throw

Unit 3
Balancing Your Life

Lesson 1, Page 37

Pronunciation Target: Pauses and Intonation in Compound Sentences

Listen to the pauses and intonation. Does the voice stop between the two parts of the sentence? Does the voice rise on the word before the comma?

Charles is a mechanic↑ *[pause],* and Maria is too. She feels tired↑, *[pause],* but she has to clean the house.

Lesson 2, Page 39

Stressed!

Listen to the conversation between Silvia and her doctor.

Silvia: I don't feel well. I have a headache and a stomachache. I also have a sore throat. I'm tired, but I don't sleep well.

Doctor: Hmmm. Let's see what's going on. Your throat looks bad. You probably have an infection. The nurse will do a test to be sure. I'm going to get you an antibiotic. Take this prescription to the pharmacy. Be sure to follow the instructions—one pill every six hours, OK? Now, tell me about your life.

Silvia: Well, . . . I work six days a week in a laundry room. I study at night to learn English. I also take care of my family. I cook, clean, drive my children to school, and help them with homework.

Doctor: That's a lot! Can your husband do some of the work at home? Talk to him. Be sure that he really understands. Your children probably could help you too.

Silvia: It's difficult for me to say that I can't do everything.

Doctor: I know. Also, try to exercise at least four times a week. Walking is good. You need to relax, Silvia. You need to balance your life.

Lesson 2, Page 40

Pronunciation Target: Sounds of *i* [I]

Listen to the different sounds of *i*. *[I]*

tired, life, night

sick, swim

Unit 4
Making a Plan for Your Money

Lesson 1, Page 49

Pronunciation Target: Sounds of *ch* [C-H] and *sh* [S-H]

Listen. Do you hear the difference between the sounds?

chart, much

shirt, wash

Lesson 2, Page 51

Saving More Money

Listen to Joseph and the bank clerk.

Bank Clerk: Good morning. My name is Cathy Reynolds. How can I help you?

Joseph: Good morning. My name is Joseph Delva. I need to open an account.

Bank Clerk: A checking account or savings account?

Joseph: Both. What do I have to do?

Bank Clerk: You have to fill out an application form. And you must provide a photo ID. Now, how much will you deposit in each account? You must deposit a minimum of 25 dollars to open the savings account.

Joseph: Here is my paycheck. I'll deposit 10 percent into my savings and the rest in the checking account.

Bank Clerk: I see that you already endorsed your check. Never endorse the check before you come to the bank. Anyone can cash an endorsed check! If you must endorse the check, write *for deposit only* under your signature.

Joseph: OK. That's good to know. When does my statement come?

Bank Clerk: You will get a bank statement the first week of every month. Use it to balance your checkbook.

Joseph: How do I balance my checkbook?
Bank Clerk: This flyer explains how to balance your checkbook. If you have any problems, just come back. I'll help you.

Lesson 3, Page 55
Pronunciation Target: Syllable Stress
Listen for the stressed syllable in the long words in the vocabulary list.
advice
apartment
emergency
compare

Unit 5
Bargain Shopping

Lesson 1, Page 61
Pronunciation Target: Sounds of *th [T-H]*
Listen. Do you hear the difference between the two sounds of *th [T-H]?*
thing, both
father, that

Lesson 2, Page 63
A Shopping Spree
Listen to the TV commercial.
Better Bargains Superstore Back-to-School Sale!
Don't miss the Back-to-School Sale at Better Bargains Superstore today and tomorrow.
Everything is on sale! Nothing is full price. Stop by and save on our products.
Brand-name clothes
Sneakers and sandals
School supplies
And much, much more!
You will also find great bargains in our appliance and furniture departments.
It's always easier and cheaper to shop with us at Better Bargains Superstore, 2555 *[twenty-five fifty-five]* East Gulf Freeway. Come on in today for the super sale of the year!

Lesson 3, Page 67
Pronunciation Target: Sounds of *s [S]* and *st [ST]*
Listen.
sale, see, socks
store, standard, stop

Unit 6
Equal Rights

Lesson 1, Page 72
Getting the Job You Want
Listen to the job interview.
Ben Sanders: Good morning. Are you Amara Mirembe [stumble over the name: *Uh-mahr-uh Meer-em-bay*]? Sit down please.
Amara: Good morning, sir. Thank you.
Ben Sanders: I see here you're applying for the machine repair position.
Amara: Yes, sir. I repaired machines in a textile plant in my country. May I show you my recommendation?
Ben Sanders: That's OK. Here you should try to start out as an operator.
Amara: But, sir, I think I could do a very good job for you as a machine repairperson.
Ben Sanders: Sure, sure. We'll call you if we have the right job. Thank you for coming in.

Lesson 1, Page 73
Pronunciation Target: Sounds of *a [A]*
Listen. Do you hear two different sounds of the vowel *a? [A]*
and, factory, ads
sales, may, age

Lesson 3, Page 79
Pronunciation Target: Reductions
Listen. Notice how the sounds change when people speak fast. Do you hear the difference?
[slowly] Would you like coffee or tea?
[quickly] Wouldjoo like coffee er tea?

[slowly] We were learning about our rights.
[quickly] We were learnin about our rights.

[slowly] Could you start working next Monday?
[quickly] Couldja start working next Monday?

[slowly] We are cooking beans and bacon.
[quickly] We're cookin beans 'n bacon.

[slowly] Amara *[Uh-mahr-uh]* is going to fight back.
[quickly] Amara is gonna fight back.

[slowly] I don't know.
[quickly] I dunno.

Unit 7
Paying Taxes

Lesson 1, Page 85
Pronunciation Target: Sounds of e [E]
Listen. Do you hear the different sounds of e [E]?
On the end of a word, the vowel e can be silent.
net, check, get
he, we, she, need, speak, agree
make, date

Lesson 2, Page 88
Pronunciation Target: Sounds of t and d [T and D]
Listen. Do you hear the difference between t and d?
tax, talk, extra
dinner, dependent, deduction

Lesson 2, Page 89
Activity B
Listen. Complete the explanation of a W-4 form with the words in the box.
Form W-4 [W four] tells how much money to withhold from your paycheck for taxes. You write how many allowances you want to claim. If no one else can claim you as a dependent, you enter one for yourself. If you are married, you may want to claim your spouse too. You can claim any children you support as dependents. When you claim more dependents, you take home more net pay. However, you may have to pay more taxes to the IRS in April.

Lesson 3, Page 90
Getting a Refund
Listen to Puri's [Pu-ree's (u as in truth)] conversation with his wife, Nadya [Nuh-dee-uh].
Nadya: Would you like some hot mint tea?
Puri: Yes, thank you. I am beginning to understand the tax system in the United States.
Nadya: You can do it. You are an accountant!
Puri: That helps, but everything is different here. I have my W-2 [W two] form from work. I need to complete our 1040 [ten-forty].
Nadya: Do we owe money?
Puri: I don't think so. I think we will get a refund.
Nadya: I hope so! We need extra money.

Unit 8
Understanding Yourself

Lesson 1, Page 97
Pronunciation Target: Sounds of u [U]
Listen for the different sounds of u [U].
public, cup, luck
humor, huge, use

Lesson 2, Page 99
Coming Together
Listen to the conversation between Carlos and Donna.
Carlos: I took a skills inventory today.
Donna: How did you do?
Carlos: It showed that my strength is working with other people. I'm worried that I won't be the best person for the new position.
Donna: Carlos, you need to have more self-confidence.
Carlos: The position is in the research department. I am going to work alone.
Donna: Carlos, don't be so negative! You worry too much.
Carlos: Donna, you aren't listening to me. I am under a lot of stress planning our future together.
Donna: You're not the only one! I had a hard day at work myself!

Lesson 3, Page 103
Pronunciation Target: Sounds of b and v [B and V]
Listen for the difference between b and v [B and V].
block, neighbor, berry
voice, divorce, volunteer

Unit 9
It Takes a Team

Lesson 1, Page 108
Working Together
Mai Lin's [May Lin's] boss congratulates her for her good work. Listen to their conversation.
Mr. Cohen: Congratulations, Mai Lin. Your team had the highest sales total this month for our factory store.
Mai Lin: Thank you, sir. I am really proud of them.
Mr. Cohen: You should be. But you should also be proud of yourself.
Mai Lin: All four of us worked together.

Mr. Cohen: Maybe you can speak at our next employees' meeting. You could tell them about your strategies for success.

Mai Lin: I am worried they won't understand me. My English pronunciation is not very good.

Mr. Cohen: Have more confidence in yourself! You're a great team leader, and you can share your ideas with other employees.

Mai Lin: I will try to do it for you, Mr. Cohen.

Lesson 1, Page 110
Pronunciation Target: Sound of *-tion [T-I-O-N]* ending
Listen.
celebration
decoration
suggestion

Lesson 2, Page 112
Pronunciation Target: Sounds of *r [R]*
Listen for the sound of *r [R]*.
respect
right
argue
proud
praise
trust

Working with Maps

Use the maps in this appendix for those opportunities when learners initiate topics about their home countries or about items in the news.

US Map

Use this US map to show learners where their state and city is located. Ask them what state they live in, what other states they know about, and in what states they have friends or relatives.

Here are some other activities you can do with the map:

- Use the map when appropriate to show where the characters in the student book live or where learners think they live.
- Addresses are referred to throughout the student book and workbook in the stories, forms, and elsewhere. Refer learners to the US map at each of these points. Ask them to find the city and/or state on the map.
- Have learners draw conclusions about life in different states based on the location of the state: e.g., north or south, near an ocean or not. Then have them write short, descriptive paragraphs about life in a certain state. Learners can write a paragraph about a state they think they might like to live in, giving reasons why, or a persuasive paragraph to convince someone to move to a certain state.
- Show learners what states are considered parts of a region (the West, the Southwest, the South, the East Coast, the Pacific Coast, etc.).
- Have learners estimate distances between major cities.
- Learners can ask questions or riddles about a city or state, such as the following: Which state is south of Georgia? (Florida) Which state is shaped like a hand? (Michigan) Which is the island state? (Hawaii) Which states border Mexico? (California, Arizona, New Mexico, Texas)

World Map

Use a world map as a way to welcome new learners into your class.

- If you have a world map on the wall of your classroom, you can have learners point to where they came from and where they are now.
- Take a Polaroid picture of each learner. Learners can write their names at the bottom of their pictures. Using a piece of yarn, pin one end of the yarn to the town they live in now and pin the other end to the town they came from, along with the picture of the learner. As new learners join your class, add their pictures to the map in the same way.

Refer learners to the world map when presenting the "Compare Cultures" portion of each unit.

As a quick review of adjectives, quiz learners with these kinds of questions:
- What language do they speak in Russia? (Russian)
- What are people who live in Canada called? (Canadians)

Learners can make up riddles about their home country or other countries they are familiar with. Here are some examples:
- In what large country in South America is Spanish not the official language? (Brazil)
- What country is shaped like a rooster? (China)

Invite learners to draw conclusions about life in different countries based on location of the country. Then have them write short, descriptive paragraphs about life in a certain country. Learners can write a paragraph about a country they think they might like to live in, giving reasons why, or a persuasive paragraph to convince someone to move to a certain country. Other learners could add to the paragraph in a chaining exercise.

Invite learners to bring to class an object or a picture that represents a country and have classmates guess what that country could be.

US Map

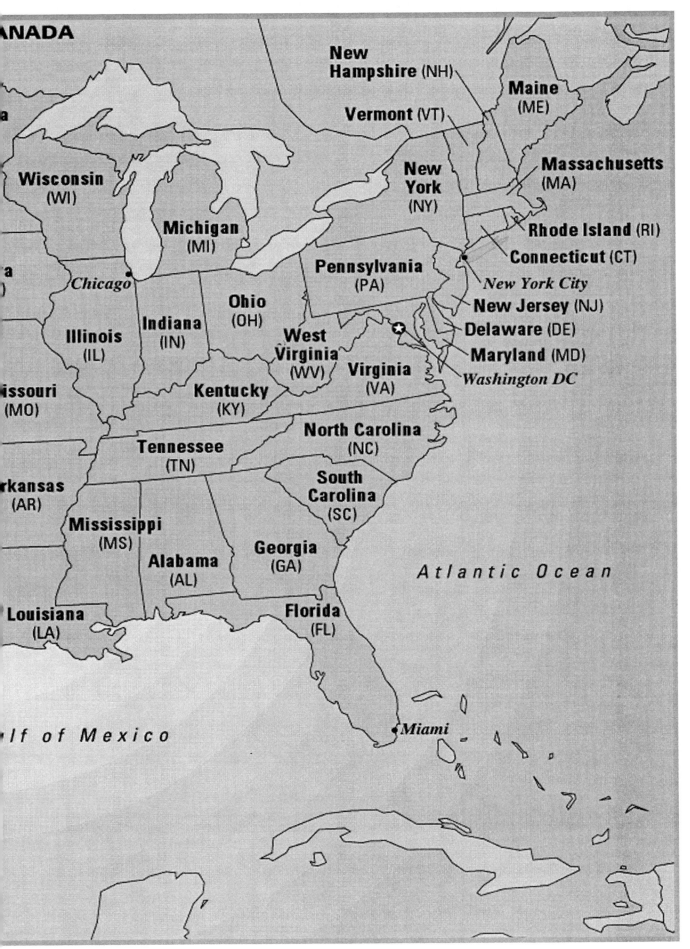

World Map

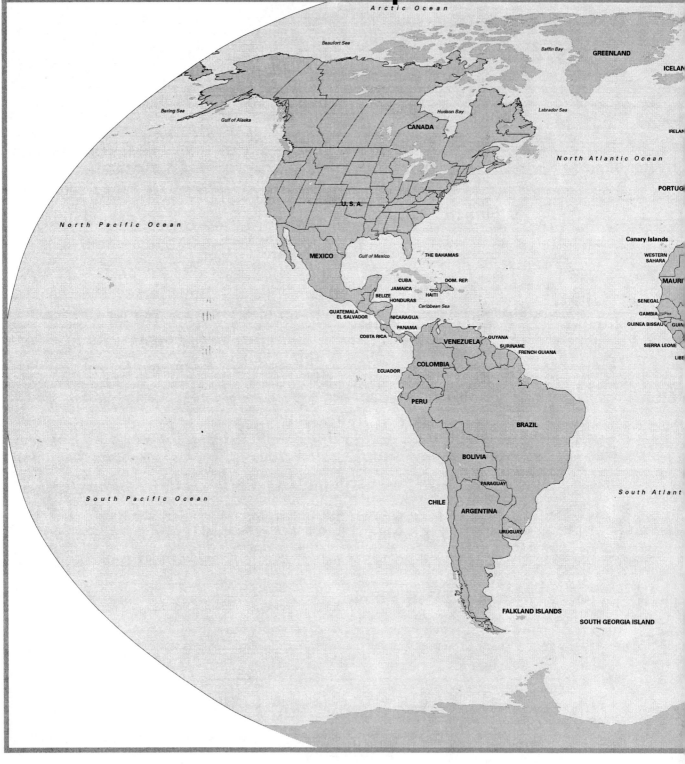

Arctic Ocean

Beaufort Sea

Baffin Bay

GREENLAND

ICELAN

Bering Sea

Gulf of Alaska

Hudson Bay

Labrador Sea

CANADA

IRELAN

North Atlantic Ocean

North Pacific Ocean

U. S. A.

PORTUG

Canary Islands

WESTERN
SAHARA

MEXICO

Gulf of Mexico

THE BAHAMAS

MAURI

CUBA

DOM. REP.

SENEGAL

JAMAICA

BELIZE

HAITI

GAMBIA

HONDURAS

GUINEA BISSAU

GUIN

GUATEMALA
EL SALVADOR

Caribbean Sea

NICARAGUA

SIERRA LEONE

PANAMA

VENEZUELA

GUYANA

LIBE

COSTA RICA

SURINAME

FRENCH GUIANA

COLOMBIA

ECUADOR

PERU

BRAZIL

BOLIVIA

PARAGUAY

South Pacific Ocean

South Atlant

CHILE

ARGENTINA

URUGUAY

FALKLAND ISLANDS

SOUTH GEORGIA ISLAND

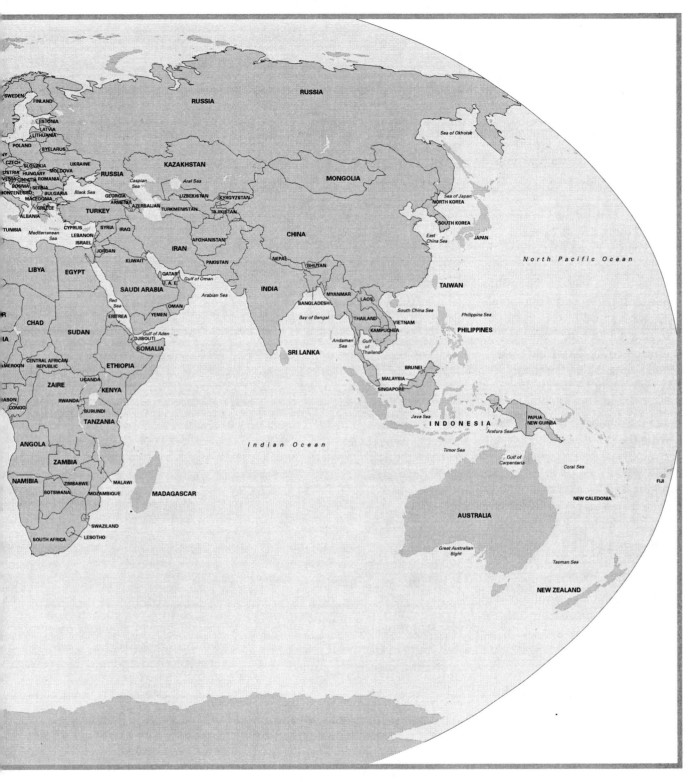

SWEDEN
FINLAND
ESTONIA
LATVIA
LITHUANIA
POLAND
BYELARUS
CZECH SLOVAKIA MOLDOVA UKRAINE
USTRIA HUNGARY ROMANIA
VENIA CROATIA
BOSNIA SERBIA BULGARIA
MONTENEGRO MACEDONIA
GREECE
ALBANIA
TUNISIA

RUSSIA

RUSSIA

KAZAKHSTAN

MONGOLIA

Sea of Okhotsk

Aral Sea

RUSSIA

Caspian Sea
Black Sea
GEORGIA
ARMENIA
AZERBAIJAN
TURKMENISTAN
UZBEKISTAN
KYRGYZSTAN
TAJIKISTAN

Sea of Japan
NORTH KOREA
SOUTH KOREA

TURKEY

CYPRUS
Mediterranean Sea
LEBANON
SYRIA
ISRAEL
JORDAN
IRAQ

AFGHANISTAN

CHINA

East China Sea
JAPAN

North Pacific Ocean

IRAN

KUWAIT
QATAR
U.A.E.
Gulf of Oman

PAKISTAN

NEPAL
BHUTAN

TAIWAN

LIBYA
EGYPT

Red Sea

SAUDI ARABIA

OMAN

Arabian Sea

INDIA

MYANMAR
BANGLADESH

LAOS

South China Sea

Philippine Sea

CHAD

ERITREA
YEMEN

Gulf of Aden
DJIBOUTI

Bay of Bengal

THAILAND
VIETNAM
KAMPUCHEA

PHILIPPINES

SUDAN

SOMALIA

Andaman Sea
Gulf of Thailand

SRI LANKA

BRUNEI

CENTRAL AFRICAN REPUBLIC
AMEROON

ETHIOPIA

MALAYSIA
SINGAPORE

ZAIRE
UGANDA
KENYA

ABON
CONGO
RWANDA
BURUNDI

INDONESIA
Java Sea

PAPUA NEW GUINEA

TANZANIA

Arafura Sea

ANGOLA

Timor Sea

Gulf of Carpentaria

ZAMBIA

Coral Sea

NAMIBIA
ZIMBABWE
MALAWI
BOTSWANA
MOZAMBIQUE

MADAGASCAR

Indian Ocean

NEW CALEDONIA

FIJI

AUSTRALIA

SWAZILAND
SOUTH AFRICA
LESOTHO

Great Australian Bight

Tasman Sea

NEW ZEALAND

World Map 127

Months, Days, and Holidays

Months and Days

The system for ordering dates in the United States is different from that used in most learners' countries. Understanding US dates is an important skill to learn.

- Explain that months are often represented by a number. Have learners practice writing each month with a number (e.g., 1. January, 2. February).
- Say "Month 4" and have learners tell you the name (April) or write it on the board.
- Write today's date on the board (e.g., 12/25/04) and write month-day-year above it.
- Read a date for the learners (e.g., December 25, 2004) and have them write the numbers only in the correct order.
- Then reverse the process and dictate the numbers. Have learners write the full date.

Calendar

Working with a calendar is a good way to review days and numbers. The calendar should be reviewed throughout the series whenever appropriate (filling out forms, writing time lines, etc.).

For continual reinforcement, write the date on the board every day (or have a learner do it) and ask: *What month is this? What day is it? What's the date?*

Use the calendar on this page for the following activities:

- Read a specific date (e.g., August 14th) and ask learners to tell you what the day is (e.g., Saturday).
- Spell a number from one to thirty-one and ask learners to say the correct day.
- Say a day (e.g. Monday) and ask learners to look at the calendar and write the dates that fall on that day (e.g., 2, 9, 16, 23).

Months and Days

Months	Abbreviations	Days	Abbreviations
1. January	Jan.	Sunday	Sun.
2. February	Feb.	Monday	Mon.
3. March	Mar.	Tuesday	Tues.
4. April	Apr.	Wednesday	Wed.
5. May	May	Thursday	Thurs.
6. June	Jun.	Friday	Fri.
7. July	Jul.	Saturday	Sat.
8. August	Aug.		
9. September	Sept.		
10. October	Oct.		
11. November	Nov.		
12. December	Dec.		

August 2004

Sun.	Mon.	Tues.	Wed.	Thurs.	Fri.	Sat.
1	2	3	4	5	6	7
8	9	10	11	12	13	14
15	16	17	18	19	20	21
22	23	24	25	26	27	28
29	30	31				

US Holidays

Day	Date
New Year's Day	January 1
Martin Luther King Day	January 15*
Presidents' Day	third Monday in February
Memorial Day	May 30*
Independence Day	July 4
Labor Day	first Monday in September
Veterans Day	November 11
Thanksgiving	fourth Thursday in November
Christmas	December 25

* Observed on the closest Monday.

124 *Months, Days, and Holidays*

US Holidays

Tell learners that this is a list of official holidays in the United States.

- If you have a calendar in your room, ask different learners to see if those holidays are listed on the calendar and what the exact date is for the current year.
- Ask if anybody knows any information about the holidays. Write some vocabulary words on the board as learners respond.
- At the beginning of each month, ask the learners what holidays are in that month.

Write the name of a holiday on one card (e.g., *New Year's Day*), and a date on a second card (e.g., *January 1, 2004*). If you have more learners, you could add a third card by writing the date in numbers (e.g., *1-1-04*) and a fourth by drawing a holiday symbol.

- Hand out one card to each learner. Have learners walk around and stand together in teams for each holiday.
- Then have each team get together in chronological order starting with the January holidays.

Irregular Verbs and Metric Conversions

Irregular Verbs

Past-tense verbs are reviewed in Units 2 and 9. As learners work on the various activities using the past tense, remind them they can refer to this page for the irregular past-tense forms.

Use vocabulary cards to practice irregular past-tense forms:

* Make vocabulary cards for the verbs, with the present-tense form on the front and the irregular past-tense form on the back.
* If learners finish activities early, they can use the cards with their partners. One partner reads the verb and the other gives the past-tense form.

Have learners write and role-play conversations about their past activities using regular and irregular verbs. Follow this model:

Student 1: Yesterday, I went to a great restaurant.
Student 2: Really? What did you eat?

Metric Conversion Table

Metric conversions are introduced in Unit 2 (weight) and Unit 5 (size). For extended practice, have learners work in pairs using these conversion tables.

Irregular Past Tense Verbs

am/is/are	was/were	leave	left
bring	brought	make	made
build	built	put	put
buy	bought	read	read
can	could	see	saw
choose	chose	sell	sold
come	came	send	sent
do	did	spend	spent
drive	drove	swim	swam
eat	ate	take	took
feel	felt	teach	taught
find	found	tell	told
get	got	think	thought
give	gave	understand	understood
go	went	wear	wore
have	had	win	won
hide	hid	withdraw	withdrew
know	knew	write	wrote

Metric Conversions

To Convert	To	Multiply by	To Convert	To	Multiply by
LENGTH			**LENGTH**		
meters	feet	3.281	feet	meters	.03048
kilometers	miles	0.62	miles	kilometers	1.609
LIQUID			**LIQUID**		
liters	quarts	1.057	quarts	liters	0.946
liters	gallons	.0264	gallons	liters	3.785
WEIGHT			**WEIGHT**		
grams	ounces	0.0353	ounces	grams	28.35
kilograms	pounds	2.2046	pounds	kilograms	0.4536
TEMPERATURE			**TEMPERATURE**		
Celsius	Fahrenheit	multiply by 1.8, then add 32	Fahrenheit	Celsius	subtract 32, then multiply by 0.555

Writing Checklists

Writing Checklist

Refer learners to these checklists for any activity that requires writing.

- Review the questions with learners and explain what each question means.
- After learners complete the checklist for a writing activity, have them assign one point for each question they can answer with a *yes*.
- Have learners work in small groups to peer-edit their writing. Each writer can then compare his or her own score to the scores given by their peer editors.
- Learners can track their progress using the checklist.

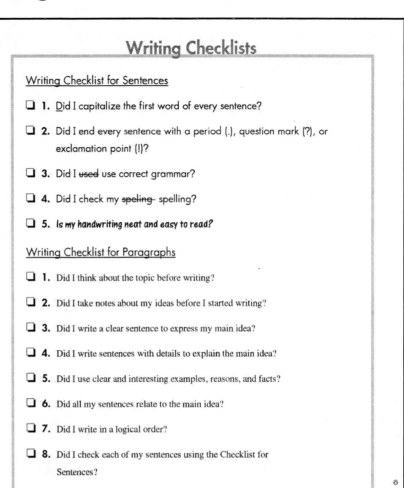

Writing Checklists

Writing Checklist for Sentences

- ❑ 1. <u>Did</u> I capitalize the first word of every sentence?
- ❑ 2. Did I end every sentence with a period (.), question mark (?), or exclamation point (!)?
- ❑ 3. Did I ~~used~~ use correct grammar?
- ❑ 4. Did I check my ~~speling~~ spelling?
- ❑ 5. *Is my handwriting neat and easy to read?*

Writing Checklist for Paragraphs

- ❑ 1. Did I think about the topic before writing?
- ❑ 2. Did I take notes about my ideas before I started writing?
- ❑ 3. Did I write a clear sentence to express my main idea?
- ❑ 4. Did I write sentences with details to explain the main idea?
- ❑ 5. Did I use clear and interesting examples, reasons, and facts?
- ❑ 6. Did all my sentences relate to the main idea?
- ❑ 7. Did I write in a logical order?
- ❑ 8. Did I check each of my sentences using the Checklist for Sentences?

Topics

Grammar and Pronunciation

A

adjectives
  comparative, 61
  descriptive, 95
  order of, 88

B

be, simple present tense, 16

C

can, cannot, and *can't*, 13
compound sentences
  with *and* or *but*, 37
  with *and . . . too* and with *or*, 67

D

do and *does* in yes/no questions and
  answers, 40

F

future with *will* and *going to*, 103

H

have, simple present tense, 16
have to, 49

I

intonation
  in compound sentences, 37
  in statements and questions, 16

M

modals: *may, should, could, would*, 73
must, 49

P

past continuous, 79
past tense (simple)
  of irregular verbs, 28, 112, 125
  of regular verbs, 25, 112
present continuous, 79
pronouns
  direct and indirect object, 109
  reflexive, 97

R

reductions, 79

S

sentence stress, 13
sounds
  of *a*, 73
  of *b* and *v*, 103
  of *ch* and *sh*, 49
  of *e*, 85
  of *i*, 40
  of *o*, 29
  of *r*, 112
  of *s* and *st*, 67
  of simple past-tense endings, 25
  of *t* and *d*, 88
  of *th*, 61
  of the *–tion* ending, 110
  of *u*, 97
syllable stress, 55

V

verbs followed by infinitives, 85

W

wh- questions and answers, 52
will, have to, and *must*, 49